ISLAND

IN THE
PLAINS

Edward
Raventon

ISLAND IN THE PLAINS

A Black Hills Natural History

Johnson Books: Boulder

For Miles and Mariah

9 8 7 6 5 4 3 2 1

Cover design by Bob Schram/Bookends
Cover photographs by Edward Raventon
Interior photographs by Edward Raventon

Library of Congress Cataloging-in-Publication Data
Raventon, Edward
    Island in the plains : a Black Hills natural history / Edward
Raventon. —1st ed.
        p.   cm.
    ISBN 1-55566-132-7
    1. Natural history—Black Hills (S.D. and Wyo.)   2. Glacial epoch—
Black Hills (S.D. and Wyo.)   3. Black Hills (S.D. and Wyo.)
I. Title.
QH104.5.B47R38   1994
508.783'9—dc20   94-17996
                                                            CIP

Printed in United States of America by
Johnson Printing Company
1880 South 57th Court
Boulder, Colorado 80301

Contents

Acknowledgments

I gratefully acknowledge the help of all the people mentioned in this book and others too numerous to list who shared their time, feelings, thoughts, and expertise on a host of subjects concerning the Black Hills.

I also wish to especially thank Ken and Kathy Rost for their unwavering friendship and generosity.

Introduction

The name Black Hills is said to have been applied to these, the only mountains of Dakota, from the fact that, as they are approached from the barren wastes of the Plains, they loom up in the distance as a dark range, black from the heavy growth of timber they support. They lie between the 43d and 45th parallels of north latitude, and between the 103d and 105th meridians of longitude west from Greenwich, occupying an irregularly shaped area about 120 miles in length from north-northwest to south-southeast, and having a width of from 40 to 50 miles.

The Black Hills are embraced between the two forks of the Cheyenne River, the Belle Fourche and South Fork . . . which join about 60 miles east of the Hills forming the Big Cheyenne. Surrounded on all sides by the comparatively unbroken sea of the Great Plains, they are entirely separated from the main chain of the Rocky Mountains on the west, to which system however, in character and structure they belong, and rise an island of rough and rugged mountains complete within themselves.

Henry Newton
Report on the Geology and Resources
of the Black Hills of Dakota (1875)

*For six years now he had heard the best of all talking. It was of
the wilderness . . . bigger and older than any recorded document.*

—William Faulkner, *The Bear*

1

Call of the Hills

In the fall of 1951, my folks took me to the Black Hills. As a three-year-old I have no recollection of it, but Mother remembers the aspens as exquisite and the autumn a memorable one. By 1956, the folks had made a regular, late summer ritual of bringing the family out to the mountains. Our vacation trips were usually undertaken in August to escape the oppressive heat and humidity of Missouri. The destination of our pilgrimage rarely varied. We always went west to the cool, mountains of Colorado, Wyoming, and Montana.

At the time, Dad drove a light tan '55 Ford station wagon, he nicknamed the "buckskin." It was a two-door, no frills, wagon with a standard V8 engine. On Friday, his last working day before vacation, Mother would be busy packing so that when the buckskin arrived home, she could load it up. Dad liked to have everything ready like a fireman so that if the mood struck him that evening, he could hit the road on short notice.

Invariably, sometime around 4 AM, the call would come. Dad would be up mumbling something about how it would be a lot cooler and there would be less traffic if we left now and my sister and I would be rousted and loaded up half asleep into the Ford.

Early afternoon would find us headed west somewhere in eastern Kansas or Nebraska, passing through small, sun-baked towns shimmering in heat. These little towns, with their canvas awning shaded storefronts, often appeared completely deserted except for an errant, solitary dog on a tongue-dragging trot down main street.

As we hit the Great Plains Dad would venture down secondary back roads to see the rural countryside. I remember old farmsteads with faded red barns and white clapboard houses surrounded by magnificent elms. The rockers on shaded porches suggested late evenings spent sipping ice tea and listening to the rasp of crickets. I also liked the shelter belts littered with hulks of old rusting machinery that once functioned as harrows, plows, planters, and threshers.

Most of the county roads then were gravel and fringed with ditches that resembled long straight moats. These roadside ditches were often choked with giant ragweed five feet tall. I can still envision their mitten-shaped leaves, laden with fine, white road dust, drooping in the heat.

In those days air conditioning in family cars did not exist, or if it did, it did not exist for us. All the windows were rolled down because, no matter how bad the dust was, it was better than the heat. Even with the windows down by mid-afternoon the air temperature in the car usually hovered somewhere in the nineties.

To keep cool my sister and I would hang out the side windows for short intervals. First our head, then our feet; then heads again until our eye lids were sore and our hair hurt. Safety belts did not exist and the rules of back-road travel were pretty informal: "Don't fall out of the car." After being thoroughly wind blasted, we would settle back and count cows and horses making up various rules as to what counted for the most.

There was usually a late afternoon stop for lunch at a small deserted rest area that had a couple of scraggly Chinese elms, a roadside picnic table, a hand pump, and two primitive out houses. Lunch was a sliced meat sandwich with American cheese on white bread, garnished with a pickle and washed down with a glass of hard, cold well water.

Evening would fall on us somewhere out on the high, short-grass plains of western Kansas, Nebraska, or eastern Colorado where the earth stretched out long and flat under an immense sky. After sunset the western horizon would glow orange, fading up into red, lavender, and indigo. If the evening was clear, there might be streamers or light pillars rising from the horizon and penetrating vertically into the darker colors. Often there would be high, windswept swirls of cirrus clouds, stained in warm colors and brush stroked against a darkening dome of purple light.

As night fell and deepened, the greenish light from the Ford's speedometer dial would slowly brighten to where all I could see was the right side of Dad's face staring intently ahead, behind two beams of headlights.

Dad was now approaching his eighteenth hour of nearly non-stop driving. Sometime after the stars had long been the only light in the sky, we would hit the foothills of the southern Rockies. It might be the Front Range in northern Colorado or the Laramies in southern Wyoming. We would arrive as we left, sleepy and in the dark. But there was a difference. Instead of unrelenting, suffocating heat and humidity, there was soft, sweet air to inhale. Breathing was like drinking cool, clear well water on a hot, dry day.

If I happened to be asleep when the buckskin finally rolled to a dead stop, I would stir awake and see Dad standing in dim lantern light by a picnic table pumping up the Coleman; above him rose a great vault of sky, immensely clear and sharp, glittering with stars. Sometimes there would be the gurgling of a stream and the deep whoosh of a night breeze scented with pine.

When I try to recall it from a perspective of over three decades, it seems like a dream experience. Dad, who spent some of his more impressionable years in Montana, still camped like a cowboy and yearned for the West. While he never pursued that life style long, he never quite left it either. He still had his old coffee pot, but instead of building a campfire he had a gas stove to put it and his black iron skillet on. He packed a few canned goods and dried items along with an old blanket he rolled out under the pines. He liked it simple and clean.

Oddly, besides what I have recounted, there is precious little in the way of specifics I can remember of those August trips except the big spruce trees. We never used motels or restaurants and rarely stopped at tourist haunts; we traveled the remote mountain roads and camped in the forest, with its campground bears behaving like huge ambling dogs with their noses stuck in cars while tourists threw marshmallows at them.

Yellowstone, its high peaks with ragged banks of snow, was a favorite destination. Like other pilgrims, we waited for Old Faithful to erupt; listened to hot vapor blow and watched the paint pots bubble. We rarely stayed long in one place. As was the custom, we stopped at the turnouts, stood in pea-size, crushed gravel and marveled at the vistas of vastness for five or ten minutes. It was too overwhelming and too far removed to be real. I guess that is why none of that majestic scenery every really stuck with me. I needed to feel it, taste it, absorb its heat and moisture into my body. The high West was too much and not enough.

That particular August of 1956, returning home from Yellowstone, we cut across the northern Black Hills. Driving east on U.S. 85 into the northern Hills, we traveled over O'Neill Pass before dropping down into Spearfish Canyon. Along the way, late afternoon sunlight streamed through a forest of tall, evergreen spruce. White canyon walls were highlighted and receded into shadow. And there was water—cool, clear and sweet. It seemed a sanctuary of serenity.

After camping near Hannah Creek that evening, we spent the next morning in Deadwood, climbing to Mount Moriah Cemetery to see Wild Bill Hickok's final resting place. His tombstone, along with Calamity Jane's, was a point of interest. I have an old photograph of my sister and I sitting quietly on the retaining wall of Hickok's grave. I remember experiencing the contrasting coolness of the pine shade as opposed to the heat of the intensely bright sunlight.

That afternoon we rolled into Rapid City, toured dinosaur park on Skyline Drive and then prepared for the thousand-mile drive home. Before we headed southeast for the central plains and the lowlands, we made one more stop at the old Prairie Market store on North Street for groceries.

The temperature hovered somewhere near one hundred degrees Fahrenheit and Dad parked the buckskin for a cooling down in the sparse shade of a stunted elm arbor. Everybody was in the store searching for something cold while I sat alone under the trees.

A breeze was blowing and it felt like nothing I could ever recall experiencing. It was both light and soft and had the sear of a blast furnace. The earth was parched and bone-dry hard with wispy bluegrass burnt to a light brown crisp. Above me the leaves, although green, were tinder dry.

I liked it all: the hoarse rattle of leaves; the comfort of their shade; the feel and smell of baked earth; the brilliant blaze of blue sky; and the hot, desiccating wind on my face. Everything was scorched and it all felt right.

Some two decades later, having forgotten the Black Hills, I headed west again for the mountains for what to me seemed like the first time. It was early in September, the temperature in the Badlands, some fifty miles east of the Black Hills, hit 104 degrees Fahrenheit that afternoon. When I arrived at Wind Cave National Park in the southern Black Hills, it had cooled only slightly. In the parking lot I could feel the blast of cold air rushing from the mouth of the cave as the pressure changed outside.

After cooling off in the cave and hydrating my body, I felt revived enough to hike out beyond Lookout Mountain that evening to wait for the elk. Near a long ridge below the mountain I hid in an outcrop of yellow rocks with my camera and binoculars and waited. A golden eagle flew overhead searching the grassland; a coyote trotted across the ridge, stopped, and momentarily looked at me before loping down the draw out of sight.

As the earth slowly cooled and evening spread her cloak, crickets began to chirp and songbirds sang vespers. Shadows lengthened imperceptibly, deepened, and dissolved into darkness. The sun set behind me and still no elk. I waited in the twilight. As the last of the light faded, a cow elk stepped out of the timber three hundred yards away. She walked south from Lookout Mountain along the top of a nearby ridge; another followed her and another and another in perfect single file. The line soon stretched unbroken over the back of the ridge for twenty yards before the lead cow dropped down into the draw below me. The procession continued and numbered some forty cows, yearlings, and calves. At the end of the file, a lone bull emerged with a magnificent antler rack.

In the east a yellow harvest moon peeped up over the horizon. The air temperature was dropping quickly. I kept my eyes on the bull elk walking through the deepening dusk calmly trailing the cows. Near the center of the ridge he stopped, tilted his head and antlers back on his shoulders, and bugled. The sound was an eerie, high-pitched tremolo squeal rising to a whistle before ending in a series of grunts and coughing.

It was a proclamation of presence that reverberated over the ridges and through the valleys. Through my binoculars I could see silver jets of vapor pump from his nostrils. He was working hard. After a short interval, he again raised his head back to open his throat. His mouth opened wide and he bugled his location and call to other elk. Never had I seen or felt anything like it.

Once more the bull tilted back his head, antlers nearly touching his shoulder blades, and opened his throat. His call again penetrated the pines and rolled over the shadowy grassland. It was filled with confidence and strength. After a pause, he followed his harem as they moved from the moonlight and disappeared into the darkness of the draw.

Silver moonlight bathed the wide, empty expanse of prairie imparting a charmed unearthly feel. Nothing stirred. The night was still. I picked and felt my way back over the earth to the campground. When I arrived I built a small campfire against the night chill and rolled my bag out under the stars. That night, curled up around glowing embers, I thought I saw Dad for a moment standing in the firelight before I nodded off to the yelping of coyotes, the grunting of bison, and the bugling of elk.

2

Black Hills Evolution

Two billion years before the present, the Earth was a fiery inferno. Due to numerous volcanic eruptions, it was becoming large enough to support and hold a chokingly hot atmosphere which was heavily charged with lethal gases, including carbon dioxide, carbon monoxide, and hydrogen chloride. This primitive atmosphere was formed as a result of the internal elemental contest between the molten interior and the cooling light granitic crust that was slowly forming and hardening on the surface. Eventually, this poisonous atmosphere cooled and stabilized sufficiently enough to allow for precipitation (in the form of rain), which immediately vaporized upon falling on the hot, rocky crust.

For thousands of years the Earth was enveloped in a vast, seamless shroud of steam vapor that formed a dense hydrosphere through which the sun never penetrated. Then over the next 500 million years, the atmosphere, together with the incessant precipitation, facilitated the cooling of the Earth's crust. Volcanic activity equalized the internal heat pressure of the Earth with crustal contraction. Earthquakes also appeared as an adjustment to crustal cooling.

With the sufficient cooling of the Earth's crust about 1 billion years before the present, the formation of the first primitive ocean began. It formed as a result of water vapor condensing on the Earth's cooling surface. This process took 50 million years and, with its completion, fresh water with a faint tint of acid covered the entire planet at an average depth of one mile. It is at this point that true geologic history begins.

Erupting across the bottom of the Pacific, deep dense lava flows depressed parts of the ocean's floor, which in compensation gave rise to the first continental land mass. This entire age is characterized by frequent and violent storms. Surface cooling alternates with the intrusion of immense lava flows that leave the Earth's crust in a continual state of flux. These new flows admix with the subsequent sedimentary deposits of early worldwide oceans.

A few ancient, pre-oceanic granitic rocks, which were formed deep within the Earth, remain intact while most are heated and recrystallized over and over again. Some of these ancient, igneous formations are up-thrusted and will eventually be exposed as the central "crystalline core" of the Black Hills. Millions of years into the future these ancient granitic core formations, eroded by wind and water into smooth, round shapes will be named the Cathedral Spires, Mount Rushmore, the Needles, and Harney Peak. The geological-type stone of this formation will be called Harney Peak granite.

Sedimentary formations, laid down by that first great ocean, eventually are heated, bent, twisted, and crumbled. Distorted and contorted again and again through these metamorphic experiences, they become the dark-slabbed iron- and silica-rich metamorphic schists scattered and exposed with the l.74-billion-year-old Harney Peak granites and the even older 2.5-billion-year-old Bear Mountain granites of the central Black Hills. These ancient metamorphic schists, exposed and intertwined at the heart of the Black Hills with the granites, make up the other major component of the Black Hills "crystalline core."

The Pacific Ocean in this early time, around 800 million years ago, covers nine-tenths of the globe and is deepening. The sheer added weight of the water, which in some of the deepest trenches approaches a depth of ten miles, increases the down thrust and overall sinking of the ocean floor while conversely operating to further up thrust the single continental land mass. In effect, the land mass begins to crack and split into seven smaller, continental masses. As these continents continue to slowly rise, they become separated by the oceans and begin to drift apart.

With the increase and elevation of the land masses, climatic variations begin to arise which, in turn, produces weather. There are now land areas that, depending on the proximity of their elevations to the sea, begin to receive either greater or lesser oceanic influences. Cosmic clouds start to form over the land and, as the continents drift farther apart, the ocean begins to more deeply penetrate the seven continents. Long finger-like extensions of the sea create shallow water inlets and sheltered bays that will soon provide suitable habitat for marine life all over the globe.

It is now 650 million years before the present, the long Precambrian era of building the Earth and preparing it to be the host for a chloride-based life system is coming to a close. Continental seas further invade the land, creating extensive shorelines of shallow water. The waters of these bays and inlets are clear, which allows the sunlight to reach the bottom. Seawater is rapidly attaining the degree of salinity essential to the development of phytoplankton, bacteria, and algae—all of which evolve rapidly and spread quickly as the Ordovician period approaches. These plants will slowly absorb the huge amounts of carbon dioxide in the atmosphere and replace it with oxygen.

The transition from vegetable to animal life occurs on the sea floor. These new creatures—which include snails, sponges, and trilobites—have soft-bodies, but soon achieve the ability to secrete hard parts. By the end of the Silurian period—400 million years before the present—and into the Devonian, the seas are dominated by thousands of species of trilobites. As the world climate grows warmer, a general marine inundation of the seashores of the various continents takes place. New oceans appear and older bodies of water are enlarged. Huge continents are successively flooded and submerged, some deeply, for millions of years before they rise up again only to be submerged, rise again, and submerge.

In the Mississippian period, 350 million years before the present, the Earth's climate is oceanic and tropical. Trilobites, while decreasing in variety, are still plentiful along with ostracods, echinoderms, and crinoids.

During this warm, pleasant oceanic interlude that lasts for 40 million years, enormous colonies of lime-secreting algae deposit huge amounts of lime that build up on the bottoms of the great inland warm-water seas. The lime eventually solidifies into thick, white limestone formations that are first identified on the bluffs of the Mississippi River. This limestone formation will become a major aquifer of the western high plains of North America. It will eventually be exposed in the Black Hills and run to depths ranging from three hundred to five hundred feet. This exposed limestone in the Black Hills will be referred to as the Madison formation. It is in the Madison that Wind Cave and Jewel Cave in the southern Black Hills will form over the intervening eons of time.

At the beginning of the Pennsylvanian period, 310 million years before the present, land masses of the world are well up after many unremarkable sinkings and elevations. The climate remains mild and equitable. Land plants are migrating farther and farther inland from the seashores while life patterns are becoming better developed and individual marine animal organisms are evolving.

During the Pennsylvanian, early mountain movements begin and the first gas and oil deposits are laid down. These deposits are derived from the vast collections of vegetable and animal matter carried down into the water and compressed at the time of the last land submergence. In the Black Hills this period is represented by the sandy, orange-and-yellow Minnelusa formation.

During the next period, known as the Permian, 280 million years before the present, much of the North American continent is again submerged by shallow inland seas. Fish become plentiful in the sea while arthropods—which include the insects, arachnids, and crustaceans—are rapidly evolving. Towards the end of the Permian, a red stratum begins to appear and extend over much of the Earth's surface. These red beds continue into and characterize the succeeding Triassic period.

In the Black Hills the red beds are classified as the Spearfish formation, taking its name from the location of the geological type site. This formation is exposed around the entire periphery of the Black Hills and generally appears as a bright red clay or shale. In the Black Hills the red beds are also referred to, topographically, as the Red Valley or the "Racetrack" and are 250 to 700 feet thick.

At the beginning of the Triassic, 220 million years before the present, ferns and cycads give rise to the first host of primitive plants that start to forest and shade the land with their delicate, leafy fronds. The fossilized remains of cycads from this ancient time will be discovered at two major site locations in the Black Hills in the late nineteenth century.

Starting in the Permian and running through the Triassic and into the early Jurassic, 180 million years before the present, continuing land elevation blocks moisture-laden oceanic influences, greatly modifying the marine climate of the preceding ages. This transitional period of increasing land mass elevation results in greater restriction of seas and moisture-bearing clouds and ushers in a drier, more variable, continental-type climate. Inland seas, which once inundated continents, are reduced to shrinking salt lakes.

Gradually, these inland lakes dry up leaving a white, chalky mineral precipitate known as gypsum. In the Black Hills, this era, which is marked by aridity and barrenness, is represented by lenses of gypsum that are forty-five feet thick in some places. These gypsum beds lie exposed as part of the red Spearfish formation. The dissolution, far into the future of a gypsum lens near Hot Springs, will play a major role in creating an entrapment for mammoth elephants near the end of the Ice Age.

About this time seed plants first appear affording a better food supply for developing land animals and insects which must evolve resting stages during the long droughts and winter periods. Insects—including cockroaches, crickets, locusts, and dragonflies—undergo radical changes to meet these demands. Amphibians, like toads and frogs, survive only because they are able to endure these long periods of desiccation by suspending their animation in the mud of dried-up pools and ponds.

There is little to find in the fossil record of the Permian-Triassic period represented by the Spearfish formation, attesting to the harsh conditions that prevailed during this period. Yet, born from these difficult circumstances, an amphibian evolves into a reptilian creature that develops a way to reproduce without returning to the water to lay their eggs. They accomplish this extraordinary feat by evolving enclosed eggs in which the embryonic animal is allowed to pass through larval and other developmental stages before being hatched in an essentially adult form. These creatures soon develop protective scales and spread unimpeded over the world, laying the evolutionary foundation for the Age of Reptiles in the Jurassic period.

In the Black Hills, the Jurassic period encompasses the Sundance, Unkpapa, and Morrison formations. The Morrison in the Black Hills, although mostly eroded away and thin, contains the richest representation of fossilized reptilian species that now completely dominate life on Earth at the close of this period.

By the beginning of the Cretaceous, 144 million years before the present, numerous species of reptiles have evolved and are thriving. They develop into a vast host of huge docile, as well as ferocious, creatures that include scaled dinosaurs, sea serpents, and flying reptiles. Some of these great reptiles, like *Camarasaurus*, will leave its fossilized bones in the northwest edge of the Black Hills to be unearthed in the late twentieth century.

In the Black Hills, the upper Cretaceous formations, with their plethora of dinosaur bones, will completely erode off the Black Hills long before time is recorded and regarded as a linear phenomena. Lower Cretaceous formations will make up the Dakota Hogback— the foothills that will eventually encircle the Black Hills proper. The Hogback sequence formations will include the Spearfish with its gypsum lenses, Sundance, Unkpapa, Morrison, Lakota, and Fall River formations. These formations (not all of which are found in sequence) will record 120 million years of the Earth's geologic history, starting at the end of the Permian, running through the Triassic and Jurassic, and ending in the middle of the lower Cretaceous. Early paleontologists will later refer to this formational sequence as the Black Hills "Mesozoic Rim."

The red-streaked Sundance and the handsome cream-colored Lakota formations which cap the Mesozoic Rim will be quarried in the late nineteenth and early twentieth centuries as building material. A handful of these beautiful Victorian Lakota sandstone structures, cut and carved from the hardened floor of what was once a Cretaceous sea, will grace the small Black Hills towns of Sundance, Whitewood, Spearfish, St. Onge, Hot Springs, and Edgemont.

At the end of the Cretaceous, 70 percent of the reptilian types that once flourished in abundance vanish from the register of living creatures, but not before they help give rise to an amazing group of hairy, shrew-like mammals and feathered, winged birds. In future millennia, evolution will naturally select animal species that exhibit intelligence, agility, and adaptability.

As mammalian species begin to evolve, continental land masses, for the most part, remain above water. Again, it is a time of tremendous crustal deformation and concomitant volcanic activity with widespread lava flows. The American continents run up against volcanic obstructions deep on the floor of the Pacific. This contention of geologic forces provides an impetus to the formation of the long north-south mountain cordillera that extends from Alaska down through North America, Central America, and South America to Cape Horn. Prior to this time there were few mountain peaks, only elevated ridges of great width. Now, with the continental drift halted by Pacific geologic obstructions, a back thrust of the continents results in the creation and elevation of the Sierras and, later, the Rocky Mountains.

This modern mountain-building episode takes about 30 million years, beginning near the end of the Cretaceous and running well into the Tertiary period. The location of the Rocky Mountain cordillera up thrusting is determined by the fact that this area is comprised of relatively lighter areas of land lying near the center of the North American continent.

During the rise of the central Rocky Mountains, sometimes referred to as the Laramide orogeny, great folding and tilting occurs coupled with enormous over thrusts of the various layers both underground and at the surface. The present Rocky Mountain system, however, is not the original land elevation. For previous ages, this mountain system, which includes the Black Hills, had experienced land elevations only to be successively covered by the sea. While some of the higher peaks in the Wyoming Big Horns and along Colorado's Front Range, like Pikes and Longs peaks, remained as islands, the present Rocky Mountain highland is a recent geologic phenomena having completed its uplifting a mere 60 million years ago at the beginning of the Tertiary.

The eastern most outlying segment of this great mid-continental orogeny—the Black Hills—is also fully elevated at a height of at least ten thousand feet at this time. It first appears as a relatively smooth, elliptical dome 125 miles long and 65 miles wide in the middle of the northern Great Plains.

During the Palocene and Eocene epochs of the Tertiary, a distinctive group of igneous bodies intrude into the older rocks of the northern Black Hills. Occurring in the northern most portion of the Black Hills, these Tertiary igneous intrusions will form an important east-west belt of peaks and domes that will later become significant to aboriginal natives as mystical/ religious sites and lithic procurement areas. At the end of the nineteenth century and into the twentieth century, this belt of igneous intrusions will become economically important to geologists and hard rock miners for their rich and extensive gold and silver lodes.

During this period, far to the north the Bering land bridge connects the two great continents of Asia and North America. Primitive insect-eating mammals, which first appeared during the Cretaceous, develop in the Eocene and gradually overrun the entire landscape which is now all but cleared of dinosaurs. Formerly, preferring the security of living in the hills and forested mountainous regions of the Earth, some of these mammals begin evolving into hoof-type, plains-grazing species.

Towards the end of the Eocene, mammalian life forms have developed into early armadillos, rabbits, rodents, weasels, and ground sloths. Along the herbivorous branch, early archaic mammals that include *Phenacodus*, *Coryphodon*, and a large six-horned, two-tusked creature, *Uintatherium*, appear. These creatures have relatively small brains, simple primitive teeth, and walk plantigrade on five toes, each of which is terminated with a small hoof. Angiosperms, now comprising most of the modern land flora, become the principal food of these rapidly increasing grazers while most of the modern plant pollinating insect families coevolve with specific plants in this era.

The Oligocene, 36 million years before the present, becomes the great age of mammalian renovation and expansion. During this epoch the Earth is dominated by an assortment of placental mammals including giant, pig-like entoledonts that grow to be the size of bison. However, the largest of the herbivores are rhinoceros-like creatures that include the ponderous *Brontotherium* with its pair of horn-like processes that grow out of its snout and *Baluchitherium* which, standing at fifteen feet high at the shoulder, is the largest land mammal ever discovered.

Like the dinosaurs, primitive mammals that grew larger in size, but had comparatively small brains, perish as distinct species. Again, larger brains and agility slowly replace size and armor as the best features in the progress of long-term species survival. Mammals exhibiting superior intelligence, agility, and adaptability possess the greatest survival advantages, and it is these creatures who finally destroy the last of their ancient reptilian ancestors to fully assume domination of the Earth. Of the saurians, only the reptilian families of the lizard, crocodile, turtle, and snake, along with the venerable amphibians, escape extinction.

The world climate 30 million years before the present remains relatively mild due to the enormous increase in the size of the tropic seas. The Black Hills are steadily being eroded down while modern types of mammals, including the camel and llama appear and evolve on the plains of North America which they soon overrun. Horses develop along with the ancestor of the swine, peccaries and hippopotamus. By the close of the Oligocene, 24 million years before the present, ruminant deer and giraffes appear while marine and terrestrial life forms appear much as they do in the present day.

At the beginning of the Miocene, ruminant bovids—including bison, sheep, and goats—appear. The climate is still mild but land elevation and sea segregation is slowly changing the world's weather patterns to one that is gradually cooling. The Rocky Mountains, now highly elevated, deposit an enormous amount of erosional material on the lowlands and create the high northern plains that slope east and surround the Black Hills.

Warm climate plants and trees soon disappear from the northern latitudes, their niche filled by more hardy plants and deciduous trees that are better adapted to the hardships and vicissitudes of a drier climate. There is a great increase in the varieties of grasses as the plains continue to rise and cool off. The teeth of many grazing mammalian species gradually broaden and alter conforming to the present-day type.

The Miocene becomes the golden age of mammals. The Bering land bridge is up again and many groups of animals use it to migrate to North America from Asia and vice versa. Included in this migration are the four tusked mastodons, short-legged rhinoceros and many species of the cat family. North America is soon well stocked with ruminants that include deer, oxen, camels, bison, and several species of rhinoceros, while the giant entoledonts become extinct.

The most impressive land creatures of this era and subsequent eras are the elephants which possess large brains encased in large bodies. Confronted by the highly intelligent life and aggressive, agile predators of these times, no animal the size of an elephant could have survived unless it had possessed a brain of superior quality. Elephants soon dominate the Earth as the largest land mammal. By the Pliocene, 5 million years before the present, elephants, along with herds of horses, llamas, and giraffe-like camels, mingle and completely dominate the northern plains of North America that surround the Black Hills. These plains animals are preyed upon by a wide host of large cats and canid species. Worldwide animal migrations are still taking place. Antelopes, bears, and mammoths are entering North America while camels and horses migrate to China and rhinoceroses migrate to all the continents except Australia and South America.

The dog family, at this time, is successfully represented by wolves and foxes, and the cat family by lions, panthers, and saber-tooth tigers. By the end of the Pliocene, the great cats dominate the Earth as predators while smaller dog and cat species increase in numbers worldwide. Small mammals—like weasels, martens, otters, and raccoons—thrive and develop throughout the northern latitudes.

It is now 2 million years before the present and the beginning of the Pleistocene. Vast lands of North America are highly elevated on an extensive scale. Simultaneous with these land elevations, ocean currents are shifting while moisture-laden seasonal winds change their directions and blow over the mountains. The combination of these conditions forces heavily saturated air to flow over northern highlands, producing an almost constant precipitation in the form of snow. Increasingly, severe cold halts animal migrations heading north over the Bering land bridge. Soon the bridge sinks again into the sea, isolating the eastern and western hemispheres which now begin to develop distinct types of life.

Snow falling over these cooler, elevated regions in North America begins to build to depths that reach in excess of twenty thousand feet. This enormous mantle of snow, compressed and metamorphosed by its own ponderous weight, becomes plastic and begins to slide down into massive creeping sheets and lobes of ice. The areas of greatest snow depth, together with altitude, determine the central points of subsequent glacial pressure flows.

There are at least four major and distinct ice invasions and retreats with scores of minor advances and recessions associated with the activity of each individual ice sheet. During the early epoch of what will be known as the ice age North America hosts mastodons, mammoths, horses, camels, musk oxen, ground sloths, giant beavers, saber-tooth tigers, sloths as large as elephants, and many groups from the cat and dog families. Towards the close of the ice age the majority of these creatures will become extinct in North America.

One hundred and fifty thousand years before the present the last ice sheet reaches its farthest point of extension in North America, carving out the present-day Great Lakes and creating major river valleys. The great glaciers come within 150 miles of the Black Hills before retreating and leaving the Missouri River as the legacy of it farthest advance.

Many animal species during this rigorous glacial period in North America are sorely tried and sifted by the severity of the cold and the back-and-forth migration necessitated by the advance and retreat of the ice sheets. Those animals which migrated with the glaciers and survived the best on the North American continent are the bear, bison, caribou, musk ox, mammoth, and mastodon.

The enforced migration of life in the face of advancing ice sheets led to an extraordinary commingling of plants and animals. With the final retreat of the last ice invasion, many Arctic species of both plants and animals are left stranded high up on remote peaks and valleys of the Black Hills as small disjunct populations. Their presence will later provide botanists and ecologists with living clues to the Earth's great changes in climate.

It is now ten thousand years before the present and the beginning of a warm period known as the Holocene or "modern age." Just prior to the opening of the Holocene, hominids with long, dark hair, dressed in thick animal hides and armed with small, deadly, stone-tipped, spearlike devices called atlatls, migrate north from the warmer southern and western latitudes of North America following herds of bison and mammoths. Their destination—the rich northern plains hunting grounds and the open valleys and canyons of the southern Black Hills. Human prehistory in the Black Hills now begins.

3

Black Hills Ice Age

When the blade of "Porky" Hanson's bulldozer sliced into a scattering of white bones and tusks on a hillside at the south edge of Hot Springs, South Dakota, in June 1974, he suspected he may have stumbled onto something significant. He stopped and called his son Dan, then a college student at nearby Chadron State, and Phil Anderson, the land developer. Based on Dan's conviction that this might be an important paleontology site, Anderson deferred construction until Larry Agenbroad, a geology teacher at Chadron State College, could render a scientific judgment on the discovery.

Agenbroad, who was working on a mammoth kill site in Arizona at the time, sent his close associate, Jim Mead, along with a crew of six excavators to examine the bones. Agenbroad and Mead quickly confirmed its value as a mammoth site that they hoped would provide an intimate view into the Black Hills Ice Age.

A 20,000-square-foot building now covers the site where at least forty-five Columbian mammoths perished in the mire of a warm water sinkhole. The Hot Springs Mammoth Site, it turned out, was a natural trap akin in its own way to the famous La Brea Tar Pits of southern California. Like La Brea with its remains of extinct mammals, the Hot Springs site offered a unique window into the late Pleistocene.

The Pleistocene epoch began about 2 million years ago and was characterized by a series of relatively rapid and repeated warm to cold climatic fluctuations. Oxygen isotopes taken from the shells of marine foraminifera indicate that at least twenty major episodes of climatic fluctuations occurred during this period. These fluctuations are most often depicted as at least seven major glacial periods, each followed by an interglacial period of warmth.

The last full glacial period began about 22,000 years ago with a warming trend that started about 18,000 years ago. The post glacial period of "real warming," known as the Holocene or present period, followed the complete decline of glacial activity and began about 10,000 years ago. Together, the epochs of the Pleistocene and the Holocene make up the Quaternary, the fourth major period of evolutionary life. The end of the Pleistocene, 10,000 years ago, is marked not only by sustained global warming, but also by the extinction of some thirty species of Ice Age megafauna.

Sometime during the last glacial extension, the continental paleotemperature of North America was at its coldest. Huge glacial ice sheets, many thousands of feet thick, compressed, spread, and slid down from the Arctic forming massive lobes and outlying tongues of ice across the North American continent.

In South Dakota, the ice sheets extended as far west as the Missouri River, a stream that would eventually be created by the glacier's melt water runoff. From the edge of the great ice mass west to the Black Hills there stretched a vast grassland steppe composed predominately of coarse tufts of grass, sedges, and herbaceous plants. It was probably a vast mosaic of open prairie, spruce forest, and bog land where for much of the year a cold wind howled unobstructed for hundreds of miles.

Pollen evidence taken from the mammoth sinkhole sediments by researchers records only shrub forms of willow and birch along with grasses, sage, sedges, and wild roses. These indicators suggest that 26,000 years ago the Black Hills was an open landscape without trees, resembling in many aspects a high Arctic tundra.

Winters during the last great extension of glacial ice were as cold or slightly colder than today while summers were short and cool. Mammalian evidence suggests that this vast grassland steppe, at least in the early stages of the Ice Age, provided more diverse and complex local habitats on a grander scale than what presently exists in the Holocene.

On what is sometimes referred to as the Mammoth Steppe, which covered most of the northern half of the world that was free from ice, there roamed horses, deer, bison, camels, musk-ox, caribou, moose, saiga, woolly rhinos, sloths, wapiti, sheep, weasels, black-footed ferrets, lemmings, shrews, voles, ground squirrels, prairie dogs, lions, hyenas, badgers, wolves, foxes, giant short-faced bears, and the great mammoths.

Columbian mammoths, the largest members of the elephant family, crossed over the Bering land bridge from Asia into North America sometime during the early Pleistocene. Adult Columbians weighed ten tons, stood ten to fourteen feet high at the shoulders and grew a pair of impressive ivory tusks that averaged twelve feet in length from the base to the tip.

To maintain their enormous size, they consumed an average of three hundred to five hundred pounds of forage, mostly rough grasses, per day. They ground up this tough, abrasive forage on four longitudinally arranged molars (two on each side of the jaw) which grew like a conveyer belt throughout their lifetime. Once the forage was masticated, it passed in their huge cecum and large hindgut intestine where microbes fermented the food, making the nutrients available for the elephant's absorption. Their simple, non-ruminant, fermentation digestive system allowed the mammoth to quickly process a high proportion of low-quality food.

Male mammoths where generally one-fifth to one-third larger than the females. Like their modern African elephant cousins, the females probably reached sexual maturity at twelve and the males a couple of years later. Reproduction was slow as females remained pregnant for two years and did not mate for another two years following the birth of their nursing calf. Both genders could expect an average life span of sixty-five years, although females tended to live longer for a variety of reasons having to do with the fact that the males experienced periods of high hormonal stress to their bodies accompanied with their sex drive and whereupon sexual maturity driven from the security of the maternal herd. This is a significant element to the story, for researchers hypothesize that most of the elephants trapped in the sinkhole were sub-adult males.

The mammoth site sinkhole was formed in the red clay of the Spearfish formation. This formation, which completely encircles the Black Hills, contains many locally thick, white lenses of highly soluble sedimentary evaporite deposits (gypsum/anhydrite).

Up warping and subsequent erosion of the Spearfish formation progressively exposed the older rocks to water infiltration which in various locales selectively dissolved the evaporite units producing karst cavities of all types and sizes throughout the Red Valley.

The mammoth site sinkhole is situated in the Spearfish formation just above the Minnelusa formation. The Minnelusa is a major Black

Hills aquifer. At this juncture, the Minnelusa once served as part of a prehistoric Fall River terrace which once carried a substantial flow of water. Whenever the river flooded, the water table would rise up into the Spearfish formation, effectively dissolving the evaporites which, in turn, created a large cavity. When the water table in the Minnelusa fell below the old Fall River terrace, hydrostatic support was reduced, and the weak, unstable cavity ultimately caved-in leaving a breccia pipe or sinkhole.

The mammoth sinkhole has another interesting twist. In the southern Black Hills there are a handful of large, warm-water, artesian springs that flow all year. Twenty-six thousand years ago, a vigorous, artesian-pressured spring found its way up into the collapsed cavity of the mammoth sinkhole. It was a strongly charged spring that created a pond that has been estimated to have been a maximum of fifteen feet deep. The spring's discharge deepened the pond floor and under-cut the relatively steep northeast side of the sink, creating a short interval of rapid wall erosion. This interval of erosion was followed by a period of pond sedimentation build-up, laying the natural elemental foundation for a trap.

With the natural trap set for mammoths, the scenario may have gone something like this: Ice Age winter; ambient air temperature is a minus ten degrees Fahrenheit. Surrounded by a low incline, steep on one side but shallow on the other, a large pond, filled with warm vaporizing water, beckons to cold and exhausted mammoths.

The water, which never freezes even in the coldest of arctic blasts, keeps the sides of the slick, red clay pond lush with a luxuriant mat of thick, green grasses. It is an oasis in the deep freeze of winter. Able to travel faster alone, young, single, half-starved, sub-adult males gravitate around the steaming warmth of the pool.

These adolescent males are at the most vulnerable periods in their life. Following sexual maturity, their female natal groups have driven them out on their own to live alone or in small, transitory bachelor bands. The young males have had relatively little experience on their own dealing with environmental stresses. Now, without the protection of the matriarchal herd and the guidance of the older, slower moving cows, many with nursing calves, the bachelor males are most vulnerable to predation and disastrous mistakes.

The warm spring exerts a tremendous attraction. A young, inexperienced male overcomes his reluctance to approach it and moves slowly into the water to quench his thirst, enjoy its warmth, and feed from the green grass slopes. In the pond he soon realizes that he must either swim or risk sinking knee-deep into the muck of the pool. At the edge of the pool he struggles to turn and free his front leg. As he does so with difficulty, he places his weight on his three other legs which become more deeply entrenched in the mud.

The shallow side of pond where he entered, while not steep, is treacherously slimy and greasy for a four-ton elephant whose movements are graviportal. Unlike most large mammals, he cannot simply throw or shift his weight forward. He must move his center of gravity as a unit; if one foot is ensnared, he simply cannot move. Feeling trapped, he trumpets a distress call that sends a shiver of panic through the group of elephants gathering at the pool's edge. They respond by coming closer to him. Another wanders into the water in a rescue attempt to push him free, only to become equally mired.

Other mammoths arrive to answer the distress call extending their trunks in a vain effort to touch the trapped duo while staying clear of the slippery mud, but there is nothing they can do except witness the young males' agony and dilemma. A late-arriving old female matriarch trumpets a warning to all others to stay back. Young cows hold their curious calves away from the pond's edge with their great trunks while other young and old males stand wild-eyed, watching the frantic struggle for life in the pond.

This scene may last for days until the once strong, trapped elephants become feeble from exhaustion and starvation. Finally, the struggle is over. The great beasts finally lie down and probably drown. Their huge, rotting corpses leave a horrendous stench repulsing the mammoth herds while attracting a host of avian and mammalian scavengers.

In a while, if the winter is particularly severe, the scenario may repeat itself again. This time with an aged male mammoth nearing the end of his life. He is arthritic and bone-weary. His teeth are badly worn and he has difficulty moving and masticating the tons of dried grass needed to maintain his strength and survive another winter. Possessing an excellent memory, he knows well the treachery of the warm pool, for elephants with their large brains are among the most intelligent of all the wild creatures ever evolved, possessing an even temperament, long memories, and a marked reluctance to panic and run. Yet he is starving and sick, and there, on the slick slope is soft, green grass. He moves into the pond, struggles briefly and succumbs.

For at least one, and perhaps two or even three centuries, mammoths periodically enter the sinkhole where all are doomed, and none escape. After three centuries the artesian spring ceases to flow, and the pond eventually filles completely with sediment and bones. Over time, the sediment layers dry and harden into a large plug that is actually harder than the surrounding, relatively softer, red shale. Wind and water eventually erode the soft shale creating a reverse topographic feature. What was once a sinkhole has now eroded into a small hill that awaits the arrival of a bulldozer and paleo-detectives from another era.

On the mid-July morning I arrived to stand on the edge of that small hill, the Black Hills could not be more different from what the mammoths experienced here 26,000 years earlier. The air, thick and heavy with humidity, carries the buzz of lawnmowers cropping rank green, irrigated bluegrass. The asphalt parking lot at 9 AM is generously sprinkled with cars and camper trucks bearing a wide assortment of out-of-state license plates. There is not the remotest hint that four-ton mammoths could ever have lived anywhere near what is now a steep, arid, sparsely vegetated hillside.

Looking southeast from the Hot Springs Mammoth Site's front lawn, the hillside has been cut by a side drainage of the Fall River. Beyond the drainage in the far distance, the ridge of the pine-clad Seven Sisters range bears the bristle of fire snags from the summer fires of 1985. What a difference 25,000 years makes stretching from the height of Wisconsin glaciation to the warmth of the Holocene.

It has been at least ten years since I first visited the mammoth site on a cold spring day in March. Back then, only a part of the sinkhole was covered by a temporary structure constructed of two by fours, rough plywood, and heavy mylar plastic. The cobbled together shelter, resembling a large outdoor oxygen tent, violently flapped and shook when the wind blew.

The change to the center is remarkable and bears no resemblance to that first makeshift shelter. Inside the front lobby are handsomely done murals that depict Ice Age Black Hills landscapes. There is also an impressive, fully articulated model of a standing Columbian mammoth. Behind glass doors that lead to the sinkhole site proper are more exhibits, an interpretive slide show, and an opportunity to take a staff-guided tour around the site.

During my excursion through the dig, Jim Mead, who functions as one of the site's co-investigators along with Larry Agenbroad, dis-

cussed the excavation findings and explained some of the finer sub-
tleties of the site regarding variations in the sinkhole pond's sedimentation. Clearly exposed in cross-section cuts of the clay sedimentation
near the middle of the quarry are stratified bands that alternate from
dark to light. Sedimentologists believe these bands, known as varves
or rhythmites, represent the periodic seasonal pulsing of the pond's
water. The light aspect of the wider varves are composed of oxidized
Spearfish formation sediments which the warm artesian pond water
reduced to a brownish color. These light bands represent one summer
season's accumulation of sediment while the much thinner, compressed dark bands represent a winter's accumulation.

The combination of one light and one dark band makes up a single varve which represents an entire year's accumulation of sediments. Throughout the sinkhole site the varves dip into the center of
the quarry indicating that everything tended to move and collapse
into the middle of the sinkhole pond.

If all the varves could be counted, it would provide a good indication of the time interval it took to fill the pond. That is impossible,
however, because the first twenty feet of cover material was not surveyed during its removal. The present depth of the quarry, including
that first twenty feet, is thirty-five feet. Mead believes there may be
twenty more feet to go before the bottom of the sinkhole is reached.
He believes the quarry in which remnants of at least forty-five mammoths have already uncovered to date, still holds the remains of fifty
or sixty more elephants. His best guess is that this sinkhole was dangerous to elephants for at least two centuries.

In various cross sections of the stratified varves, there frequently
occurs what appears to have been a hole about the width of a cedar
fence post punched down through the evenly layered sediments.
Along the sides and above the "post hole" indentations are swirls of
laminated varves that disrupt the otherwise uniform, horizontal sedimentary stratigraphy. Mead explained that these swirling, sedimentary disruptions around and above the "holes" are mute evidence to
the locations where a mammoth had managed to extricate a leg up and
out of the sucking muck.

We walked around the perimeter of the sinkhole which, outlined
by the red clay of the Spearfish formation, is easily discernible from
the tan, cinnamon-colored sediments of the sink. The evidence of
heavy sand grains and erosive cutting action on the northeast wall of

the dig indicates the area of the main spring head where the pond was deepest and the water velocity the greatest. The sedimentary evidence indicates that the south and west side of the pond had two small spring feeders and was the quiet, shallower environment where the mammoths most likely waded into the pool.

At the bottom of the sinkhole quarry, you look up at a fifteen-foot wall of stratified pond sediments filled with a mass of mammoth bones and skulls in various stages of exhumation. The bones present themselves in every direction imaginable. Mead likes to view this contorted welter of bones, tusks, and skulls as an enormous, three-dimensional jigsaw puzzle.

One curious aspect of this mammoth bone puzzle is the evidence of an inordinate number of single tusks that have turned up near the shallower outer edge of the pond. Mead postulates that as the sinus cavities of the dead elephant skulls filled up with gas, they detached from the skeleton and floated to the surface. Many of these skulls eventually lodged in the pond shallows and lost their tusks. Due to the tusks' high tendency to roll, coupled with the powerful thrust of artesian springs, an inordinate number of them washed up on the highest, shallowest areas of the pond. Mead expects to find a number of tuskless skulls buried deeper in the sediments as the dig proceeds.

To date, the excavators have recovered ninety-one mammoth tusks as well as a tooth from each of the following: camel, wolf, peccary, and coyote. Mead believes these teeth were probably washed into the hole and do not represent trapped animals. One animal however that seems to have been a victim of the trap was a giant short-faced bear. The presence of this extinct, enormous Ice Age bear that stood 5.5 feet high on all fours (a grizzly stands at 3.5 feet) and measured almost 10 feet in length (a grizzly is 6 feet 7 inches) is somewhat of a different puzzle. It is possible that the omnivorous bear, attracted to the sinkhole by the cries of an entrapped mammoth or perhaps by the odor of a decaying carcass, became a victim himself. Once within the pool, this scavenger-hunter may have become injured by a thrashing elephant and subsequently drowned or was crushed into the mud. It is just one of the mysteries of this site that both Mead and Larry Agenbroad like to ponder.

Agenbroad, who heads the Quaternary Studies Program at Northern Arizona University, recalled the time he spent in 1974 sitting on that "pile of dirt" and bones wondering what he should do with it, not knowing the mysteries of the bear and mammoths it held. He did know that it was probably a one-of-kind site and a once-in-a-lifetime opportunity to study mammoths. He believed it merited a better fate than an alleyway and a basement for an apartment condominium and decided to make and effort to save it.

He spoke to the people of Hot Springs and presented his vision of developing the site as a world-class research center and museum. In the end it was the senior citizens of Hot Springs that generated the funds to buy the site which Phil Anderson generously agreed to sell at his cost with only one stipulation: that all the bones stay on the site. Anderson believed, like Agenbroad, "that the value of the bones is here in their original context." Over nearly two decades and under Agenbroad's guidance and support, the mammoth site, against all odds, has grown and prospered to become a world-class paleontology site, museum, and research center.

Now in his fifties, Agenbroad is a man of wide experience and education with a rural western background, all of which has served him well in his various endeavors as a geologist, engineer, educator, archaeologist, paleontologist, and mammoth site director. His integrity as a scientist, along with his openness and passion for his work, pervades the site and is felt and shared everywhere on all levels. He always seems accessible and moves throughout the complex visiting with earth watch volunteers, gift shop clerks, foreign scientists, ranchers, writers, and tourists. But first and foremost he is a teacher who likes to share what he knows about mammoths.

In the afternoon, sitting on a bench in front of the museum while sprinkles of rain drift over head, Agenbroad talked about his family and his connection to South Dakota. "My father," he said, "was born and raised in Huron, South Dakota. When he left home, he moved to Belle Fourche, South Dakota, to ranch and [was], ultimately, starved out." Agenbroad recounted how the same thing happened to his father in Montana and California. Eventually his father homesteaded successfully south of Nampa, Idaho, where Agenbroad grew up on a farm/ranch operation.

Agenbroad began his professional career as a geologist and an engineer working in the Permian Basin "oil patch" of Texas and southeastern New Mexico. He also spent some time working with underground nuclear explosions before deciding to go back to school and earn graduate degrees in archaeology and geology. While working as an archaeologist in the Southwest, he began to develop an interest in the paleo-hunters who roamed that country at the end of the Ice Age and successfully hunted and killed mammoth elephants using spears and atlatls. In the mid-1950s, he was working as an archaeologist in Cochise County, Arizona, at the Murray Springs mammoth kill site and at the Lehner Ranch kill site. Both sites were places where people and Ice Age animals had congregated for millennia. Both sites also produced clear evidence, in the form of spear points lodged in the bones of elephants, that mammoths had been killed and butchered here by hunters 12,000 years ago. The Murray site produced eight dead elephants and Lehner thirteen.

These hunters, known commonly as the Clovis people from an earlier artifact type site discovered near Clovis, New Mexico, were, according to Agenbroad, well adapted and highly skilled in hunting Pleistocene megafauna, particularly the mammoth. He envisions them as the first explorers to successfully penetrate and populate the New World.

What stuck in Agenbroad's mind and rankled him as a field archaeologist was the discarding of a perfectly articulated mammoth skeleton in Arizona once it had been exhumed and examined. "That mammoth skeleton was the largest one I have ever seen," he said recalling his feelings of that dig long ago. "It was just left and discarded like so many other ones in the field." Agenbroad felt it was a disgrace to the animal, remarking that, "They (archaeologists) just left these magnificent animal [remains] in the field—animals that had fed humans." He believed that "we were not giving them their due."

It was an epiphany of sorts when Agenbroad switched his focus from the hunter to the prey and decided to learn more about mammoth evolution and the cause for their ultimate extinction. How could these large, intelligent creatures have failed to survive, he wondered.

He searched for a plausible answer through the geological and archaeological record of Pleistocene North America. His theory hinged, finally, on the arrival of hominids on the new continent. Man in the New World, he believes, sent "a shock wave" through the populations of the large Ice Age animals, particularly the mammoths, which because of their intelligence and size had never had to contend with any serious predators. Agenbroad believes that the Ice Age hunters proved so adept at hunting immature and young adult mammoths as to virtually eliminate them and ultimately perform the coup de grace on a species probably already under intense environmental stress with the oncoming of the warmer Holocene period. It is a theory that is gaining acceptance as evidence of more large mammoth kill sites are discovered.

Agenbroad, who continues as the principle investigator at the Hot Springs Mammoth Site along with Jim Mead, is convinced this is one the best sites for studying mammoths in the world. He bases his belief on the fact that many of the elephant remains contain tongue supports that normally would not be preserved. This is because the elephants at the mammoth site stayed where they died as opposed to other sites where disarticulated remnants of an animal may have washed down a stream for a great distance before being buried naturally in sediment.

The natural trap at Hot Springs, with its large number of relatively intact specimens, makes it a statistically valid representation of mammoths in terms of measuring for comparison all the physical characteristics of this animal. It provides, according to Agenbroad, "a match of data beyond a probability of chance."

All of the mammoth data and much of the bone preservation is done in the preparation lab adjacent and behind the main museum. Earlier that morning, I watched Judy Davids squirt down mammoth bones with an ethanol butvar mixture. It is her job to seal coat all the bones with the butvar as a preservative against oxygenation. Formerly, mammoth bones at the site were treated with a thick, exterior coat of a shellac-like substance known as glyptol. It gave the bones the slick, semi-gloss shine of varnish. Unfortunately, after a period of time, the varnish cracked, exposing the interior cancelleous bone to air and allowing it to rot. All bones prepared this way will ultimately have to be redone.

The prehistoric bones at the mammoth site are extremely delicate since they have not been mineralized, calcified, or petrified. Technically, they are not fossils but actual bones. The warm water in the sinkhole simply leached away the protein and calcium in the bone leaving only a thin, fragile fossil shell lacking any kind of elasticity. Exposure to air breaks these ancient bones down rapidly.

Over the last eighteen years, fifteen hundred bones have been removed from the site and remain in storage at the lab. Since 1974, about one thousand of those bones have been prepared. There are another thousand bones presently exposed that Davids periodically squirts down. "They only dig here two weeks in the summer every year," she said, "because it takes me the rest of the year to prepare what they have unearthed."

Back inside at the quarry I catch up with Mead again. A young volunteer who has been screening sediments all morning from a nearby cave for snails and animal bone fragments tells him that she believes she has also unearthed some prehistoric cultural material. It means her work may have to stop until an archaeological survey is done.

Mead is surveying other nearby caves in the southern Black Hills to gain more information on the presence of flora and fauna from which he hopes to more accurately reconstruct plant communities and environments during the Wisconsin Ice Age period. He hypothesizes, as many scientists have, that there should probably be closed spruce forests occurring in the Ice Age Black Hills. Pine and spruce pollen, he explains, can travel one hundred miles, but to date he has yet to discover any paleo-botanical data confirming this at the mammoth site and he wonders now if the Black Hills was simply a stressful environment consisting only of grassland steppe/tundra or is it just a lack of pollen in the mammoth site sedimentary layer fossil record.

All the pollen evidence Mead has gathered at the mammoth site indicates that the southern Black Hills Ice Age environment was probably a grassland steppe consisting of sage, roses, sedges, and various species of ranunculus (buttercups) along with dwarf willows and birch. Megafauna are poor indicators of change and it is the small plants and mollusks that tell the story of temperature and climate change.

Twenty-six thousand years ago the Black Hills were located midway between two large ice masses. One hundred and sixty miles east, a huge lobe of ice stood stagnating at the edge of the Missouri River; one hundred and fifty miles west, the Big Horns were completely ice capped down to six thousand feet, at which point a steppe tundra with clusters of dense limber pine forests began. From the pollen evidence to date, it appears that the entire country from the eastern side of the Big Horns to the thick ice wall east of the Missouri was grassland.

Focusing in tighter on the immediate mammoth site area, screen washing of quarry sediments has turned up two species of snails that can live in a warm body of water between the temperatures of ninety-five to one hundred degrees Fahrenheit, indicating the warm sinkhole pond water was decidedly here. If the water was cool, Mead said there would be evidence of between ten and fifteen other existing varieties of mollusks. The scarcity of mollusk species is consistent with a warm body of water and the circumstantial pollen evidence indicates that the mammoth site was in fact a warm-water oasis in a grassland plant community.

By the beginning of the Holocene, ice sheets had retreated well back to the north where they remain today surrounding the earth's north pole. The Aleutian low, which dominated the last ice invasion, moved farther north and was replaced by the milder Bermuda high which ushered in a substantially warmer climate. With the warming, summer precipitation increased and plants like the ponderosa pine were able to migrate up from Mexico and establish forests in the Black Hills that in turn attracted their associated fauna of birds, tree squirrels, and chipmunks.

The warming also had other effects. The two dozen or so species of megafauna that flourished on the grassland steppe and survived the relatively cold, wet Pleistocene began to overheat. Their large size, hairy bodies, and layers of insulating fat, once necessary insulation and protection from intense cold, produced heat stress as well as other serious repercussions that may have affected ovulation and ultimately reproduction.

Due to rapidly accelerating changes in climate, plant communities shifted, changed, and disappeared. Large herbivores had to contend with a host of new biotic mosaics and patterns or perish. The biological options for each species of Ice Age megafauna were clear: either migrate with their biotic niches or adapt quickly to the new ones. Some species like the saiga, emigrants from Siberia to North America, turned around in Alaska and returned to their native home on the Eurasian steppe. Others, like the American horse and camel, abandoned their native continent and survived in Eurasia. Caribou and muskox retreated to Ice Age tundra pockets in the far north on both continents.

Other animal species, like the bison and the beaver, relied on genetic variability and selectively survived as considerably smaller subspecies by down sizing body mass. The Ice Age woolly rhino of Asia and the mammoth of both continents disappeared from the biological record forever. Their disappearance, particularly the mammoths, is strongly linked to the carnivorous appetites of hunting humans who appear on the North American continent at the same time.

Starting five thousand years ago and developing over the next millennia, the present Black Hills biotic community evolved into a mixed, coniferous pine-spruce-aspen forest with an understory of drought and fire tolerant prairie shrubs, forbs, and grasses. Deer, elk, pronghorn, and a smaller sub-species version of the prehistoric *Bison occidentalis*, *Bison bison*, began to flourish on the northern plains and Black Hills along with a host of carnivorous cats and dogs that evolved to prey on them.

The on-going research at the Hot Springs Mammoth Site continues to provide a fascinating window on the animal creatures of that frozen, ice-bound time who flourished and died out during one of the most traumatic evolutionary periods in the Black Hills.

4

A Geology Road Log

On the campus mall of the South Dakota School of Mines and Technology, there is a small plaza shaded by an old American elm. The plaza is laid out in right triangular fashion adjacent to the sidewalk that leads from the mall to the Geology Museum. At the apex of the plaza's right angle, there is a large, built-in planter flanked by two comfortable wooden park benches. The floor of the plaza and the face of the planter are constructed of flat, reddish brown and gray slabs of Black Hills schist. Set on the face of the planter is a bronze plaque that reads:

DR. J. PAUL GRIES
PROFESSOR OF GEOLOGY
1936–1986

EDUCATOR
GEOLOGIST
FRIEND

"It was an honor and a nice way to be remembered," Dr. Gries tells me when I mention the plaza to him in his campus office which he still maintains as geology professor emeritus. For a half century, Gries has studied and taught Black Hills geology. At eighty-one, he is still active as a consultant and considered to be one of the foremost authorities on Black Hills hydrology and mining geology. His hobby is looking at old mines and historical sites in the Black Hills. On this particular morning in late June, he agreed to take me on a field trip and share some of the lore and knowledge he has acquired over his lifetime.

Our Black Hills field trip took an entire day and began early in the morning on the campus of the South Dakota School of Mines and Technology located on the southeast side of Rapid City. I chronicled our day-long journey through Black Hills geologic time with stops and mile markers for those who might wish to follow our path. Our trip begins at mile 0.0 on the campus of the School of Mines at J. P. Gries Plaza.

Leave the campus and turn left (west) on East Main (South Dakota 79); turn right (north) on East Boulevard at the post office and proceed to East Omaha (South Dakota 44) and turn left (west) again. As you proceed west, on your right (north) is the broad green meadow of Memorial Park along with the channel of Rapid Creek. You are driving over relatively recent alluvium deposited by Rapid Creek over the last five thousand years.

Crossing the intersection of West Boulevard, you enter a wide water gap cut into the Dakota Hogback by Rapid Creek. At mile 2.2, enter the parking lot off to the right of West Omaha. The Dakota Hogback forms the outer rim of the Black Hills uplift and rises several hundred feet above the surrounding area. The hogback separates the Red Valley just to the west from the plains proper to the east. The hogback was created when the Black Hills dome was thrust up from the surrounding plains about 60 million years ago and has been eroding down since that time. The Black Hills are the farthest outlying segment of a great mid-continental uplift known as the Larimide orogeny. This orogeny also elevated the great Rocky Mountain cordillera 150 miles farther to the west.

Geographically, the Black Hills, as viewed from a satellite from five miles up, appear as an elliptical dome measuring 125 miles long and 65 miles wide. The oldest rocks lie in the center and consist in part of a huge mass or batholith of granite that was cooled eight to ten miles below the earth's surface and then gradually pushed upward. This massive core of granite, referred to as the Black Hills crystalline core, makes up the eroded outcrops of Harney Peak, the Needles, the Cathedral Spires, Bear Mountain, and Mount Rushmore.

The entire crystalline core area was once covered with many thick layers of sedimentary rock. These formations include from oldest to youngest, the Deadwood, Englewood, Madison (Paha Sapa), Minnelusa, and Minnekahta. Prior to the uplifting of the Hills, an additional 3,500 feet of sediment was present above the Minnekahta. These sedimentary formations eroded off the Black Hills over the ensuing millennia, exposing the granite. Today they are present as remnant layers at the edge of the Black Hills and farther out on the plains.

In Black Hills geology, there are five more or less distinct sections, each with its own distinctive geologic and geomorphic characteristics. From the center of the Black Hills outward they are:

1. The central core of granite and metamorphic rock
2. The Madison limestone plateau outside the central core
3. The Red Valley encircling the outer edge of the Black Hills
4. The Dakota Hogback encircling the Red Valley
5. The Tertiary belt of intrusive laccothic mountains in the northern edge of the Black Hills

If you divide the Black Hills dome in half, east and west, the dip of the east side is much greater than the west. This has resulted in more erosion taking place on the east side of the Hills, leaving more rivers flowing in that direction and more deeply incised canyons cut through the sedimentary formations. The west hemisphere of the Black Hills is still primarily covered with Madison limestone. The part of the Dakota Hogback directly to the north, just across the creek, is known locally as "M" hill or on the quad maps as Cowboy Hill. The part of the hogback directly behind you to the south is called "Hangman's" or Dinosaur Hill. On Cowboy Hill the sedimentary beds of Lakota sandstone tilt up on the west and dip to the east away from the dome as a result of the initial up thrust of the Black Hills dome. This type of long, low ridge with a relatively steep face or escarpment on one side and a long, gentle slope on the other is geographically referred to as a "cuesta," from the Spanish meaning shoulder or sloping land.

The tributaries of the Rapid Creek basin begin high on the west side of the Black Hills draining a large section of the western limestone plateau. Rapid Creek and nearby Boxelder Creek have cut a series of deep, winding canyons through the sedimentary formations.

Here, located on the first terrace of the Rapid Creek flood plain are the remnants of a gallery forest composed primarily of cottonwood, willow, boxelder, green ash, and American elm. Along the creek is a dense thicket of willow. This groomed flood plain was a residential area until the night of June 9, 1972, when a fourteen-inch downpour farther up Rapid Creek created a flash flood which swept many homes and businesses out of the gap. The storm covered an eight-hundred-square-mile area taking in large parts of Pennington, Meade, and Lawrence counties. The National Oceanic and Atmospheric Administration reported it in their "Storm Data and Unusual Weather Phenomena" annals for June 1972, as follows:

> Heavy rains of up to 14 inches over the east slope of the northern Black Hills causes flash flooding in the area. Much of the area from Keystone to Sturgis received 6 inches or more of rain which fell in a period of 4 hours or less. Most of the damage occurred in Rapid City but other areas along the creeks that drain the east slopes of the northern Black Hills also suffered flood damage. Damage was compounded by the collapse of Canyon Lake dam located just above Rapid City and caused a wall of water to rush down Rapid Creek through the city.
>
> Other creeks along which extensive damage was reported were: Bear Butte Creek which flows through Sturgis; Battle Creek and Grizzly Creek which flow through Keystone; Spring Creek which flows through Rockerville; Boxelder Creek and Little Elk Creek which flow near Piedmont.

The report added up the morbid statistics of the night, noting there were 237 deaths with 5 missing and presumed dead. Nearly 3,000 people were injured, 750 homes were destroyed with major damage to 2,261, along with well over 1,000 cars completely demolished beyond repair. Following the disaster, the city council re-zoned the flood plain as green space to avert any future flood disasters and named it Memorial Park in commemoration of the deceased.

Proceed west to the intersection of Mountain View and West Omaha. Here, West Omaha changes into West Chicago. Stay on West Chicago, cross Rapid Creek to the intersection of Deadwood Avenue. At this point you are climbing out of the Rapid Creek valley and onto the red Spearfish formation also known as the Red Valley.

Rapid Creek now bends away to the south and west. Over millennia the creek has cut, spread out, and cut again, creating a meandering maze of alluvial terraces and benches. On the north side of the road, the red shale of the Spearfish formation can be seen exposed around the tank farm. The white chunks of rock laying in and around the clay are gypsum.

In the distance to the northwest many quarry operations are mining the Minnekahta limestone sedimentary layer. The Minnekahta is the uppermost layer of the Black Hills dome proper. It is a massive, gray limestone that was deposited in the late Permian period about 250 million years ago and ranges from 30 to 50 feet thick. The younger Spearfish formation was deposited above it in the Triassic period and ranges between 250 to 700 feet in thickness. As a general rule of thumb on this geologic journey, the closer a formation is to the center of the Black Hills, the greater its relative age.

Proceed down West Chicago past Sturgis Road (I-90 alternate) to mile 4.8 (44th Street). Turn right (north) down 44th for three blocks to Wilderness Park and the old city springs. Directly to the north through the tree thicket and below the parking lot is a low, moist depression covered with sedge and bulrushes.

This was the site of City Springs. A century ago Rapid City derived most of its water from a group of artesian springs that poured forth from this spot. Dr. Gries noted here that the Minnekahta formation lies just to the north and described the park area as an "anticline that has created a sharp, little double fold in the Red Valley (Spearfish formation) with the Minnekahta peeking through. The rocks are broken (fractured) all the way down," he said, "which allowed the water to come up."

The springs flowed until 1988, when the last one dried up during the fierce drought of that summer. In 1990, the spring started to run a little again but went dry leaving just the low damp area below the old weir choked in bulrushes.

Return back to West Chicago and turn right (west) on to South Canyon Road. At mile 6.4 you leave the city limits and South Canyon Road becomes Pennington County Road 234. At this point it is locally referred to as the Nemo Road. Here, just beyond the city limits the road enters South Canyon.

On the right (north) is the Minnelusa formation recognized by its wavy appearance and its yellow to red cross-bedded sandstone and limestone. The wavy stratigraphy was created as gypsum layers or lenses dissolved during the weathering process. The Minnelusa formation is an important aquifer in the Black Hills transporting water over great distances via its porous sandstone and fractures.

Proceed up South Canyon to mile 7.5. The mountainside on the left and right was burned in 1988 by the Westberry Trails Fire. The fire was set by an arsonist. The outcrops up the canyon are Minnelusa. At the top of the ridge the road climbs out of the South Canyon drainage and drops down into the Boxelder Creek drainage.

Mile 11.2 is the Boxelder Creek bridge. To the west and to the east, the smooth, red canyon walls have been carved out of the Minnelusa by Boxelder Creek. The top of the canyon wall tends more to sandstone while the lower canyon wall tends more to limestone and dolomite. The top of the ridge affords an excellent view to the east of the canyon wall.

Leaving Boxelder Canyon, the road travels over the top of the Madison or Paha Sapa formation. This is a massive, light-colored limestone. The greatest share of it lies underground and covers a vast area running nearly the whole width of the great plains from western North Dakota south into the Texas Panhandle. It is one of the most important aquifers in the West. In the Black Hills, all the major underground caves and caverns are located in the Madison.

Mile 13.6 is a historical grave. It lies in a meadow to the west of the highway just across a barbed-wire fence. The grave is that of James A. King who served with General Custer in his 1874 Reconnaissance Expedition of the Black Hills. The marker commemorates King as a private in Troop H, 7th Regiment Calvary, born 1849, and died on the morning of August 14, 1874.

At mile 15.3, located on the north (right) side of the highway, is the Custer Gap pull off. The gap appears as a narrow ravine in the north canyon wall of the white, buff-colored Madison. It is actually a huge fracture in the formation.

Custer's expedition camped in the Boxelder Valley, just above the gap, on August 12, 1874. The expedition had followed the southeasterly course of Boxelder Creek from present-day Nemo. On the next morning, August 13, Lieutenant Godfrey, with an escort, was dispatched several miles down the creek to determine its course and to ascertain his position from bearings in relation to Bear Butte and Harney Peak. At 2 PM that same day, the main party broke camp, crossed Boxelder Creek at the gap, and proceeded up the narrow gulch. Some of the wagons reportedly capsized while navigating the tight ravine.

This location where Custer turned north was later positively identified in 1901 by Dr. Cleophas O'Harra, one of the first presidents of the South Dakota School of Mines. According to Gries, O'Harra reported finding rope burns on the rocks and trees on top of the gap twenty-seven years after the expedition had hauled their wagons through it to get up on the high ground of the Madison formation.

The Madison formation here is between four hundred and five hundred feet thick. Near the mouth of the gap an old beaver check dam has created a shallow pool of clear water in Boxelder Creek. Just below the dam the stream splits into two channels. The first channel of water that flows over the dam immediately disappears into the bed of stream gravel.

The second channel flows a hundred yards farther over riffles and through a braided willow thicket. This channel feeds small, shallow pools which in the summer teem with minnows, water striders, and blue darner dragon flies before it, too, seeps without a trace into the stream bed. It is an odd and curious phenomena.

At the mouth of Custer Gap, Boxelder Creek is a vibrant, mountain stream that flows into a cool deep pool; two hundred yards below the gap it becomes a mud-stained, bone-dry, boulder-strewn stream bed. Such is the fate of most Black Hills streams and the insatiable thirst of the great Madison formation in dry years.

Dr. Gries noted that the Madison takes all the water it wants and then burps it back up in springs. The spring-fed streams after running a ways might disappear again into the stream gravel. Run-off water in the Black Hills is constantly circulating above and below the ground through a vast array of springs, stream channels, and caverns.

Henry Newton, in 1875, described the Black Hills as "an extremely well-watered country. Springs are found in almost every ravine. Nearly all the small head-branches of the creeks are running brooks of pure water and streams of considerable size and, but a few miles apart, drain this region, affording a constant and regular supply of water. . . ."

Unaware of the vast underground cavern system in the Madison, Newton was nonetheless aware that most of the water originating in the Black Hills disappeared before reaching the Red Valley and the foothills (hogback). He writes: "From the character of the geological formations outcropping in the foothills and along the edge of the plains, all the streams rising in the Black Hills sink in their beds and disappear before passing through the Carboniferous limestone (Madison formation), with the exception of Rapid Creek, which flows into the Cheyenne, and Spearfish and Redwater, which empty into the Belle Fourche." Two other perennial streams, Whitewood Creek which flows into the Belle Fourche and Fall River which flows into the Cheyenne, also manage to exit the Black Hills.

A number of years ago Dr. Gries conducted some dye experiments at the Custer Gap location. He poured a dye into the stream water and waited. It took an hour and eleven minutes for the dyed water to resurface in a spring in another drainage about a half mile away.

Other mysteries of Black Hills water come to mind. In the pre-white settlement days stories abounded about great booming noises in the summer that often emanated from the Black Hills. The Sioux were frightened of the noise and ascribed them to thunder beings while early pioneers were without clues as to their reason or occurrence.

The booms may have been the result of a vast, intense rush of water moving underground as might occur from a localized, spring downpour. Theoretically, a great force of run-off water would create enormous pressure as it moved from the surface into half-filled underground chambers of water. This rush and pressure of water would have created a forced explosion of air sounding a lot like thunder. Since the Black Hills are literally honeycombed by a maze of caves and caverns, the boom could have traveled for miles before surfacing at some distant location where the sun may have been shining gloriously.

The mysterious booming noises stopped shortly after the turn of the nineteenth century, probably for a number of reasons. At that time a great deal of underground water was beginning to be pumped, diverted,and drained from the aquifer, most notably by deep-shaft, hard-rock mining operations like Homestake's in Lead, South Dakota. Later, agriculture and other industries took a big share so that many artesian springs, once a source of abundant fresh water, permanently ceased to flow.

With the concerted effort by foresters to suppress forest fires and stimulate more production of timber in the 1920s, ponderosa pine was able to proliferate in great numbers—increasing their density and acreage by as much as 50 percent overall. This explosion of conifer trees also absorbed vast quantities of run-off once gulped and stored in the Madison. Finally, the climate on the northern plains, which by most indications appears to have been in a relatively dry cycle over the last century, has further aggravated the water situation.

So it breaks down something like this: water levels in the Black Hills aquifers and underground caverns are probably at all-time lows and by some indicators are still gradually dropping. The century has been one marked by relatively long-term heat and dryness with few occasional, massive downpours. Therefore, no water—no boom.

At the gap Dr. Gries recalled how the flood plain area appeared during the great June flash flood of 1972. He noted that the same massive downpour that flooded Rapid Creek also scoured Boxelder Creek. "There were large cottonwood trees growing here then (next to the creek)," he remarked. "When I came here after the flood a lot of them were 'barked-up'—had the bark beat off of them—to a height of twenty-eight feet. The highway department cut them all down," he said in some disgust, "so that the next time we have a flash flood the water can run even faster through here."

Mile 16.5 is again at a Boxelder Creek bridge. To the east, the canyon wall exhibits the buff Madison on top, the Englewood, which is the slope covered with vegetation, and the Deadwood formation at stream-cut level.

The Englewood is a pink to buff limestone formed 400 million years ago in the Devonian when the sea, high with suspended red mud particulates, inundated the Deadwood formation just below it. The Deadwood formation here is a purple and red sandstone that has been cemented together with a lot of "bubbles" caused, as in the Minnelusa, by the dissolution of other minerals once present in the layers.

Mile 17.9 is another stop at a Boxelder Creek bridge just past the Pennington-Meade county line. To the left, on the west side of the road, is an outcrop popular with geologists because it graphically shows the Cambrian Deadwood formation sitting on top of Precambrian Boxelder quartzite.

The Boxelder quartzite is about 2 billion years old and is tilted at a seventy-degree angle. Originally, it was horizontally laid down as sedimentary sandstone, then metamorphosed (compressed) into a fine-grained quartzite. Sometime, during the intervening one billion years, it was tilted.

On top of the Boxelder, laying in a horizontal fashion, is the Deadwood formation. The Deadwood, at 600 million years old, is the oldest recognizable sedimentary formation in the Black Hills and serves as "the floor" of the Cambrian, separating it from the twisted, metamorphic schists of the ancient Precambrian period.

For geologists, who have literally beaten a trail to the site, it is an outstanding record of the dramatic meeting of two ancient geologic eras. The lower—Precambrian, twisted and wild; the upper—Cambrian, even and level. It is a graphic record of earth forces beginning to settle down.

There are about "one billion years of pages missing here from the geologic register," Dr. Gries casually remarks as we relax in the shade of some scraggly pines and gaze at this record of geologic time. "The geology of the Black Hills is relatively straightforward," he explains, "until you get down into the Precambrian unconformity."

Unconformities in the discipline of stratigraphy are gaps in time. In the geologic history of North America there have been at least two dozen alternating sea invasions of the land, each lasting millions of years. Their deposition of sediments can be read as progressive epochal pages in the earth's crustal history. Down in the Precambrian basement of earth history, however, the pages have been compressed, twisted, and tilted, distorting their record so much as to make their story cryptic. Gries describes the Precambrian outcrops in the Black Hills as "a wild assortment of sedimentary and igneous rocks faulted all to hell." It is for this reason that he likes this geologic example of the very, very old meeting the truly ancient. "There are very few places where you can see it (the Deadwood) so graphically in contact with the Precambrian."

Mile 20.0 is the Steamboat Rock picnic grounds—so named because of a handsome butte just to the east of Boxelder Creek that must have caught someone's imagination as resembling a steamboat. Steamboat Rock, like the last stop, is a geologic classic. "It is," Dr. Gries says, "the best place to see each particular aspect of early Cambrian geology." Starting at the bottom of the butte at stream level, the dark rock is a sill (igneous intrusion) some three thousand feet thick. At the railroad grade level the sill, once basalt, has metamorphosed and weathered into a low-grade talc. Above the sill, laying in a horizontal formation is the Deadwood. Above the Deadwood, again sloping and hidden by pines and vegetation, is the Englewood. On top of the Englewood, capping the butte and distinguished by its typical, buff-white color is the Madison.

In the picnic grounds there is a large sign announcing a trail that goes up to the top. The sign notes that the trail is steep and rugged. From the sign, the trail leads down through a waist-high willow thicket to the creek. I picked my way across the creek, jumping from one smooth, flat stepping stone to another. A kingfisher chattered overhead and perched on a pine snag to overlook the water for minnows. On the other side of the creek, the trail climbs up a steep, gravelly embankment of talc to the old railroad grade. The bank is rank with poison ivy.

On the grade, the trail turns south (right) to a barbed-wire fence and follows the fence a short way up the slope. On the brow of the ridge, I climbed over the fence and followed a narrow path as it wound up the slope in the direction of the butte.

As the trail winds upwards it comes into contact with the red and purplish outcrops of the Deadwood formation. The color of the Deadwood here is indicative of a heavy concentration of iron. Near the top of the formation, I encountered canyon wrens flitting around the crevices. I also discovered one large crevice with evidence of a smoke patina on the ceiling, suggesting that it had been used at some point as an aboriginal rock shelter.

Above the Deadwood formation lays the upper Englewood which appears a pink to reddish limestone formation. Scattered about the steeply sloped surface of the Englewood are white limestone boulders. These boulders have eroded off the top of the Madison formation just above the Englewood and are slowly working their way down to Boxelder Creek.

Near the top of the Englewood, the trail vanishes. I continued to proceed around the west side of the butte following game trails, eventually picking my way up onto the buff-colored Madison. In the highest most inaccessible rock crevices of the Madison I found evidence of a few pack rat middens. The Black Hills are the farthest eastern range limit of this western mammal which is also known as the bushy-tailed wood rat. Their middens, which also serve as nests, are generally made of twigs and grass built in crevices and under rock ledges.

On the northwest edge of the butte I climbed up through a large crevice in the Madison which gave me access to the summit. Turning around to catch my breath and survey the country, I caught a fleeting glimpse of a pair of hawks performing aerial acrobatics in the strong northwest wind. The summit is as flat as it appears from the valley and covers a couple of acres of solid limestone rock. The soil is thin but supports a relative abundance of hardy vegetation.

The south and west edges of the butte, which catch the prevailing summer winds the longest and hardest, feature areas of smooth, wind-eroded, bare, white limestone. However, tiny fractures in the rock have very sharp, cutting edges.

The plants growing here along the western edge of the butte in the sunniest areas are the most drought tolerant and include at the south edge blue grama grass, sideoats grama, little bluestem, junegrass, and wheat grass. Also present are small, stunted specimens of shrubby cinquefoil, skunkbrush, wild rose, and currant. Like the grasses, the forbs include common plants found on the western plains including western yarrow, fringed sage, and rabbitbrush.

As for trees, there is one specimen of ground juniper and a few Rocky Mountain junipers. Ponderosa is the dominant tree and there are a couple of ancient ones on top. One of the oldest ones grows near the east edge of the butte and bears a nasty eight-foot-long fire scar on its southwest flank. It is difficult to image a fire of the intensity necessary to scar a tree that dramatically up here since fuel is minimal, but the scar is an ancient one suggesting that other conditions may have prevailed here a century earlier. This is borne out by the fact that there are also a half-dozen old, swirled pitch snags that stand stark and gray like wizened sentinels against the backdrop of a hard, blue sky. It must have been a very hot fire to take all these yellowbarks and leave only one alive to tell the story.

The north and east sides of the butte support a thick dog hair stand of ponderosa that may be forty to fifty years old. They probably came in sometime after the big blaze that took the old ones out.

The center of the butte's summit features elements commonly associated with a mature pine forest community. There are a handful of trees, well spaced, shading an understory that features flowering plants typical of the forest floor including a carpet of kinnikinnick (Bearberry) and bluebells. For fauna there was a small flock of juncos flitting about the ground where the edge of the butte's "forest" meets the "prairie." Juncos throughout the Black Hills are commonly present in ecotones that feature a blend of forest and openings.

The summit of Steamboat Rock provides a microcosm of life typical of both the mountains and plains. There are the elements of the mountains typified by the small ponderosa forest grove with its complementary understory of plants on the north end while the south end supports elements of the plains with its varied community of prairie grasses and forbs. Interspersed are shrubs of both communities.

Ecotones are the crossroads where plant communities intermingle. According to the terms set by sun, wind, rain and fire, some species of plants spread and prosper for awhile while others diminish only to return to dominance when conditions for their success prevail. The summit of Steamboat Rock, because of its relative isolation and inaccessibility, provides a microscopic picture of a native botanical community that is still virtually intact and under the complete management of nature.

As for the view, it is spectacular. To the east, the great plains stretch out into the blue haze of infinity. Tracing the curve of the earth from the northeast to the southeast, the horizon erupts into what appears like small, asymmetrical, worn, old teeth. These are the Badlands.

Black Hills Biotic Communities

Two Top
Butte

MONTANA

WYOMING

LITTLE MISSOURI RIVER

Limit of Dakota
Sandstone Hogback

GRASSLANDS

BELLE FOURCHE RIVER

LOWER HILLS

Devil's
Tower
NM

Bearlodge Mountains

Belle Fourche

Spearfish

Bear
Butte SP

MIXED
FOREST

*Crow
Pk.*

NORTHERN ECOTINE WITH OAK

Warren Pk.

Sundance

Keyhole
Res. SP

Deadwood

Sturgis

Spearfish Canyon

Lead

Terry Pk.

*Eagle
Buttes*

*Inyan
Kara
Mtn.*

HIGHER
HILLS

Custer Pk.

SOUTHERN ECOTONE WITH JUNIPER

SPRUCE FOREST

Rapid City

GRASSLANDS
with Sagebrush

SCATTERED SPRUCE

MIXED FOREST

Hill City

Mount
Rushmore NM

SCATTERED ASPEN

Bear Mtn.

Harney Pk.

Custer SP

Newcastle

*Elk
Mtn.*

Jewel
Cave
NM

Custer

Wind Cave NP

PINE
FOREST

CHEYENNE RIVER

N

Hot
Springs

SCALE:
MILES

SOUTH DAKOTA

Edgemont

0   5   10   15   25

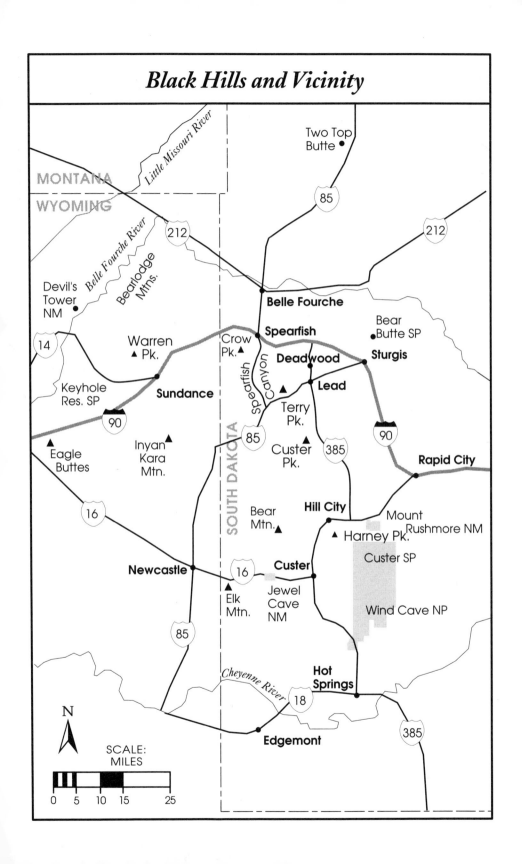

Black Hills and Vicinity

On the other side of the butte, looking to the northwest, the small conical mountain standing alone is Custer Peak. West are rolling, pine-covered ridges with a few showing gray, talus slides. These slides indicate their igneous character and origin. Southwest, the long blue mountain in the distance is Harney Peak.

Harney Peak is the highest point in the Black Hills at 7,242 feet above sea level. Its handsomely sculpted, curvilinear outline sits near the middle of the great Harney Peak batholith. "Batholith" is a geologic term used to describe the largest bodies of magmatic rock with an exposed surface of at least forty square miles and no known bottom. The Harney Peak batholith is made of pegmatoidal granite and has been estimated to be 1.74 billion years old. Its deep and ancient presence forms the heart of the Black Hills core.

Scouting around the southeast side of the summit for another way down I ran across three half-filled cans of Budweiser. Assuming the Bud-heads found the path of least resistance, I scouted the crevices at this end of the butte for a descent path. Not far from the cans I found a slickened, well-used crevice where the beer climbers probably made their ascent.

Descending this slick crevice, while tricky, went without incident and the hike back down to the picnic area took about twenty minutes. The climb up to the top of Steamboat Rock, while not particularly difficult, is strenuous and at places challenging.

The area around Steamboat Rock also has the distinction of being recognized by the U.S. Forest Service as Case #1. This label refers to the fact that it was the first timber sale made by the Forest Service to a private entity, in this case the Homestake Mining Company. A Forest Service sign notes that in 1930 the forest was thinned by the Civilian Conservation Corps (CCC) and in 1960 it was thinned commercially for timber. The sign also states that Case #1 produced the 2 billionth board foot of lumber taken from the Black Hills and was last commercially thinned in 1990.

At mile 22.0 to the east (right) there is a low, dark red hill being mined. Its redness indicates it to be rich in iron and it is being mined for this mineral. This hill is located below the Deadwood formation in the Precambrian.

Mile 23.8 is the town of Nemo named after the captain in the Jules Verne novel *20,000 Leagues Under the Sea*. The old town is now a guest ranch. Nemo was constructed as a company town about the turn of the century by Homestake and had a store, sawmill, and cabins. These structures housed and served the hired men who lived and worked here for a number of years harvesting the timber from Case #1.

On the west (left) side of the road as you climb the ridge and head north out of town, the sea that deposited the Deadwood formation formed coarse bars and sand dunes which overlay the iron-rich Precambrian schists. Gries noted that there are a lot of "glory holes" (gold prospect holes) still left here from the gold rush days of 1876.

Four miles down the road at mile 27.5 is the Safe Investment Mine. The mine site is located on the west side of the road very close to where a bridge again spans Boxelder Creek. The name of the mine is one of those wonderful gimmicks promoters would use to lure unsuspecting investors from back east. There was hardly a mine in the West that could be considered a "safe investment" since mining has always been a business plagued by the vagaries of extent and richness of wandering and disappearing ore deposits.

The Safe Investment is a mine frequently mapped as an exercise by students from the School of Mines. It consists of two to three holes and a shaft on the west side of the creek where the tailing piles are and an open cut on the east side of the creek. The mill stood on the east side of the road and ore from the open cut was hauled by a tramway across the creek. Gries noted that the Safe Investment operated from 1900 to 1910. Gold at this site was mined from a deposit in a very ancient conglomerate. On a human note, Gries added that this mine was located in a "kind of no man's land. It was too far from Rapid City to the south," he said, "and too far from the bars in Deadwood to the north."

At mile 29.5 an old dilapidated log cabin stands to the north and east side of Boxelder Creek next to the bridge. The cabin is the last remains of the old hamlet of Benchmark. The hamlet probably took its unassuming name from the fact that there is a benchmark here that registers an elevation of 5,022 feet above sea level. At this point Nemo Road bends to the northwest and leaves Boxelder Creek to follow a small tributary known as Hay Creek. The sedimentary layers of the Madison and Deadwood have long since been eroded away from this part of the Hills leaving only Precambrian schists. Schists are not good aquifers, which means that finding any subsurface water here is a matter of luck in locating a fracture in the rock. As the road winds up Hay Creek, Black Hills (white) spruce and aspen appear among the ponderosa pine, indicating a gradual rise in elevation.

At mile 34.0 the road crosses Windy Flats at an elevation of about 5,500 feet. To the west a conical mountain appears. This prominent landmark is Custer Peak and stands at 6,804 feet above sea level. Custer Peak is an igneous laccolith intrusion into the Deadwood formation.

In another mile the road crosses Elk Ridge and drops into the Elk Creek drainage. The hamlet of Roubaix is located at mile 35.6. Here, Dr. Gries noted that in 1878 miners picked up and followed a rich, wandering quartz vein of gold. The vein dipped down seven hundred feet, eventually forcing the miners to dig shafts to get at it. The mine was variously dubbed the Elk Creek, the Uncle Sam, and the Cloverleaf by its host of owners. According to Gries it produced some very rich ore.

In 1900, Pierre Wibaux, a cattle baron who had already made a handsome fortune by that date in the cattle business in eastern Montana, bought the town which was then named Perry and operated out of the old two-story log house which still stands. During his tenure Wibaux did two things, he renamed the town Roubaix after his hometown in France and then went to work mining gold. By the time he quit working the mine four years later, it had produced $400,000 worth of gold at a time when the going rate per ounce was $20.

In 1930, optimistic investors reopened Wibaux's mine believing the old boys before them may have missed something. Gries said the late comers got "about $10,000 worth of gold and probably spent $100,000 to get it." The old timers had already mined the mother lode. This was more often the case in the Black Hills mining business rather than the exception, particularly in the twilight years of the 1920s that followed the initial gold rush of 1876.

At the intersection of Nemo Road and U.S. 385 turn north (right) to mile 37.7 and enter the front gate of the Tomahawk Country Club. In 1875, the Newton-Jenney expedition came to the Black Hills from Laramie for the primary purpose of studying its geology and natural history. Just to the east of the club house on a small knoll, the geologists found an interesting and unique geologic feature in the Black Hills, a volcanic neck.

Dr. Gries explained its formation this way: "Water got down real deep into a fissure, heated up, and blew the hell out of a square mile, scattering around a lot of debris which eventually came back down and fell deeper in the hole." Quiet molten activity followed this explosive geologic episode and blistered up the sediments creating a neck of volcanic glass (obsidian) and pitchstone. Dr. Gries describes this episode as the only evidence of molten lava activity to take place in the Black Hills some 10 million years ago and praised those late nineteenth-century geologists who had found the site and correctly interpreted what had transpired there. Leave Tomahawk and continue north on 385 to the Galena turnoff.

On the way to Galena, Dr. Gries explained the difference between the two types of gold found in the Black Hills. Precambrian gold is found in the ancient Precambrian beds (created over 600 million years ago) of Roubaix and the Homestake Mine while Tertiary gold was formed much later and came up with the volcanic intrusions of the Tertiary some 30 million years ago. Tertiary gold basically seeped up through cracks and fissures into the Deadwood formation. Tertiary gold is the type discovered at Galena.

At mile 39.7 turn right (east) off U.S. 385 at the sign that says "Galena, 3 miles." Galena means lead sulfide. Galena in other parts of the country is mined for lead and is also attractive for an impurity found in it, silver.

At mile 41.4, a hillside on the left shows evidence of a tree blow down that occurred many years ago. A blow-down is indicated in the way all the old, dead tree snags were snapped off about halfway to two-thirds up their trunks.

Blow-downs in the Black Hills are not uncommon and occur when high, strong straight winds, which are not infrequent in the higher elevations of the Rocky Mountains, hit an exposed stand of timber. If the trees are firmly rooted, saw-log-size trunks like the ones on this hillside are snapped like match sticks. On other occasions, if the trees are shallow rooted (i.e., over rocks and heavy gravel) or already dead, the wind may actually blow over the entire tree or stand.

Wind gusts that snap or flatten forests reach velocities in excess of 100 mph. This phenomena tends to occur most often on hillsides directly exposed to the force of the west wind or, in this case, at the edge of a high clearing where the wind funneled down the valley.

Henry Newton in his 1875 *Black Hills Resource Report* observed that "on the tops of the ridges and hills, where the trees are exposed to the violence of the storms, the timber is wind-shaken and injured in quality; but on the more sheltered hillsides, the broad level mesas, and in the numerous valleys and parks, the trees are free from this evil, and are remarkably straight and regular in growth. Pines were sometimes encountered, blown down by the wind across the narrow ravines, the trunk of the tree, even when one or two feet in diameter, being broken short off by the violence of the fall on the rocks."

At mile 41.8 turn right on U.S.F.S. Road 534 and proceed to mile 42.1 and the Silver Queen Mine. During the Tertiary period of mineralization, gold was carried up by hot solutions (igneous sills) from deep within the earth until it could find a host rock to move into. Around Galena the first host rock available to this intrusive igneous sill was the Deadwood formation. Depending on the properties of the Deadwood formation at any given place, the gold solution would tend to move either into the upper or lower contact host zones of the formation. It might follow a fracture or seep into a transition zone from sandstone to coarsely crystalline dolomite where it replaces the dolomite extending for a few inches or feet into vertical fractures. Understanding the nature of this process, prospectors would look for vertical fractures in the Deadwood and dig in after them hoping to find a gold vein. Once the vein was located, the trick was trying to divine and follow the direction of the fractures.

The Silver Queen Mine consists of a number of old drifts (horizontal tunnels) dug into the base of the Deadwood's lower contact zone a few feet above where it meets the Precambrian schist. This was pretty much standard gold mining procedure around Galena. Little prospecting was done in the area of the upper contact zone since most of the upper contact areas within fifteen to twenty feet of the top of the Deadwood formation have been eroded away. In this area the upper and lower mineralization contact zones of the Deadwood are about 250 to 300 feet apart.

Silver is also found in these two mineralization zones and some of the galena here proved to be very high grade. The first prospectors at the Silver Queen mined the ore with teaspoons. They then put the ore on ox-hide covers, dragged and hauled it down to the road where they loaded it into wagons bound for Deadwood's smelters.

Other early prospectors who mined the Silver Queen shipped their ore all the way from Deadwood by ox wagon to Fort Pierre and then by steamboat to smelters as far away as Omaha. It was fantastically rich ore.

In 1878, when the first miners reached Galena, some of the smeltering was done near the town in a method that employed a crude salt smelter using evaporated water salt from Newcastle, Wyoming. The earliest miners never let the fact that there were few wagons and no railroads around to stop them from turning raw ore into gold and silver.

In the early 1950s, Gries was employed by the U.S. Bureau of Mines to map the old drifts at the Silver Queen Mine. He said that some of the drifts went back fifty to two hundred feet into the Deadwood formation.

A couple hundred yards back from the road are the two main drifts of the Silver Queen. These drifts appear to drop at a 5- or 6-percent grade as they enter the hillside. It was hard to tell since they were caged shut with iron bars. This did not bother me since I had no desire to get in, my impression being that they were likely caved in farther down the runway.

Strewn around the work staging area that had obviously been dozed flat not too long in the past was a collection of debris that included tires, cans, rusted cable, rotted timber, and assorted junk from more modern eras. The most conspicuous hulks of abandoned equipment included an old straight-six engine block, the black, oxidized corpse of a 1950s vintage International pickup, and a yellow, rusted Allis-Chalmers bulldozer.

When the wind blew there was the haunting, random flap of tin on the old roof of what had once been the machine shed. The Silver Queen had the uneasy feel of hundreds of other abandoned mines and ghost towns that now fill the West; places where people brought with them great hopes and expectations and left with broken dreams.

Growing about the yellow, relatively sterile clay soil of the flat was a carpet of wild strawberries, daisies, sorrel (*oxalis*), a few raspberries, and tall stalks of mullein. I tried to imagine the scene here a century ago with the first miners squatting down, backs aching as they laboriously hand sorted the ore they had painstakingly dug out of the rock.

On the west side of the flat I followed Gries up a narrow winding track to some smaller drifts in the lower contact zone. The road was littered with basal quartz conglomerate schists; metamorphosed relics of the first seas of so very long ago. The road was originally cut for oxcarts well over a century ago. Gries recalled negotiating it with a small military jeep forty years earlier. Now it was thickly overgrown with doghair stands of ponderosa eight to ten feet high. The pines were just the right height to be difficult and irritating to pass through easily. Their long, limber branches would snap back after I passed them, stinging the sides of my face and head with their sharp needles.

About midway up the side of the hill we stopped at a drift Gries recognized as the Alice. It appeared smaller than the two below but, unlike the others cut into the lower contact zone, it appeared to be very stable. After bending around a little initially to crawl in, we could stand up inside. The tunnel was cool and damp and had the strong, sickly smell of mold. The old drift curved down slowly to the right, no doubt having been dug following a fracture. Dr. Gries said it went for a few hundred yards. We walked only as far as the light coming in from the mouth of the drift allowed us to see. Gries said the Alice was worked in the late 1870s and early 1880s by miners using a single jack. Single jack is a Cornish term applied to one man who worked alone using a small sledge hammer and a chisel. The early miners used candles in pointed wrought iron holders which they could jam into fissures in the drift's walls for light. The ore was hauled out of the drift with wheelbarrows and then either dragged on hides by hand or transferred onto ox-carts for transport down to the main area. It was hard, back-breaking work. As for the Alice, she was in good shape having stood open to the elements for over a century.

While Gries was mapping the Silver Queen complex back in the early 1950s, he assayed the Alice to see what, if anything, was left. His remark was simply that, "those old boys got absolutely everything here to be got." Gries admired those early miners who, in spite of primitive equipmen and no formal training, knew exactly what they were doing.

From the Silver Queen return to the junction (mile 42.4) and turn east (right) towards Galena. On the right, the dark, brownish stone formation is the Deadwood. If you look closely there is evidence of a road and rock tailings from another mining operation at the lower Deadwood contact zone.

At mile 42.7 the road runs right into a large igneous outcrop of stone that juts out in front of it. The rock is fine grained and appears smooth and billowy. Gries described it as a Precambrian submarine lava flow.

At mile 43.2 on the left side of the road there is a large outcrop of banded schists that have been folded, twisted, and faulted. The relic banding of the schists attests to its ancient sedimentary ancestry.

The old Galena assay office stands at mile 43.8. Situated in close proximity to the office and all along the banks of nearby Bear Butte Creek are numerous stone wall remnants, foundations, and depressions, evidence of where the many town structures and residences of Galena once stood a century ago. Back when it was booming in the late 1870s and 1880s Gries said there were ten thousand people living in the Galena vicinity.

The biggest mine at the time was the Double Rainbow which was operating east of town in the upper Deadwood contact zone. In 1883, a lawsuit was initiated against the owners of the Double Rainbow who wanted to pursue a vein of gold under the property lines of another mining concern. The court action stopped the mining activity and the lawsuit dragged on for years. In the meantime the town went bust. By 1891, the action had still not been decided in the courts but it no longer mattered. The price of silver had plummeted to the point that the question became academic. By this time Galena, like hundreds of other western ghost towns, had now been deserted.

A mile or so down a rough road below Galena, Dr. Gries pointed out a head frame where Homestake Mining Company sank a shaft into the lower contact zone in the early 1950s. Gries explained that at that time the U.S. Bureau of Mines was offering a fifty-fifty cost split for any company exploring for gold. Homestake found some ore at the site but not enough to cover their investment. The company pulled out leaving a huge ore pile of iron pyrite to oxidize next to Bear Butte Creek. Gries explained that iron pyrite breaks down into sulfuric acid, adding that this pile of waste rock has been polluting Bear Butte Creek for the last forty years. It is an old mining story all too common in the western mountains of America.

The old cemetery at Galena is located on the edge of Vinegar Hill, past the assay office. The road is rough and washes out periodically, making it tough to get to. Upon seeing the old assay office and the cemetery, Gries recalled attending the burial of Charlie Bentley there in the early 1970s. Bentley was the assayer at Galena for many years before he went to work for the School of Mines. Gries described him as a good wet chemist of the old school. Back then "they worked you till you dropped," he said. He recalled being at a School of Mines award dinner for Bentley when he was eighty. "They gave him a glass plaque for service," he said, "but he was so shaky, he dropped it when they handed it to him and it shattered to pieces."

Before Bentley died at the age of eighty-five, he requested to be buried at Galena. It was a muddy day when they put his casket in a jeep since a hearse, even on a good day, could not possibly negotiate the steep grade. Gries said the pall bearers had to hold the tailgate up by hand to keep the wet casket from sliding out on the trip up. It was nip and tuck as the pall bearers slid around behind the jeep trying to stand up and keep the casket from falling and spilling out Charlie.

A few years later Bentley's widow died and it was the same kind of story. Except that on this occasion it was so wet and muddy prior to and on the day of her funeral that only half of the grave could be dug. The undertaker decided to set the casket down into the hole temporarily anyway. While they were lowering the casket into the half-dug grave the dolly jammed. The undertaker, while bending over trying to unjam it, lost his silver pen in the mud. He jumped in after it and the whole affair became another kind of unholy muddy mess.

Of historical interest is the fact that Custer's Negro cook from his 1874 Black Hill's expedition, Sarah "Aunt Sally" Campbell, lived and spent the final days of her life in Galena. Aunt Sally was a frontierswoman in her own right who claimed to have cooked on one of the first steamboats up the Missouri. She is described as a kind, faithful servant of General Custer and during the 1874 expedition was assigned as the sutler's cook.

Near the site of Custer, South Dakota, where gold was discovered on French Creek during the expedition she was interviewed by the reporter of the *Chicago Inter Ocean* newspaper. Her story appeared in the same news dispatch that included the discovery of gold in the Black Hills. In the interview, Aunt Sally stated that she had wanted to see the Black Hills for a long time so she seized the opportunity to join it as a cook.

Having seen it, she made up her mind to return at the next opportunity, eventually moving to Crook City (near Whitewood, South Dakota) and then Galena where she died in 1887 and was buried in the Galena Cemetery on Vinegar Hill. The epitaph above her grave reads as follows:

AUNT SALLY SARAH CAMPBELL
Colored
Died 1887

As a member of the Custer Expedition to the Black Hills in 1874, she ventured with the vanguard of civilization. Erected by her friend and neighbor 1874-1934.

Fred G. Borsch, a life-long Galena resident, is also buried on Vinegar Hill. Borsch acquired the Galena town site and cemetery in 1931. His claim to fame has to do with an orphaned coyote he raised and kept at his Galena home. Borsch was often seen in the Deadwood Days of '76 parade in the company of "Tootsie" and gained a certain notoriety with his unusual pet. It was through his efforts that the coyote eventually came to be designated as South Dakota's state animal and the silhouette of the howling coyote that appears on old historical markers throughout the state is adapted from a picture of Tootsie. As a lasting reminder of his link with Tootsie, Borsch had a bas-relief silhouette of Tootsie chiseled into the upper left corner of his own tombstone.

The Galena cemetery is a melancholy place with many old, unmarked grave depressions enclosed by decrepit picket fences. Not even the abundant display of wildflowers—including daisies, yellow and purple asters, goldenrods, bluebells, yarrow, bergamot, and sunflowers—that grow in abundance on the cemetery grounds can dispel the dismal somberness that hangs there on an overcast afternoon.

From Galena return to the intersection of U.S. 385, turn right (north) and drive up Strawberry Hill. Winding down the hill, Gries described the outcrops on the east as "shot up with porphyry (igneous rock) into schists and black graphitic slate; a lot of unconformity rock." Just over the top of the ridge and to the north, the terraced slope of the Homestake Open Cut is visible. Farther down the hill, the silver head frame of the Homestake Mine's Yates shaft appears on top of a gray terraced slag pile.

The Pluma junction at U.S. 385 and U.S. 85 is at mile 53.4. On the left side of the intersection stands of row of old tourist cabins that date back to the late 1920s. Tourist camps like this were the precursors of motels which replaced them in the 1940s and 1950s. Turn left and follow U.S. 85 up the hill to Lead, South Dakota.

At mile 54.2 is King's Grocery. King's is one of the few places you can buy a hot, authentic miner's pastie lunch. Pasties are a beef, onion, and potato pie that served as the standard fare for miners. The pastie was brought over from Europe by Cornish miners.

Across the highway from King's Grocery is the Homestake Mine cyanide plant. Huge vats located both inside and outside the building are filled with ore that has been pounded into the consistency of flour. After the ore powder has been placed in the vats it is leached with cyanide which dissolves the gold out and allows it to be recovered.

Mile 54.7 is the Homestake Open Cut. This is the best place to see certain aspects of Black Hills geology. Looking north into the cut the black schists are the Precambrian Homestake and Poor Man's formations. The long, yellow vertical sills are rhyolite, a later intrusion which came in and followed the grain of rock at a tilt until it hit the

Deadwood formation and flattened out. The Deadwood formation, which has now been completely removed by the mining operation, was thrust up by the intrusion of the rhyolite sill creating a geologic domal structure.

The discovery of the Homestake lead or lode was made on the 9th of April in 1876 by Hank Harvey and Moses and Fred Manuel. The gold discovery by the Manuel brothers has now become almost mythic in proportion, and there are different stories about how they found gold shot through the quartzite sills in the Deadwood formation.

Initially, placer gold was discovered around and below the Lead dome first in Deadwood, then Bobtail and Gold Run creeks. Harvey and the Manuel brothers traced the placers to the Lead dome using their gold pans to find color and eventually located the mother lode in the lower contact zone of the Deadwood. Feverish mining activity ensued on the Lead dome with over a dozen mining companies quickly forming to remove and process the ore. To serve the needs of the mining operations, the city of Lead was first laid out near the mines in July 1876.

William Randolph Hearst quickly bought out Harvey and the Manuels in 1877 and named his company Homestake after the name of the claim. Hearst and his Homestake investors were eventually able to secure all the mining claims adjacent to the Homestake claim and eventually consolidated all their activities into two large operations that include the open cut and the underground mine. Homestake's hardrock underground operation is serviced by two main shafts and numerous drifts. The main shafts probe the earth to a depth of six thousand feet while secondary shafts are now as deep as eight thousand feet.

Homestake's open cut operation has generally been more profitable to mine than the hardrock in terms of ore quality and relative ease of removal. In the early days, fourteen mining companies dug into the mountain where the open cut is now. Some of their old drifts are still apparent on the side of the cut which is nearly a mile long and a quarter of a mile deep.

The heart of Lead's first mercantile district was initially located about where the center of the open cut is today. As mining progressed through the end of the nineteenth and into the beginning of the twentieth century, the city of Lead slowly began to subside. Beginning in 1919 and due to subsidence from the encroaching open cut and hardrock (underground mining) operations, the oldest section of the city which included many homes, businesses, and milling operations had to be torn down and the mercantile and residential districts relocated.

Proceed through Lead to South Dakota 14A. Turn right towards Central City. Past Central City at mile 58.7 turn off to the left into the parking lot of the Broken Boot Mine. The Broken Boot, formerly known as the Olaf Seim, was dug into a vertical north-south iron dike full of pyrite or flux. Flux is used in the smelting process where it is mixed with ore to help reduce its melting temperature.

In the winter of 1943, Gries was doing some work for the Bureau of Mines that included sampling the flux in the Broken Boot. He recalled spending the afternoon far back in the mine and knee deep in water. When it was time to leave, he passed the dog leg to go out and, to his surprise, where there should have been light there was only complete darkness. For an anxious moment he thought the mine had caved in and he was trapped. Later he discovered that while he spent the afternoon back in the mine, the mouth had been completely snowed shut.

Proceed .1 mile and turn left onto Deadwood's old Main Street down to the front of the Franklin Hotel (mile 59.5). It was down this stretch of road that the Cheyenne to Deadwood stagecoaches rolled into town in the 1870s and 1880s.

On the left side of the Franklin Hotel flows a rivulet known as City Creek. City Creek once flowed through the site where the hotel is now located. The creek flows in a culvert under the street and then alongside the old Franklin Hotel garage beyond which it joins the confluence of Deadwood and Whitewood creeks.

In 1875, the year after Custer announced to the world the discovery of gold in the Black Hills, Frank S. Bryant, a sawyer from Iowa, was in the northern Black Hills prospecting for gold. He entered Deadwood Gulch, which at that time was dammed by a series of beaver dams. All the water had flooded and killed a lot of trees which, as one story goes, is how Deadwood Gulch received its name.

In the early 1960s Robert Bryant, Frank Bryant's son, pointed out the location to his son-in-law, Linfred Schuttler, where his father made the first gold discovery in Deadwood. Schuttler said that according to Robert Bryant, the spot was "a little sandbar point in City Creek near the site where the hotel now stands." That point, now long gone, would have been somewhere between where the library and the Deadwood Middle School parking lot is now located.

Bryant built a sluice box there and worked his claim for a short time before eventually selling it. According to Schuttler, later miners came in, drained the beaver ponds, and struck a few sizable fortunes of placer gold.

After selling his placer claim, Bryant went up to Bobtail Gulch, located just below Central City, and made the second big gold strike in the Black Hills. But that could not hold him either and he sold out again to miners who would make another small fortune there. From there Bryant went up to Carbonate Camp near Terry Peak to stake another successful claim which he again sold acquiring the handsome sum of $60,000.

According to Schuttler, Bryant was nicknamed the "Lamplighter" because he "always lit the way for others to follow but could never stay." Eventually Bryant settled in Spearfish where, during the intervening years and through a series of poor investments, he lost most of his money.

In 1900, Bryant contracted yellow fever while in Cuba checking over a hemp investment. That trip took his health while the investment erased the last of his fortune. In 1910, at the age of sixty-two, he was broke and died in Spearfish from complications brought on by his yellow fever.

Bryant's story was positive in the sense that he was one of the few that actually struck it rich. Retired Deadwood librarian, Marjorie Pontius, who has done a great deal of research in old newspapers on the life and times of early Deadwood pioneers, discussed what she found in the *Lawrence County Book of Deaths* from 1876 to 1897.

"So many people came here unprepared for the rigors of a gold camp and frontier South Dakota," she said. She described the people that arrived in those early days as "lonely, desperate, and destitute," hoping to make it big in one last effort. "Many of those people committed suicide," she added, noting that "the people who made it came as carpenters, storekeepers, and salesmen."

At the Franklin, turn left and drive up Shine Street. This street was the last leg of the old Centennial Wagon Road. Ox-drawn wagons enroute from Bismarck and Fort Pierre entered Deadwood in the early days via this alleyway. At the top of Shine Street turn left, then right, and proceed up Denver Street.

Denver is a narrow, one-lane street that turns into a gravel road at the edge of town and then winds its way up to Mount Roosevelt. This route also serves as a scenic, alternate way to get to U.S. 85. It does, however, contain hair-pin turns and is not recommended for trailers or large RVs.

Just above the town the mountain sides bear the scars of the Deadwood forest fire that roared over these ridges in September 1959. As the road climbs to the crest it offers spectacular views of Whitewood Gulch to the southeast and the back side terraces of the Open Cut to the south.

The Mount Roosevelt Memorial parking lot is at mile 62.8. There is a short trail that goes up to the memorial for Seth Bullock named Friendship Tower. The tower was built in 1919 at Bullock's request as a lasting legacy to his good friend, President Theodore Roosevelt. Bullock, who briefly served as an early Deadwood sheriff and the first superintendent of the Black Hills National Forest, was a businessman who became a prominent figure in Deadwood's pioneer history.

In the early 1880s Seth Bullock and Theodore Rooseve became acquainted while he was sheriff of Deadwood and Roosevelt was ranching up in the North Dakota Badlands. The two outdoorsmen served together in the Spanish-American War of 1898 and maintained close contact throughout the rest of their lives. Roosevelt liked to refer to Bullock as "my ideal typical American."

At the time of Roosevelt's death, Bullock, who was ailing himself, had the small stone tower hastily erected in Roosevelt's honor. Shortly after Friendship Tower and the Mount Roosevelt Memorial dedication in July of 1919, Bullock passed away. He was laid to rest across Deadwood Gulch, above Mount Moriah Cemetery near the white rocks and in view of his friend's monument.

Mount Roosevelt, geologically speaking, is part of the Tertiary igneous intrusion into the northern Black Hills. In the 1920s and 1930s it was a popular area for picnics and outings. Today, far off the beaten path, it is of more interest to geologists and mountain bikers than historians.

Proceed down the gravel road east to the junction of U.S. 85 and turn left (north) towards the Centennial Prairie and Spearfish. The highway winds north down Polo Gulch and out of the Black Hills. The road cuts along the way are in the Minnelusa formation. At the mouth of the gulch it passes through the Minnekahta which is being quarried on the east side of the highway.

At mile 70.4 stop at a pull-off near the gate of the Centennial Prairie Ranch. You are back in the middle of the Red Valley again and at the entrance to one of the oldest privately owned and operated ranches in the northern Black Hills. The ranch's history, according to Glen Baker, the present owner, begins in 1873 when a man named Mike Burton and two other partners came down from the Gallatin Valley in Montana to start a stock ranch. Burton staked his claim near a six-inch spring just northeast of here, not far from the foot of Elkhorn Mountain which lies directly to the east.

Burton's ranch became an important watering and rest stop for herds of cattle that came down the Montana Beef Trail from Miles City, Montana, to Deadwood. It was also an important stop for rest and repairs for the bull team trains out of Fort Pierre and Bismarck in the 1880s. They would regroup here for the last pull over the mountains into Deadwood.

In prehistoric times the spring at the foot of Elkhorn Mountain and the Centennial Prairie hosted herds of bison and elk. South of the spring, many old buffalo wallows which appear as shallow scooped-out bowls in the prairie are still faintly visible to the trained eye.

Elkhorn Mountain was named for two racks of antlers, one elk the other deer, that once stood about midway up the mountain. These piles of antlers were placed there by native peoples who also erected burial scaffolds that held the bones of their dead on top of the mountain.

To the southeast, the long mountain is Crook Peak. The mountain was named after General George Crook who actively campaigned against the plains Indians in the Powder River country. Below Crook Peak there was also a town named Crook City which flourished during the ox team days and was promoted as a boom town in the 1880s. It is now gone.

The small peak to the south is Whitewood. The peak to the southwest on the west side of the highway is Green Mountain. Following the line of hills west to the next high, single peak is Spearfish Mountain. Early maps of the area referred to it as Black Butte. The large double-humped mountain far to the west is Crow Peak.

All of the above named peaks are laccolithic intrusions from the Tertiary and form a major part of the eastern belt of igneous mountain peaks on the northern edge of the Black Hills. The western part of that belt includes the peaks of Inyan Kara, the Black Buttes, the Bear Lodge Mountains, Little Green Mountain, Sundance Mountain, Devils Tower, and the Little Missouri Buttes in Wyoming.

At mile 71.6 turn east (right) on to Interstate 90 and drive to Sturgis. Take the first exit and drive east through town following the signs to Bear Butte State Park. Bear Butte is one of the most significant aboriginal cultural sites on the northern Great Plains. Cheyenne legend tells the story of how on this mountain, over two centuries ago, Sweet Medicine received the knowledge and spiritual precepts associated with the Four Sacred Arrows.

The mountain itself represents the farthest eastern extension of the Black Hills laccolithic belt and is composed of phonolite porphyry. The intrusion of this igneous material thrust the Madison formation above it up 2,500 feet. Ridges of the shattered Madison appear on the north and east slopes of the mountain.

On the west side of Bear Butte, scattered about in the grass, are eroded remnants of the Madison along with other sedimentary layers associated with the Black Hills uplift and include pieces of the Minnekahta, Minnelusa, Lakota, and Fall River formations. Bear Butte mirrors on a small scale the entire process of mountain building and erosion that is taking place in the Black Hills proper just to the west.

Returning back to Sturgis and taking the interstate south will take you via the Red Valley back to Rapid City. As you return this way, the Dakota Hogback will be to the east (left) and the dome of the Black Hills to the west (right).

I was tired when I arrived back at the School of Mines with Dr. Gries late in the afternoon. It was a satisfying kind of exhaustion. I had a thick sheaf of notes, a couple of rolls of exposed color slide film, and memories of an outstanding day spent on geologic exploration with one of the most interesting and eminent geologists of the Black Hills.

5

The Search for Fossil Cycads

On a shallow, sloping road cut between Hermosa and Buffalo Gap, South Dakota, Dr. Mark Gabel and I stop to poke around for evidence of ancient fossilized plants. Gabel, a paleobotanist and earth science instructor at Black Hills State University in Spearfish, has spent his last few summers on the high plains researching fossilized plants and focusing specifically on the hackberry tree *(Celtis oxidentalis)*.

Gabel has been analyzing the ratio of carbon 12 to its isotope carbon 13 in the fossilized remains of hackberry trees that lived as far back as the Oligocene period some 30 million years ago. The carbon ratio present in the fossilized remnants of hackberry seeds functions as a kind of barometer that represents the amount of atmospheric carbon which can then be used as an indicator of climatic change. According to Gabel, the preliminary evidence suggests a long-term trend towards a hotter and dryer climate moving slowly up from the southern high plains to the northern plains and Black Hills.

Today Gabel and I are traveling back beyond the Oligocene on a trip to the site of an ancient Jurassic fossil forest that flourished as late as 130 million years ago in an area that is now part of the southern Black Hills. The Jurassic was a time when the free carbon in the earth's atmosphere was much higher than it is today; a time when a group of plants, known collectively as cycads, flourished and dominated the earth. This trip is a search for the last known remaining fossil cycad in the "wild" from that ancient time.

During the Jurassic the earth had a relatively uniform temperate climate with a wet, soggy atmosphere thick with humidity. This rich carbon environment created the conditions necessary for the evolution and development of an array of tropical plants. There were swamps around inland seas that hosted vast gymnosperm forests dominated by cycads and cycadeoids along with horsetails, gingkoes, sequoias, and huge ten-foot-high ferns. These shallow, foetid swamps teemed with large flower-eating beetles and cockroaches eighteen inches long while the air hummed with the buzz of giant dragonflies with three-foot wingspans. In the setting of these swampy forests reptiles evolved into a plethora of size and form. Rain was a constant—dripping off dark green fronds and needles—as was the lapping sound of shallow water on nearby shores and beaches.

Conditions like this prevailed for tens of millions of years into the Cretaceous when great inland seas rose again and flooded the swamps, depositing sand and silt on those early primitive forests and entombing them as pages in the Jurassic chapters of geologic history.

The species of cycads preserved in those fossilized sea sands were many and varied, but their story goes back farther to an even more primitive plant called *Cooksonia psilotum* which made its way on land from sea algae about 430 million years ago in the Silurian period of the Paleozoic (ancient life).

Cooksonia is the prototype of all terrestrial plants and is interesting from the standpoint of its sheer simplicity—it had no leaves or roots; it was all stem. It may have washed ashore as a long filament of algae managing to survive long enough to harden and establish itself on land. Part of its stem adapted itself to grow above ground while the other part grew below. The plant consisted of a simple dichotomous branched stem with chlorophyll that reproduced sexually or asexually by spores. *Cooksonia* appeared the same above ground as it did underground; its root simply being its stem inverted.

The roots of higher plants today are still basically unchanged inverted stems. However, above ground there has been a great deal of evolution and modification regarding the stem structure. As time progressed *Cooksonia* evolved in two distinct ways. Its descendants developed a microphyll (small leaf) that was in actuality a flattening out of the stem. The plant was simply evolving a way to produce more tissue and generate more energy. It is a very primitive system that can still be seen in lycopods like club mosses and equisetum (horsetail).

The other aspect in terrestrial plant evolution was the development of a macrophyll (big leaf). Macrophylls have a different system than the microphyll, which was just an extension of the stems plumbing system over a wider area.

A macrophyll is characterized by a place in the stem where the leaf trace has been torn out of the main vascular bundle and the stems plumbing is run in another divergent direction (i.e., into a leaf). It is a more advanced anatomy that is seen in ferns, cycads, cycadeoids, gymnosperms, and angiosperms.

Sometime in the Jurassic, 200 million years after *Cooksonia* emerged from the salt sea, cycads and cycadeoids evolved. Primitive cycadeoids resembled palmettos and pineapples with squat, lumpy stems that supported leafy, fern-like fronds of foliage. While both cycads and cycadeoids have many of the same physical characteristics, they differentiate from each other in the aspect of reproduction.

Cycads have separate male and female cones while cycadeoids have male and female organs on the same fleshy cone. Cycadeoids may have also been self-fertilizing, which is a distinct advantage if times are good and all climatic variables remain the same. However, if, for instance, climatic conditions change abruptly, self-fertilization limits your ability to react and be variable enough to successfully survive the shift. Cross-fertilization also enabled cycads to experiment with a much broader mix of their entire gene pool allowing for greater possibilities for the recombination of different and more adaptable strains of DNA.

Fossil evidence seems to point out that cycadeoid self-pollination may have been helped along by beetles that munched on the bare, fleshy cones. If so, it was a primitive method of reproduction, but these were primitive plants in primitive times.

Gabel believes that cycadeoids, with their male and female parts appearing on modified leaves of the same plant, are a convenient group to examine when searching for a group of plants that functioned as the ancestors in the divergence and origin of the angiosperms.

The first people to stumble upon the fossilized cycads of the Black Hills were early gold prospectors enroute from Rapid City to Deadwood in 1878. What they found as they trekked up the Red Valley near Black Hawk were huge fossilized cycad trunks which they described as "petrified beehives." It was an apt description for the lumpy, ball-shaped blocks of stone which did in fact resemble huge, insect combs reminiscent of the egg nests constructed by bees and wasps.

In February of 1893, a local collector from Minnekahta, South Dakota, sent six silicified Black Hills cycad specimens to Professor

Lester F. Ward at the United States National Museum. Ward later described them as cycadeoids (cycad like). According to G. R. Wieland, who wrote an exhaustive two volume report entitled *American Fossil Cycads* (published in 1906), these six specimens were the first of the "marvelous trunks to come from the Black Hills Mesozoic Rim."

Later, in the summer of 1893, Professor Thomas H. MacBride of the State University of Iowa collected twenty more trunks which he described as *Cycadeoidea dacotensis* for that university's museum in Iowa City. That same year he published his findings in the *American Geologist* of October 1893, igniting a great cycad rush of paleobotanists to the Black Hills in the later part of that decade. Professor Ward visited the Minnekahta site that fall to personally collect more specimens which he later described as *Cycadeoidea minnekatensis*.

Information of these discoveries soon came to the attention of Professor O. C. Marsh of Yale, who promptly made every effort to visit the two great cycad "patches" in the Black Hills and secure from them a collection for the Yale Museum. Collecting both from the Black Hawk and Minnekahta sites, Marsh managed to remove seven hundred well-preserved trunks before the nineteenth century ended, effectively cleaning them out. Wieland managed to gather another twenty specimens for the American Museum of Natural History in New York in 1900 and 1901 along with the remainder of some fossilized branches which he donated to the Yale collection.

Following the removal of nearly all the cycads and cycadeoids, Wieland described the Mesozoic Rim of the Black Hills of South Dakota (i.e., the Dakota Hogback) in his 1906 quarto as "the most important of all the American cycad horizons." Ironically, by this late date most had been removed far from the site.

In 1922, President Warren G. Harding proclaimed a rugged area west of Minnekahta flats and north and west of old U.S. 18 as Fossil Cycad National Monument. What, if any, old fossilized trunks where still around at that time is hard to say. A newspaper article appearing in the *Rapid City Journal* in the early 1980s stated that by 1937 "every last cycad had been smuggled out of the monument." The article also reported that "twenty years later the monument was quietly de-authorized by Congress."

In 1981, U.S. 18 was rerouted straight through the old Fossil Cycad Monument to bypass the numerous curves in the old road. According to the *Rapid City Journal*, "construction was often halted to uncover buried cycad trunks." During the construction, part of a cycad trunk was discovered embedded in a rim of Lakota sandstone. Not far from the cycad, a fossilized log also laid entombed, another remnant of that same Jurassic forest that was submerged eons ago in sand and rising water.

It was this last remnant fossil cycadeoid still in context that Gabel and I sought to locate that morning. Fortunately for me, Gabel had already located the fossil a few years earlier and recalled the site as being under the new highway bridge on the east side of a narrow, nameless draw that drains as a minor tributary into Chilson Canyon. The draw also happens to be near the center of the old defunct Fossil Cycad Monument.

After parking the car near the edge of the bridge, we scrambled down a long, steep, shaly bank to the top of the Lakota sandstone formation. The Lakota marks the end of the Jurassic and the beginning of the lower Cretaceous. We are on the top of Wieland's Black Hills "Mesozoic Rim" and the final natural resting place of the great fossil cycad forest.

At the ledge of the Lakota, the bottom of the draw abruptly cuts down thirty or forty feet perpendicular into grainy, cream-colored sandstone. Situated along the edge of the draw are a scattered handful of old, yellowbark ponderosa pines approaching the two-century mark.

The bottom of the draw supports a rank, heavy growth of poison ivy with some wild grape covering a scattering of large boulders. Interspersed in this growth is a representation of late twentieth-century cultural detritus consisting of old tires, silver Coors Light beer cans, bits of plastic debris, an assortment of containers of all colors and shapes, broken glass, a length of black stove pipe, and a smashed TV set.

Making our descent to the bottom of the draw, we picked our way up along the east side wall. Assessing the situation for the best route around the poison ivy (there was none), I finally had to decide where I wanted to step in it. I watched closely as Gabel made a precarious effort to stretch and touch a spot on the rim of the sandstone wall while two hundred feet above us the highway bridge periodically rumbled with traffic.

"It should be right here," he said, looking up and pointing to a round, shallow indentation near the top of the ledge that he can just barely reach. "It was hard to see and nearly impossible to take a picture of, but now I can't find it at all."

He searched around the ledge some more by touch. From my perspective perch, about midway up the opposite side of the narrow gulch, I could see a chunk of rock embedded near the indentation Gabel has his hand in. It appeared to be the end of a large petrified log laying cross ways to the edge of the smooth sandstone rim. When I mention what I see to Gabel he adds that the petrified log confirms this as the right location, noting that the fossil cycad was embedded very close to it.

Eventually I join Gabel on the east sandstone wall. After crawling along the wall and ledge for a while longer we both have to admit the obvious. The fossil cycad is gone. With a good deal of effort and deliberation, some collector has managed to chisel it out of its sandstone tomb. Since it probably weighed in at a few hundred pounds, it had to be winched out and up to the highway grade. While I am disappointed, I have to admire the engineering effort that went into its removal. The last known fossil cycad in the wild is probably languishing in some distant suburban flower garden or it may be the centerpiece of a rock pile.

Moving back along a narrow ledge, we both stop to examine a crevice climbers refer to as a chimney in the sandstone wall that earlier attracted my interest. There is a slight overhang of rock above the crevice. On the underside of the overhanging rock I notice it is covered with a black charcoal patina, indicative of having been exposed to smoke from numerous campfires. It is a tight, sheltered space but large enough to provide moderate shelter against the elements. With a small fire banked next to the wall, you could wait out a storm or spend a cold evening out of the wind and weather.

The sandstone along the edge of the crevice, with its smooth even grain, is cool and pleasant to my fingertips. On the sandy ground below the crevice there is a random spacing of small ant lion holes and a pair of Cecropia moth wings, the tell-tale remains of a bat meal.

Three feet above the ground in a tiny wall fracture there is a white silk sac of spider eggs and the discarded end of a Cecropia cocoon. If the wings are circumstantial evidence, the Cecropia that popped its cocoon here did not get very far in his life as an adult.

Moving around the ledge away from the crevice, we encounter a series of weathered, cross-bedded strata in the Lakota formation. Cross-bedding is a common feature in continental deposits that usually results from the action of wind or water pushing sand. Cross-bedded strata invariably dips in the direction of the current which deposited them. Due to the irregularity of the mass over which the sand has been laid and/or the inconsistency of the depositional agent, the beds are crossed at varying angles and in different directions, presenting an interesting pattern reminiscent of icing swirls on a cake.

Past the cross-bedded strata we encounter a half-dozen, deep vermilion striations about the width of a pencil running a few inches apart parallel through the sandstone. The red lines begin straight, then undulate up at forty-five degrees in a graceful wave before running straight again, suggesting that perhaps water subsided and then rose again, depositing sediments over an irregular beach. Above this curious irregularity in the sandstone formation, everything is smoothed over again by parallel-running striations. A few feet farther around the sandstone ledge, the red striations bow up in one big bulge that somehow seems to overwhelm us. It is time to crawl off the Mesozoic Rim, out of the draw, and back to the highway.

We decide to return to Spearfish, our point of origin, by heading back along the west side of Black Hills via Edgemont, South Dakota, and Sundance, Wyoming, in order to search another area at the edge of the Bear Lodge Mountains for fossil plant imprints.

Edgemont is a small, depressed community situated on a low floodplain south of the Cheyenne River. It was originally plotted by the railroad in the late nineteenth century and since then, like most small isolated western towns, has gone through its share of economic booms and busts. Back during World War II it served as a munitions center employing hundreds of people. After the war it went bust. In the late 1950s it experienced another short boom when uranium, then in great demand, was discovered in small quantities in the southern Black Hills. Some uranium milling went on for a time near Edgemont that left piles of low-level radioactive waste around to pollute the atmosphere and surface water. Most recently Edgemont finds itself perennially in the midst of controversy for wanting to serve as a host for out-of-state garbage and radioactive waste from a variety of states and corporations who see the area's isolated location as prime for dumping all manner of waste.

The Cheyenne River, east of Edgemont, is a shallow, braided stream with large, handsome gallery groves of cottonwoods. At Edgemont we leave the river and drive in a northwesterly direction up over the Greenhorn limestone cuesta which is particularly rich in fossils and out along the Niobrara chalk cuesta. On top of the Niobrara, seventy-five yards from the highway, a pronghorn doe watches her week-old kid frolic on the side of a low, grassy hill. Behind her, twenty miles to the north across a wide windswept plain, the Elk Mountains which are actually part of the Dakota Hogback of the Black Hills, stretch out in a purple haze with a high, billowy cluster of afternoon nimbo stratus building overhead.

At Mule Creek junction, across the state line in Wyoming, we are on the eastern edge of the Thunder Basin which stretches out beyond the horizon to the west. To the east, the high, southwest slope of the hogback looms in the distance. The Thunder Basin is a high, dry grassland steppe, rich in oil and gas and drained by numerous coulees that feed into the Cheyenne and Belle Fourche rivers. Rain, when it comes to this country, is usually accompanied by wild displays of lightning, ear-splitting thunder, fierce winds, and torrential flash floods.

Driving north over the basin, the country is open and desolate. After we re-cross the Cheyenne, we enter an area where the wind has stacked tumbleweed fence-high up along the barbed-wire that parallels the highway right-of-way corridor. The tumbleweed is thick here because this area is presently under cultivation.

One tumbleweed escapes the west fence, bounces, and rolls across the right-of-way and, with a dull thump, slams into the front of Gabel's Honda Civic. It holds tight to the grill. I have run into a few tumbleweeds myself, or to be more exact, they have run into me. More air than substance, it is an odd sensation when they thump into your car.

Tumbleweed is a generic term for the dried stems of Russian thistle *(Salsola kali)*. At maturity the stem of the thistle breaks from its roots and moves freely across the plains or fields pushed by the wind. The bouncing and rolling motion of the plant disperses the seed, sowing the next generation of thistle.

The tumbleweed, a romantic symbol of the old West, is a tough, drought-resistant, alien annual weed that was inadvertently imported with seed grains from the steppes of Asia. In actuality, the tumbleweed is a symbol of the sodbusters who broke the great western grasslands. Where it blows, the land has been cut open.

During the severe drought years of the late 1980s, the town of Mobridge, in north-central South Dakota, was literally inundated with them. They piled up roof-high against houses in town and all but buried them, creating a serious fire hazard.

The stretch from Mule Creek junction to Newcastle, Wyoming, is thirty-four miles. The road parallels Stockade-Beaver Creek a dozen miles or so farther to the east which drains a large part of the central west side of the Black Hills. Along the way of this high, dry open country we encounter numerous herds of pronghorns that number from five to twenty animals.

Pronghorns are commonly called antelope and sometimes "goats" in western South Dakota slang but are actually neither. Antelope live in Africa and the term "goats" probably goes back to the journals of Lewis and Clark who, never having seen any creatures quite like them before, mistook them for wild relatives of the domestic goat.

Pronghorns are members of the Antilocapra family and are unique to North America. While they live primarily on the great plains where their keen eyesight and enlarged windpipe make them hard to run down, they are also found in parts of the foothills, the southern Black Hills, and the Red Valley.

In pre-white settlement days their population was estimated to be between 30 and 40 million, with the greatest concentrations of them on the western great plains. While agriculture and market hunting was the ultimate cause for the reduction of their great numbers, they were also susceptible to winter starvation and possibly die-offs from virulent epidemics.

W. J. Hoffman, who visited the southern half of Dakota Territory in 1873, believed that a fatal epidemic raged among them in the summer of that year and estimated that three-fourths to nine-tenths of the population may have been killed-off. Coincident with this great die-off, he reported that an epizootic disease killed most of the government stock and the Indian ponies in western South Dakota, noting that if the horse epidemic was not the cause of massive pronghorn fatalities, "it is at least a very remarkable coincidence."

Ronald W. Turner in his Ph.D. dissertation paper "Mammals of the Black Hills," noted that epizootic diseases also had a terrible affect on the local Indian population. "Indians," he wrote, "procured their drinking water from the same pools where the ponies drank. Nearly 64 percent of the Indians at this time were affected with cerebrospinal meningitis and suffered a 10- to 12-percent mortality."

However, Colonel William Ludlow in his 1874 *Report of a Reconnaissance of the Black Hills* noted that while antelope were scarce around Fort Lincoln, North Dakota, due to local hunting pressure there, they became more abundant as the expedition approached the Black Hills. "As we proceed [south]," he wrote, "the antelope become more numerous, until finally there is no hour of the day when they are not to be seen either running gracefully off over the prairie or curiously watching the command from the top of some distant bluff."

"The antelope," he continues, "is regarded by hunters as the most difficult to kill of any animal found on the prairie or in the mountains. In proportion to its size, it is more tenacious of life than the grizzly bear, and its astonishing speed often enables it to escape even after receiving a wound that would have immediately brought a deer or an elk to the ground. A specimen, shot by Charles Reynolds, had one foreleg broken at the knee and one hind leg broken just below the knee. Notwithstanding these wounds, it ran much faster than a horse could gallop for over two miles and a half, when, becoming exhausted, it lay down and awaited the approach of the hunter, who gave it the coup de grace. I have seen several specimens wounded in such a manner that their entrails dragged along the ground as they ran, but even under such conditions they can outstrip a horse, until exhausted by loss of blood."

By 1925, after decades of overhunting, only 680 pronghorn were estimated to be living in the entire state of South Dakota. Like the native deer, they had all but disappeared from the Black Hills and surrounding plains. Throughout the 1920s efforts were constantly being made to establish a small population of pronghorn in Custer State Park. After numerous attempts at restocking and exhausting work aimed at controlling disease and predation, a small herd of forty individuals finally took hold in the 1930s and grew to 150 animals by 1948. On the western South Dakota plains, pronghorn refuges were also established in the 1930s in an effort to increase their numbers statewide. By the 1950s and 1960s the pronghorn population had successfully been reestablished and the animals were no longer in danger of extinction here.

Pronghorn on the plains are a wonder to watch. They are a true herd animal—cueing off a lead animal like a school of fish and running in exact unison as a group at speed bursts that can approach 50 mph over rough country. Gabel makes the observation that their simultaneous group movement, akin to the true antelopes and zebras of Africa, is one of the ways they distract and elude predators. "All you can see is a blur of movement," he said, "making it confusing to pick out one animal to attack." Their defense is in their speed, coordinated movements, and their numbers.

In 1985, western South Dakota had a very severe winter with extensive snow and extended periods of intensely cold temperatures (-10 to -20 degrees Fahrenheit). North of the Black Hills out on the plains in places like Butte, Harding, and Perkins counties in South Dakota, winterkill of pronghorn was estimated to be in the area of 90 to 100 percent. In some places conservation officers went out and mercy shot the ragged, starving beasts, remnants of herds that had once roamed extensively over the western third of the state.

The winter of 1991 to 1992, on the other hand, was the second warmest in recorded history in western South Dakota and the pronghorn herds did very well. However, in some areas north of the Black Hills, they still have not recovered enough to return to their old haunts.

Dave Junek, a rancher who grew up and ranched all his life in southern Harding County some sixty miles north of the Black Hills, recalled watching pronghorn migrate across his ranch in a southwesterly direction in the fall. Looking today at the many small herds ranging along the southwest side of the Black Hills, which receives the least amount of snow in the winter, it seems plausible that this mild area is where they have wintered traditionally for millennia. There is also some good proof for this.

On October 16, 1804, Indians told Lewis and Clark, who were at that time on the Missouri above the mouth of the Grand River in northern South Dakota, that the pronghorn were currently on their fall migration west to the Black Hills to spend the winter.

In 1862, naturalist F. V. Hayden, who accompanied many early military expeditions into the Black Hills, Badlands, and Upper Missouri River country wrote: "In the beginning of winter they (pronghorn) may be seen for days following each other in files . . . , leaving the prairie country for the more rugged portions of the country near the Black Hills (foothills). In the spring, usually about March, they may be seen returning again, and distributing themselves over the open prairie." Naturalist writer Ernest T. Seton also reported that pronghorn of the open country move to the Black Hills "from all points on the compass" to winter there.

Junek has not seen any pronghorn on his ranch since the last big winterkill of '85. Looking at these herds in Wyoming suggests that they are the offspring of the surviving remnants of the last winterkill that were either resident or migrants that stayed or migrated down here and have not yet reached population numbers that will force them to disperse farther out and back into northern ranges above the Black Hills.

As we travel north, away from the Cheyenne and the irrigated fields, the tumbleweed noticeably disappears from the fence lines. Eventually the one in the car's grill also bounces off to propagate its seeds. We begin a slow ascent towards Newcastle, Wyoming, where we will re-enter the Black Hills. The country we are now crossing is shrubby steppe dominated by big sage *(Artemisia tridentata)* and greasewood *(Sarcobatus vermiculatus)*. It is wide, windswept country that belongs to pronghorn, jackrabbits, and golden eagles.

As we draw closer to Newcastle I recognize a long, white, diagonal slash, like half of a chevron across the dark green forest of Elk Mountain where the Whoop-up Canyon fire raged back in 1985.

The combination of sitting and driving in the afternoon tends to make me drowsy. Needing fresh air, I suggest taking a walk to survey the country up close, turn over rocks, poke the holes, see what's lurking in the mud. Gabel understands this need implicitly and pulls the car off on the shoulder near a nameless black, gumbo wash that meanders east across the Pierre shale. It could be, by almost anyone's definition, the quintessential "middle of nowhere." Over the fence there is absolutely nothing man made in sight for as far as anyone can see. It looks perfect. Gabel seems to fully appreciate the nature of my mission here: to see nothing and look at everything.

The first sense of the community I feel as we amble down into the greasewood is how tough these plants are. The tallest plant, greasewood is a deciduous native shrub that grows two to five feet high. It has numerous spiny tipped twigs and narrow pale green leaves. Its flowers are green and inconspicuous with male and female flowers growing on different plants as well as in separate locations on the same plant.

Greasewood is characteristic of saline or saline alkaline plains, frequently becoming the sole dominant plant on soil textures ranging from sandy to clay. It is among the most alkali resistant of native shrubs and, while sheep and cattle can browse it, it has a high alkaline content in its leaves and can be lethal to livestock if eaten in large amounts or without the supplement of other feed. In one instance, one thousand sheep were poisoned when they were turned out to feed in a nearly pure stand of greasewood.

Randomly interspersed among the greasewood is big sage. It is the classic signature plant of the high, dry West, suggesting elegance, ruggedness, and fragrance. Big sagebrush is a stout, native plant that normally grows to a height of three to five feet but may attain ten feet in very old plants. While its primary range is in the Great Basin province of North America, it is found in all eleven far western states as well as both Dakotas and Nebraska. Here on the eastern edge of Wyoming, as well as southwestern South Dakota, it grows about three feet high. North of the Black Hills it rarely grows above eighteen inches.

In much of the American West, particularly farther south, during fall, winter, and early spring, cattle and sheep regularly browse it. Its nutritive value is considered to be exceptionally high but because of bitter resins, it is low in palatability. Sage grouse and many large game animals, including elk and mule deer, browse it while pronghorn particularly depend on it for forage. Since the advent of heavy livestock grazing, sagebrush densities have increased while the more palatable associated forbs and grasses have decreased in abundance. Such changes have precipitated extensive sagebrush eradication projects in the West that have been criticized by many people for possible adverse effects on native wildlife.

Big sagebrush with its pleasant, bitter, aromatic odor is the state flower of Nevada and is used almost universally by Native American peoples as a spiritually cleansing/purifying agent. It was also used by Indians as a source of medicine, yellow dye, and fuel.

Growing closer to the ground are patches of blue grama grass (Bouteloua gracilis), buffalo grass (Buchloe dactyloides), and clones of plains prickly pear cactus (Opuntia polyacantha). All are common plants native to the driest aspects of the short grass plains. Also present here are stands of western wheat grass, a taller mid-range grass more common on the east side of the Black Hills.

While walking through these shrubs and grasses Gabel points out black patches of algae growing in the soil on areas strewn with pebbles. Algae are important in establishing a biotic crust on this barren soil and eventually preparing the way for a succession of future plant communities.

Since it has been a wet, cool spring, the wash has intermittent pockets of standing water. Some of the pockets are choked with sedges that echo with the sourceless chirping of frogs. On the east side of the wash above the cutbank is an ant hill which I walk over to examine. Perfectly conical and made of tiny, uniform grains of sand, it resembles a large pile a child might make on the beach. Scattered around the ant hill are tiny claws and the bleached, discarded shells of land snails. At the edge of the ant hill Gabel finds a small skull that once belonged to an immature jackrabbit.

Examining the organic minutiae of the area reminds Gabel of a young student of his who did a study on how ponderosa pine reclaimed a highly acid coal slack site just east of Aladdin, Wyoming, in the Bear Lodge Mountains. The young woman discovered that the pine was not able to reseed itself under these very specific environmental conditions without the interaction of an unusual fungus, *Pisolithus tinctorius.*

Piscolithus tinctorius was discovered on this site in 1980 and is a type of mycorrhizal fungi that forms close, mutually beneficial relationships with plant partners. This fungus is rare to the low, acid soils of the Black Hills and occurs only at this site because of the high acidic condition of the coal slack.

Nutrient levels in the coal slack ranged from 60 to 70 percent less than normal for soils in this region and a level far below nutrient levels necessary for the survival and growth of ponderosa pine and bur oak. However, the mycelium or growing strands of fungi that inhabit the area in and around the roots of the pine and oak aids these trees by absorbing nutrients from the coal slack for them, especially phosphorus. It then makes these nutrients available for use by the trees.

The trees in turn furnish beneficial nutrients produced by their photosynthesis to the fungi creating a partnership whereby the trees are able to survive in nutrient-poor soils. As the trees produce needles and other organic litter, the soil environment gradually becomes less acidic and more favorable for the growth of a second mycorrhizal fungus *(Scleroderma)* which eventually replaces *Piscolithus tinctorius* and continues the partnership with the trees.

Native grasses will eventually return and become established on the site and, with time and the absence of new disturbances, the Aladdin coal slack will be bioremediated and appear much like any other unmined site with a twist involving a seemingly insignificant plant that made a sterile slope suitable for the Black Hills' most conspicuous and dominant tree species.

In the natural scheme of things, its seems no one aspect or process is really more significant than the other, just different. While it is true some are grander or larger and may act as a "keystone" for others, all have their place. Ecosystems, when disturbed, have the tendency to fill a vacuum and re-establish an equilibrium through the coordinated response of its parts to any disruptive situation or stimulus. If bioremediation is not done one way, it will be done another, and the more natural checks and balances in place, the healthier the ecosystem and the more effective the healing.

There is also a cultural analogy to this concept. In the Taos Pueblo of New Mexico there is a small group of Indians who, by choice, occupy the main adobe structure. Residence is free of charge here but there is a catch: the great adobe is without running water, gas, or electricity and the residents there must, in the traditional way, procure their water from the stream and their fuel from the forest.

There is a point to this. The people who live in the big adobe pueblo maintain direct contact everyday with the source of their sustenance. They act as environmental monitors and serve as an alert system when the water turns bad or the forest is ravaged. Everyone in the pueblo depends on them to know when and where their life support system is breaking down. Aldo Leopold stated it another way when he wrote, "There are two spiritual dangers in not owning a farm. One is the danger in supposing that breakfast comes from the grocery, and [secondly], that heat comes from the furnace."

In our economic/social system resource managers are charged with overseeing the removal of great quantities of specific biomass that have an economic benefit, like grass and timber, from the Black Hills forest ecosystem. Scientists and resource managers, by definition, are forced to equate that the sum of all the parts is equal to the whole. This is never completely the case because natural relationships, even if we knew and understood them all, are constantly changing as they respond to a host of variables and climatic stimuli. As regards the earth's biosystems, not everything can be measured with a tool of our invention.

To understand the workings of drought, wind, fire, and floods on a natural community, a good working copy of the original ecosystem blueprints in the form of wilderness areas that receive only minimal disturbance needs to be maintained in order to reconsider at every juncture the grand and subtle relationships of all the parts.

While Nature is forgiving and her biological systems are capable of great renewal in the face of abuse, there is a limit; continuous unabated use without time to rest and heal eventually means fewer parts are replaced, resulting in depletion of natural biodiversity and genetic variability. Biodiversity is the forest or the grasslands immune system; the part of the equation that cannot be factored into the sum.

Walking back to the car, I consider how fossil cycads might get factored into the grand scheme of things. Maybe it's only a philosophical point since most have been gone from the Black Hills for a century and no one seems the worse for it. But then maybe we are. Who knows what positive economic impact tourist development could have had on the people and the community of Edgemont if seventy years ago there had been someone with the foresight to protect and push for the development of Fossil Cycad National Monument.

About a dozen handsome fossil cycad specimens reside in the geology museum of the South Dakota School of Mines, while two huge specimens lay in repose on the outdoor grounds. Remembering them there out of context leads me to think that after one hundred years, perhaps it is time to reconsider creating a cycad national monument and advocate that the preponderant share of "stolen" cycads be returned to the monument site and tastefully "restored" in some way.

After a century of being removed and hidden away, it seems appropriate that the majority of cycads should be returned to the light of day again and afford many of us an opportunity to study and stand amongst them. This would serve as a reminder that this area was once a Jurassic forest environment with a warm, shallow sea, primitive tropical plants, dinosaurs, and a host of buzzing insects flying over soft, wet sand.

6

Black Hills Dinosauria

My fascination with dinosaurs began when I was eight and found a book lavishly illustrated with pictures of the great reptiles. I remember marveling at the forty-ton, eighty-foot-long *Brontosaurus*, with his long neck and small head, standing placidly in a cycad swamp. On the next page was his eighteen-foot-tall nemesis, *Allosaurus*, with glinting reptilian eyes, and teeth dripping with bloody gore. Everything about these primitive creatures was completely out of proportion and bizarre like a hairy apple or a square wheel.

It was all very exotic knowing that they were virtually mindless and have been extinct since the end of the Cretaceous period some 65 million years ago. As a child I tried to imagine what the Cretaceous period was like when I played with my friend Jimmy and his plastic dinosaurs thirty-five years ago in the dry dirt under my grandmother's back porch. It was difficult to conceive of being huge and reptilian, and in the end I abandoned that daydream in favor of others and eventually drifted away from thoughts of larger-than-life, extinct monsters.

That was how I was remembering dinosaurs as I drove west on Interstate 90 headed for Sundance, Wyoming, to meet Dr. Phil Bjork. Bjork is the director of the Geology Museum at the South Dakota School of Mines and Technology in Rapid City and an advisor to a young paleontologist graduate student named John Foster. Foster is a boy who grew up and maintained his fascination with dinosaurs. His interest has taken him to a bone quarry west of Sundance on the edge of the Black Hills.

At the Sundance Mountain View Campground I linked up with Dr. Bjork for the trip to the dig site. The campground is where Bjork,

Foster, and their volunteer crew of five women have been camped for the last week while they excavate the dinosaur quarry. Following a short drive west, we reached the Little Houston Quarry site. The site, located on the interstate right of way, takes its name from nearby Little Houston Creek.

It is mid-July and the morning temperature is a chilly fifty-eight degrees with a light wind and rain clouds scudding ominously over the pine-studded ridges to the northwest. When we arrive, Foster and his crew are just beginning to settle down to a morning's work of dusting and scratching around two piles of fossilized bones.

Foster is a tall, slender young man with light, blond hair and fair skin. He wears a low crown, slouch hat, loose, baggy trousers, a heavy pullover shirt, and a light vibram sole boots. In this weather it is more or less standard outdoor garb for all. The crew will spend most of their day either kneeling or reclining alongside the bones and digging them out with ice picks and hand trowels. Foster is from San Francisco and has an undergraduate degree in geology from Occidental College. This dig is part of his master's thesis project. His goal is ostensibly to explore the Morrison formation surrounding the edge of the Black Hills for vertebrate fossils.

The Little Houston Quarry site consists of two shallow depressions, both about the size and depth of a child's wading pool. In these two depressions lay a matrix of bones embedded in the light gray shale of the Morrison formation. The crew is clearly enjoying the camaraderie and their license to casually recline in the fine, gray dust around the two depressions and casually pick at the matrix. The women are for the most part in their thirties. Three of them are elementary teachers on vacation from Cape Cod. One lady is a businesswoman from Denver and the other is a young paleontologist from the West Coast.

The teachers plan to use this experience to teach about dinosaurs in their classes next fall. One of them tells me that a large number of her students begged to go with her and work on the dig. Some students even offered to cook and clean if she would take them. I suspect most of these extravagant promises were made by desperate children ensnared by their fascination of dinosauria and the West.

The Morrison formation at the quarry site consists of finely laminated sedimentary beds of light green to gray siltstones and green mudstones laid down during the late Jurassic period about 156 to 144 million years ago. While the Morrison shale beds in the Black Hills are generally the color of elephant skin, there are some luminescent bands of pale green and maroon that run through them. There are also some amazing shades of yellow and purple. Color, however, is not its main attraction. For paleontologists, the Morrison has proven to be one of the best-known repositories of dinosaur fossils in the American West.

The Morrison formation derives its name from Morrison, Colorado, where in 1877, a professor named Arthur Lakes, discovered bones of a huge sauropod he named *Titanosaurus montanus* (giant reptile). Later *Titanosaurus* was rechristened *Brontosaurus*, *Atlantosaurus*, and finally *Apatosaurus*. Many of these names were in use during the same period of time since early paleontologists, working separately, believed they had all discovered different creatures. Once the dust finally settled, it became apparent that all these monsters where in fact the same creature and that *Apatosaurus* would be given priority.

Lakes's discovery started an intense rivalry in the West for great dinosaurian trophies which were the current goal of every major Victorian-era museum around the country. The chief rivalry developed between O. C. Marsh of Yale's Peabody Museum and E. D. Cope of the Philadelphia Science Museum. Their rivalry lasted until the end of the nineteenth century when both men died. Cope and Marsh collected and described some of the best early dinosaurian specimens to come from the West and their work ultimately set the pace and the standard for early American paleontology .

Twenty types of dinosaurs have been found in the Morrison beds of Colorado, Utah, and Wyoming while only three of these types have been unearthed in the Morrison around the Black Hills. A major part of Foster's project is to discover how many of these types occur in the Black Hills Morrison, which he estimates to be an average of eighty feet thick as opposed to four hundred feet thick at places like Dinosaur National Monument in northeastern Utah.

In early June of 1991, Foster started searching the Morrison formation for fossils at the southern end of the Black Hills near Hot Springs, South Dakota. From there he worked his way west and north by car around the Black Hills periphery, stopping at various outcrops and road cuts where the Morrison was exposed. One afternoon in late June, while working his way back east on Interstate 90 from Moorcroft, Wyoming, he and co-worker Greg Goeser pulled off to investigate a deep road cut through the Morrison a couple miles east of Inyan Kara Creek. Laying on top of the shale, about midway up the slope, they noticed a small, scrap pile of fossilized bones. To the untrained eye, a scrap pile of dinosaur bones in the Black Hills Morrison formation appears to be nothing more than a group of nondescript, round, gray pebbles that are virtually the same dun color of the shale. Both men, however, quickly recognized them as pieces of bone fragments.

Foster pointed out a pile of bone fragments for me like the ones he first spotted a year ago. They were laying together in a small cluster under a clump of straw-colored crested wheat grass. Altogether the cluster spread over an area no bigger than a dinner plate and was completely unremarkable in color and shape. Upon closer examination, however, one could easily recognize the unmistakable cancellate, sponge-like structure of the stones, typical of the interior of large limb bones and evidence that marrow had once flowed through them.

"These bone fragments are indicators," Foster said. "They tell us that there are probably large limb bones around. We know they have to be large bones to have interior fragments of this size." Foster squatted down next to me as I picked up a bone fragment from the small pile for closer examination. "This pile suggests a strong possibility of finding the remains of a large, extinct reptile near this site," he added.

A few paces west of this scrap pile is where Foster recalled seeing a bone eroding out of the shale. It proved to be the humerus of a *Camarasaurus* that lived and probably died nearby about 150 million years ago. *Camarasaurus* (chambered reptile) was a huge herbivorous sauropod that stood about forty feet high at the head, weighed up to thirty tons, and could attain a length of sixty feet.

Camarasaurus were abundant in the late Jurassic and died off at the beginning of the Cretaceous period, about 144 million years before the present. The Cretaceous itself lasted about 70 million years, during which time great reptilian land monsters climaxed their evolution into a host of species, shapes, and sizes to roam and dominate the earth in vast numbers.

The largest of these "terrible lizards" originated in North America where their fossilized remains have been found buried throughout the high plains and Rocky Mountain region. Many theories—ranging from catastrophic global climatic changes, asteriod impact, and cosmic supernova explosions—have been advanced to explain the demise of these creatures that once dominated life on earth for millions of years.

The least dramatic and simplest theory for their extinction hypothesizes that these huge creatures, growing ever more plentiful as well as massive, became correspondingly more sluggish and less active and strong over succeeding millennia. Their gargantuan size required an enormous amount of plant food for sustenance. Over time, the land simply could not support their numbers and they literally starved themselves to death.

The scenario may have gone like this: The biological collapse of sauropod populations quickly lead to the population collapse of the great carnivorous theropods like *Tyrannosaurus* and *Allosaurus* that preyed on them and gorged on their dead carcasses. As living sauropods became more scarce, their declining numbers were, in turn, hunted even more aggressively by the now half-starved theropods. When sauropod populations reached the point where all their young were quickly devoured, both types—unable to adapt and break the biological chain of events—died out.

As for *Camarasaurus*, their remains were first unearthed at Como Bluff, Wyoming, in 1877. Como Bluff, regarded as one of North America's premier nineteenth-century dinosaur graveyards, is about three hundred miles south and west of the Little Houston Quarry. The Bluff is actually a long, prominent ridge consisting of Morrison shales. It is a few miles east of Medicine Bow, Wyoming, near the old site of Como Station on the Union Pacific Railroad. The quarry site was inadvertently discovered by two employees of the Union Pacific, named Carlin and Reed, while pronghorn hunting in the fall of 1877. Both men believed the bones they unearthed were those of huge crocodiles. They had, in fact, uncovered bones belonging to the skeletons of *Diplodocus*, *Apatosaurus*, and *Camarasaurus*, three of the most massive creatures ever to walk the earth.

The diplodocids were a closely related group of sauropods which include *Diplodocus* (double beam) and *Apatosaurus* (deceptive reptile). *Apatosaurus*, previously more commonly referred to as *Brontosaurus* (thunder reptile), was 69 feet long, stood over 12 feet high at the hips, and weighed in at 30 to 40 tons. *Diplodocus* could out stretch him at 88 feet, but weighed considerably less at a mere 10 tons. *Camarasaurus* fit somewhere in between these two giants in size and stature and as a result was often confused by early paleontologists with *Diplodocus* and *Apatosaurus* in Como Bluff's fossil record. A nearly intact skeleton of *Camarasaurus* was eventually discovered in 1925 at Dinosaur National Monument. This discovery made *Camarasaurus* one of the best-known specimens of its type of dinosaur in North America.

Foster describes *Camarasaurus* as one of the most common sauropods in this formation. The sauropods were a group of gigantic, quadrapedal, herbivorous dinosaurs that include the diplodocids, the brachiosaurids (*Brachiosaurus*), and the camarasaurids (*Camarasaurus*).

The body configuration of these huge beasts all resembled one another. They were characterized by long necks attached to a bulbous-shaped body and counter balanced with long tails. Skeletally, *Camarasaurus* had cleft spines like the diplodocids but lacked the diplodocids tail skids (a flat extension of bone on the bottom of the tail vertebrae). *Camarasaurus* also had relatively long forelimbs and the broad teeth of the brachiosaurids.

The other distinguishing characteristic shared by the sauropods was the location of their large nostrils. All were located above their eyes on the top of their head. Because of the location of their nostrils, it was once hypothesized that these great reptiles lived in the swamp and spent a great deal of time submerged underwater. A model based on physics, however, has pointed out that submersion in a depth of sixty or seventy feet of water would have, theoretically, created enough exterior hydro pressure to collapse their lungs. More recent theories place these creatures completely on land where they probably employed their long necks in browsing shrubs and the crowns of trees much like modern giraffes. Their massive bulk suggests that these great reptiles probably moved graviportally like elephants.

It has been suggested from evidence of vast fossilized trackways recently uncovered in North America and Asia that sauropods behaved socially in the manner of herd animals. These trackways also suggest they may have migrated great distances and were strong and efficient walkers.

Other evidence suggests that dinosaurs practiced communal, social behavior. This theory was derived from the discovery of a group of dinosaur nests in Montana that were found by Robert Makela and John Horner. These nests, built on mounds, were found to contain the fossilized remains of fifteen baby hadrosaurids. Fossil evidence of young dinosaurs found around the nest showed they had well-worn teeth and were considerably larger than hatchlings, implying that the dinosaurs had stayed together for some time and were receiving parental care. Noting this behavior, Horner named this species *Maiasaura* or "good mother lizard."

Further exploration and excavation of the Egg Mountain site revealed another six unoccupied nests with lots of fossilized, crushed egg shell fragments. The nests were spaced twenty-three feet apart—about the size of an adult *Maiasaur*. This relative spatial arrangement, based on adult bird size, is typical of avian colonial nesting behavior where eggs are laid close enough together for maximum mutual protection, yet far enough apart for access past neighbors.

Horner found other nests at a different site which seem to be those of a different smaller dinosaur, hypsilophodontid. These remains clearly show that these animals returned to the same nest annually and also reveal the way in which their eggs were laid, with the pointed end directed into the soil so that the hatchling could emerge from the rounder end of the egg.

Once the hatchlings reached a size where they could defend themselves, they would have to search out their own food and deal with predators. Hadrosaurids, which were bipedal vegetarians, were probably better able to outrun the predatory theropods that hunted them while the enormous mass of the larger, heavier quadrapedal sauropods would have probably been their best defense, making them extremely difficult to stop or pull down.

Theropods make up the other famous group in the order Saurischia. Theropods, which include the carnosaurs like *Allosaurus* and the tyrannosaurids, were the bipedal, carnivorous contemporaries of the sauropods and undoubtedly lived off their flesh. Trackways of theropods like *Tyrannosaurus* suggest they moved along briskly at a pace of somewhere between 3 to 6 mph and may have been able to run at speeds up to 15 or 20 mph. Multiple sets of *Tyrannosaurus rex* tracks suggest they also traveled in groups and may have hunted using ambush along with a mass attack stratagem whereby they rammed their victim, preferably a smaller juvenile sauropod, and quickly proceeded to crush its neck with huge powerful jaws. Carnosaurs and tyrannosaurids also probably scavenged dead sauropods as much as they actively hunted them.

According to Foster, Little Houston Quarry is only the third major site in the Black Hills to yield a relatively large number of dinosaur bones that include remnants of sauropods and theropods. In 1889, O. C. Marsh unearthed the first *Barosaurus*, a type of diplodocid, on the north side of Piedmont Butte just east of Piedmont, South Dakota, and subsequently removed the bones. In 1935, parts of a *Camarasaurus*, two *Apatosaurus*, and a femur from an *Allosaurus* were uncovered from a site near St. Onge, South Dakota.

A century later, fossilized remnants of crocodilians and turtles were unearthed in the Piedmont area along with another partial *Barosaurus* skeleton. It is the smaller creatures as well as the smaller theropods that Foster is most interested in finding. He believes that the Little Houston Quarry holds the biggest promise for small creatures and hopes to find new types of animals and creatures similar to the ones in the Morrison formation of Utah and Colorado.

Taking a closer look at what Foster has found in the bone matrix of the quarry reveals fossilized teeth, ribs, humerus, radius, ulna, sacrum, ilium, and tail vertebrae chevrons of *Camarasaurus*. He estimates that there may be three, possibly four specimens of *Camarasaurus* including a juvenile about half the size of the adults.

Along with the majority of *Camarasaurus* bones, Foster has also unearthed an *Apatasaurus* metatarsal; a femur from a *Diplodocus* or *Barosaurus*; *Allosaurus* teeth and skull fragments; *Dinochelys* (turtle) fragments; unidentified actinopterygian fish teeth; small theropod teeth and footprints; and possibly *Goniopholis* (crocodilian) fragments.

The elements preserved at the Little Houston Quarry are more varied than other localities with most of the fossils, along with abundant layers of plant debris, appearing in the siltstone layers. This quarry unit occurs immediately above a crossbedded channel sandstone in which isolated bones and fragments of the *Allosaurus* skull were found.

The channel sandstone is mostly very fine-grained quartz with occasional rounded clasts of green mudstone and caliche. This indicates that there were periods of low to non-existent water current flow when the channel was probably abandoned and occupied by a pond of more quiet water at which time silt was deposited. Occurrence of the mudclasts in some layers of the siltstones indicates that the channel was occasionally reactivated by relatively strong floods.

What killed these great creatures at this site is a mystery. Since there is what Bjork calls a "weird jumble of bones" in the gray, siltstone matrix, the most expedient explanation is that the animals drowned in a downpour and were washed a short distance to this site during the ensuing flood. Their carcasses were then immediately interred in alluvial sediment and thus preserved.

Bjork notes that the pelvis of one of the *Camarasaurus* is upside down and has been crushed underneath, again suggesting the work of a great natural force like a torrent of water that was able to contort and deposit three or four enormous corpses down stream.

In the following millennia after the flood, silica in the sediment slowly replaced the minerals in the bone and hardened it into stone. A thick layer of sandstone was eventually deposited over the Morrison shale sealing it for 140 million years until the early 1970s when bulldozers cut through this ridge crypt of dinosaur bones to make a path for Interstate 90.

It is now close to lunch time and the storm squall that has been threatening since early morning closes in, forcing the excavators to bring out the blue plastic tarps which are quickly thrown over the quarry pits to protect the fragile bones.

While the excavators head back to the two vans for shelter and lunch, I take a walk along the crest of the sandstone cap ridge to get another perspective of the Little Houston Creek valley. Little Houston Creek drains a small area of broken, pine-covered table land southwest of the Bear Lodge Mountains. Just west of the dinosaur quarry, Little Houston joins Houston Creek which nearly parallels Little Houston draining the other side of a long ridge. Past the confluence of the two creeks, Houston Creek meanders about a mile farther before flowing into Inyan Kara Creek.

The Bear Lodge range proper lies to the northeast of this area. Topographically, the dinosaur quarry is located at the edge of a small uplift known as the Houston Dome. The Bear Lodge Mountains themselves are an extension of the Black Hills that reside entirely within the boundaries of Wyoming. This range is approximately twenty miles wide with a spine that runs in a north-south direction for about thirty miles. The Bear Lodge Mountains were uplifted by vulcanism at the same time the greater Black Hills dome to the south and east was pushed up. The most famous geologic features of Bear Lodge include Devil's Tower and the Little Missouri Buttes, both of which are landmark igneous intrusions into the surrounding sandstone table. They lay on the northeast periphery of the Bear Lodge and are about twenty miles north of the dinosaur quarry.

The ridge above the quarry itself is low and unremarkable. It trends in a north-south direction for a few hundred yards and is covered with even-aged ponderosa pine about saw-log size in diameter (eight to ten inches). Few pines here reach a height above forty feet. I estimate the average age of the pines to be close to one hundred years, but in this dry habitat looks can be deceiving and without the aid of an increment borer for a positive age determination, they may be twice that age.

On the southwest side at the tip of the ridge there are huge blocks of exposed sandstone. This part of the ridge, bearing the direct brunt of prevailing westerly winds, has been scoured and eroded the most. Closer examination of the exposed sandstone reveals crossbedding and ripple marks, clear indications that this ridge was once the floor of a braided stream about 140 million years ago. This information concurs with Bjorks' theory that the dead *Camarasaurus* were washed down a stream course.

Gathered on the southwest edge of the ridge that overlooks Little Houston Creek are a handful of ancient ponderosa pines. Generally, the oldest pines in the Black Hills tend to grow on the driest, rockiest slopes that face south and west. These trees reach the greatest age because conditions are such that they manage to survive the longest here. Ironically, it is not because this is the best place to flourish, but just the opposite; while it is initially more difficult to survive in this environment there are other amenities.

Rock outcrops create a micro-habitat more difficult for competing shrubs, grasses, and pines to grow, ultimately allowing only a handful of the hardiest trees to colonize it. This lack of vegetation and bare earth also works as a natural wildfire break for all but the hottest of fires, thereby protecting the trees when they are most vulnerable.

This rocky advantage is a major reason a grove of ponderosa can attain Methuselan ages. Recently, a ponderosa growing in Reno Gulch on a rock outcrop facing southwest in the central Black Hills was determined to be 695 years old; nearly twice as old as their average life span. This pine which is south of Hill City, South Dakota, is only a few years younger than the oldest ponderosa pine known to exist in California and it is virtually indistinguishable from a host of other ancient trees that grow beside it.

Old growth pines can be recognized by their flattened crowns that are reminiscent of bonsai trees and their large, flat limbs that often occur high up in the tree. In the small vicinity of less than a half acre, stretching from the foot of the ridge to about midway to the crest, there are a half-dozen old growth pines. The oldest trees are probably between two and three centuries old, based on the site and seeing their old growth characteristics including flattened, thinning crowns (old growth trees die from the top down). Had you accompanied the Custer Expedition that passed about fifteen miles east of here in 1874, you would have seen a bare ridge. Only on the extreme southwest side would there be a handful of then medium-age ponderosas.

Laying stretched out on the very south edge of the ridge with trunks uphill are the skeletons of two ancient pines. From the looks of it they also attained great age, died perhaps from a lightning strike, and eventually fell with their crowns pointed down towards the valley. The biggest trees growing on the crest of exposed ridges generally are struck during their life by lightning. The chances of surviving to great age as a pine are better if the location is on the side or the foot of the ridge.

From the looks of these two skeletons, now completely denuded of bark with no trace of that plated armor in sight, they have probably been slowly rotting away in this position for centuries. In this arid climate and at this particularly dry site, dead snags can stand for centuries shedding all their bark before they fall in a windstorm, and then take centuries for the trunk to finally breakdown and rot away.

Looking out from the tip of the ridge to the south, a narrow ribbon of green, meanders down a shallow valley from the east to the west, outlining the run of Little Houston Creek. At the foot of the ridge is the edge of the creek's cutbank, the slope is dominated by big sagebrush with clumps of western wheatgrass. Even at this height of some seventy or eighty feet above the valley, the bank of the creek is cut too deep into the clay to tell if it has water in it.

Pausing about midway down the slope, I turn to look back at the ridge above me and consider the millennia old stream bed, now hardened and eroded into a ridge that juts out like a crooked index finger above the meandering coils of the Little Houston. The softer shales have long ago been eroded away from the sides of it, creating a reverse topography where the ancient stream bed has been elevated far above the land. Then there are the dinosaur bones interred in its north end. First a stream in a swamp; now a dry ridge with pines.

Walking down to the creek, I find numerous water holes in the stream bed. The water holes have a luxuriant growth of submerged algae with duckweed on the surface; some of the water holes look to be about three or four feet deep and obviously spring fed. Growing on the bottom of the stream course are large, thick stands of sedges, cattails, and rushes—indicating that the water table is very close to the surface. Just above the water's edge on the slope, milkweed are blooming pink and white as are yellow coneflowers.

On the south side of the creek the bank is gently sloped, as opposed to the precipitous north side which is actively being stream cut and eroded. Growing between the riparian creek vegetation and the top of the terrace are a couple of old, squat willows. It is apparent that they all started as mere shrubs because now, in their old age, they have thick branches radiating from a gnarled hide bark, old trunk. The branches are splayed out in graceful swirls about the tree trunk while most of the old crowns have long since been battered and snapped off by the wind.

Above the willows, unlike the north terrace which is a sagebrush flat, the south side of the stream terrace is completely choked by buck brush. At the edge of the terrace where it meets the slope of the next ridge, there are occasional thick stands of hawthorn and wild plum; these stands are entirely absent on the north side. The more luxuriant vegetation on this side of the creek which faces north suggests more moisture and probably enjoys slightly cooler temperatures at various times of the year. It stands in contrast to the bare edge of the ridge I just walked off of that faces south.

Upon closer inspection of the old shrub copses I notice that the plums and hawthorns have grown up intimately intertwined together suggesting a mutually beneficial close-knit relationship. All the thickets in the valley are large and very old having reached their maximum height of about eight to ten feet. They have developed a thick canopy with no leaves growing below about six feet where the cattle have been able to reach up and browse them. There are no young thickets growing on this terrace, which is also due to the heavy browsing of them by cattle.

Moving back up alongside the quarry ridge again I head for the bone holes to see if anyone is still around. The site is abandoned and quiet except for the occasional, low muffled rumble of traffic on the interstate. The shallow pits are covered with blue plastic tarps. I sit down in front of the small pile of fossilized bones Foster pointed out to me earlier that morning and try to imagine how paleontologists or archaeologists, 10 million years into the future, are going to interpret the remains of wheeled, metal boxes on the ribbon of concrete that will someday be buried in the ridge below me.

7

Black Hills Biodiversity

Mid-July—high summer in the mountain parks and valleys of the Black Hills. At this time of the season the ambient light is brilliant and the tenor of life rich and vibrant. Whitetail deer stand out with slick, reddish coats against lush, green aspen groves while rusty barbed-wire fence lines host pairs of turquoise-feathered mountain bluebirds. At the higher elevations, either at or above six thousand feet, mountain meadows along with native riparian plant communities are at their peak of floral display. These parks and valleys, if they have been left ungrazed, teem with a biodiverse assortment of plants, breeding insects, birds, small mammals, and reptiles living in close interrelated association.

MCINTOSH FEN

One riparian plant community with these unique characteristics is located near the small hamlet of Deerfield in Castle Creek valley. Known as McIntosh fen, it survives as a rare remnant plant community stranded at the end of the Pleistocene.

Castle Creek valley was so named because of its highly eroded limestone formations that appear as castellated ramparts bordering the valley. The most prominent of these limestone buttes is called Castle Rock. The rock, which resembles a tower, is a landmark in the central Black Hills and was first described in 1874 by Colonel William Ludlow, chief engineer attached to General George Custer's Black Hills Reconnaissance expedition into the Black Hills.

Custer, who commanded twelve hundred troopers, including two companies of infantry and ten companies of the soon-to-be-infamous

7th Cavalry, lead one of the largest reconnaissance expeditionary forces to date into the heart of the Black Hills. The expedition, which left Fort Abraham Lincoln, North Dakota, on July 2, also included a small civilian contingent of Indian scouts, frontier guides, newspaper correspondents, miners, scientists, a sutler, a wagon master, and one photographer, William H. Illingworth. To keep the expedition rolling, 110 wagons and ambulances were provided along with 700 mules to pull the wagons, 1,000 cavalry horses, and 300 head of cattle to slaughter along the way if needed for meat.

The movements of this caravan along the 833-mile route were meticulously recorded on glass plate negatives by Illingworth. Illingworth, who owned his own studio in St. Paul, Minnesota, was considered an expert photographer of his day and was specifically hired by Colonel Ludlow to make the first visual record of the sites and landscapes of the then relatively unknown Black Hills.

The army provided Illingworth with a stereoscopic camera as well as a "traveling dark room" wagon since all negatives had to be developed immediately after their exposure to light. With this cumbersome equipment, Illingworth produced eighty 4.5-by-8-inch, high-resolution glass plate negatives. The majority of Illingworth's glass plates, which are now housed in the South Dakota state archives, feature a fascinating look at historic Black Hills landscapes.

These old plates have become an invaluable resource for historians and scientists interested in tracing Custer's route through the Black Hills. Biologists have used these photographs as permanent "study plot" records against which they have measured ecological changes to the Black Hills environment over the last century.

One of the most productive photographic sites Illingworth recorded was done while the expedition was camped on July 26 and 27 at the foot of Castle Rock. While the command remained in camp for two days in order to give the surveyors and gold prospectors time to thoroughly examine the surrounding country, Illingworth took a series of six photographs in the Castle Creek valley that provides haunting, nineteenth-century panoramic views of the encampment, the vegetation, and the escarpments. The 1874 photographs graphically document a wide, lush valley meadow with sparse stands of mature ponderosa pine growing on the upland areas.

The surveyors discovered that each tributary valley along Castle Creek bubbled with numerous springs of very cold, pure water that kept the small streams flowing for most of the year. They described the soil everywhere in these valleys as moist and the vegetation as fresh and luxuriant. The valleys they reported were heavily grassed and filled with wildflowers while all the streams were then actively occupied with beaver in great abundance.

In 1924, a half century after Custer's visit, Arthur McIntosh, then a biology professor at the South Dakota School of Mines and Technology, found near the vicinity of Custer's Castle Creek camp a rich association of plants growing in zones above a wet, boggy fen. His photographs taken at that time, when compared to Illingworth's, document the invasion of ponderosa pines that were beginning to cover and dominate the upland areas.

McIntosh described his findings extensively in the 1930 issue of the *Black Hills Engineer* in which he wrote, "As a specific and more complex example of vegetational zonation let us consider Castle Creek valley at a point approximately two miles northwest of the Deerfield post office. Here Castle Creek meanders southeastward down a magnificent valley approximately one mile wide. Locally a beaver dam has impounded a considerable pond, drowning willows and converting several acres of low meadowland into marshy sedge moor."

McIntosh, fascinated by the diversity of plants he found growing there, described in detail what they were along with their zonation (relative location) in the valley and on the north facing slope. He noted in his article: "A streamside shrub zone; a sedge moor 150 yards wide; a willow zone; an aspen zone; and a yellow (ponderosa) pine forest (zone)."

Sedge moor zones were not unusual in low mountain valleys of the Black Hills, McIntosh observed that "the water may come from seepage on the slopes above or beaver dams may flood considerable areas. These types of conditions serve to keep the ground wet and boggy for most of the year." He further noted that "various species of sedges and rushes with interlacing rhizomes (underground stems) typically form a mat-like turf on the water-soaked soil."

In his article, McIntosh explained that "in the lowest areas of a moor, the sedge mat actually may be floating on the surface of water a foot or more deep. He added that "walking on such a quaking bog is apt to be an unpleasant experience as one may break through into the cold black water."

In the 1960s, biologists from as far away as Sioux Falls tried repeatedly to relocate this rare Black Hills bog community but were consistently unsuccessful, even though they scrupulously followed McIntosh's directions of "two to three miles above the Deerfield post office."

In the early 1980s Dave Ode, a botanist/ecologist with the South Dakota Department of Game, Fish, and Parks, along with John Pearson, another botanist working with the Nature Conservancy, managed to rediscover what by then had become an illusive botanical site.

Like the other unsuccessful botanists, Ode following McIntosh's directions, found what the other botanists had—an over-grazed pasture and an oat field. Still convinced, however, that the rare and diverse plant community McIntosh had discovered fifty years earlier had not been obliterated, he searched for other clues to its location.

In 1984, after a little detective work, he learned that when Deerfield Reservoir was built in the 1930s, the old town of Deerfield, which McIntosh had used as a reference point, had to be relocated about two miles farther up the valley. Allowing for the shift, he relocated the fen about a half mile above present day Deerfield, South Dakota.

The changes in the bog plant community using McIntosh's photos and report fifty years earlier were dramatic. The aspen grove McIntosh described had been reduced to a few old trees with no regeneration and the willow grove was almost completely obliterated. Ode believed that the integrity of the fen as a viable biotic community was in serious peril.

Most of the changes to this relic, Ice Age fen community were brought on primarily by a number of man-related land use changes that Ode believes probably occurred during the 1940s. The changes included the building of a temporary road just above the fen; the digging of ditches to purposely divert water and drain the fen; the elimination of beaver dams and the heavy grazing of cattle that like to browse tender young aspen and willow. These uses left the meandering fen in the Castle Creek valley in a much-reduced and degraded state.

Fens, like McIntosh, are a rare and distinctive type of wetland plant community that dates back at least one million years to the middle of the Pleistocene Ice Age in the Black Hills. This information becomes impressive when you consider that much of the present-day dominant Black Hills floral community dates to about the middle of the Holocene and is only about five thousand years old.

McIntosh fen probably developed as a result of groundwater seepage along the southwest side of the valley where artesian ground water slowly seeped out of a hillside. The seepage still keeps alive such water-loving plants as horsetail *(Equisetum)* on the hillside while the fen proper harbors only a relic population of the unique plants McIntosh described sixty years earlier. In his 1985 summary report, Ode described McIntosh fen as having "an organic substrate (peat) and noted that it is characterized by groundwater saturation high in carbonate and sulfate salts." He described the fen with its springs "as the source of life that helps sustain upper Castle Creek."

In the early 1980s, using Federal Land and Water Conservation Funds (LWCF), the Black Hills National Forest acquired the property of McIntosh fen from a private land owner. At that time the Forest Service was primarily interested in the property for fishing access to Castle Creek, unaware that they had also acquired a unique and relic plant community.

Ode sent them a copy of his 1985 report citing it as a perfect project for the restoration of an endangered riparian community. Since that time, due primarily to the removal of grazing pressure by the Forest Service, a healthy clone of aspen trees has re-asserted itself and some of the willows are coming back.

Standing in the heart of the fen one late spring afternoon, Ode noted that "this particular fen is one of only three locations that supports the Autumn willow in South Dakota." The Autumn willow, which grows to a height of six feet, is unique in that it flowers in the summer rather than the spring. While it is common in the Arctic reaches of Canada, at this latitude it is found only in micro habitats like McIntosh fen.

Besides the Autumn willow, McIntosh also supports the sage or bog willow which grows to a height of three feet and occurs only at this particular site in the Black Hills. Three other willow species that occur at McIntosh include the plain leaf willow which grows to a height of about four feet, a few specimens of peach leaf willow, and Bebb's willow. The latter two willows can attain heights of twelve to fifteen feet. Bebb's willow is the most common willow in the Black Hills but because of recent drought conditions, willow borers, and grazing it has also decreased in abundance.

Rare flowers growing on or near McIntosh fen include the northern gentian, once abundant but on the decline, and the cottongrass and rush aster. Two of the rarest plants, the bog buckbean and the green sedge, described by McIntosh in his 1930 article, appear to be gone from the site.

Along with its rich plant association of stream and riparian zones,

Castle Creek provides habitat for not only hundreds of plant species but harbors many rare Black Hills insect and animal species—one of which is the tiny redbelly snake, a subspecies endemic to the Black Hills. Redbellies are about the size and girth of a pencil and, as its name implies, have a reddish belly and a pine-bark-colored back. It is one of the state's smallest snakes.

Directions: McIntosh fen is approximately one half mile northwest of Deerfield. Drive northwest past Deerfield, turn left (west) onto U.S.F.S. Road 110. The heart of the fen is just south of the junction. Drive a quarter of a mile farther and park at the first turnoff. Walk through the fence access down to the creek. There are no trails and the site is undeveloped. Follow the creek downstream. When you reach the plank bridge you are at the fen.

BOTANY BAY

Science instructors from Black Hills State University in Spearfish, South Dakota, refer to it informally as Botany Bay. It is a tiny refuge that harbors a small host of primitive plants located in the narrow limestone neck of Robison's Gulch. The plants are not particularly rare, just primitive from the standpoint of evolutionary development and unusual, relatively speaking, to the high, dry setting of the Black Hills.

Dr. Audrey Gabel, a biology instructor from the college, describes it as "going back in geologic time," when she stops to examine the lush growth of ferns, mosses, and liverworts in the heart of Botany Bay. "You could be back 300 million years," she adds, admiring the variety of ferns that surround her.

Ferns and their allies once dominated the Earth during the Carboniferous period that began some 350 million years before the present. They are considered primitive because they do not produce seeds. All of these primitive plants require a relatively constant, shady, moist micro-habitat to thrive in like that of the Carboniferous period. Botany Bay provides this. It is shaded nearly all day long from the hot sun and the limestone walls seep life-sustaining water.

Liverworts grow on the large boulders situated at the edge of the gulch's moist limestone walls. These plants take their name from their liver-shaped body which consists of one asymmetrical leaf about the size of a coffee-cup saucer with rhizoids (tiny plant hairs that serve as primitive roots). Many botanists believe liverworts were among the first terrestrial plants.

Growing on the limestone walls and covering boulders situated in the center of Botany Bay are mats of thick, lime green mosses. Mosses are also considered to be important evolutionary transition plants that first made the change from life in the water to life on land. While they appear to have stems, leaves, and roots like higher plants, these structures are superficial, lacking the true vascular tissue necessary for the movement of nutrients and water through the plant body.

Mosses of many varieties often cover bare rock and ground and as such are considered primary soil builders. Moss protoplasm has the amazing ability to survive long spells of heat and dryness, so while a clump of moss may look dead and dry, following a good rain it will again become green and active. It is this characteristic perhaps more than any other that has allowed mosses to spread profusely and to successfully colonize the earth from the humid tropics to the cold, barren reaches of the Arctic.

However, the dominant plant in the small wet throat of Botany Bay is the fern. Gabel refers to two dominant genera growing here: shield fern *(Dryopteris)*, a large fern with big fronds that grows to be about eighteen inches high; and fragile fern *(Cystopteris)*, a smaller species that grows only four to six inches above the ground.

Ferns are vascular plants that reproduce by spores. They probably evolved into the first true seed-bearing plants. Botanists consider them to be an important transition plant between the early primitive spore-bearing species and the later seed-bearing types. These early seed ferns became extinct millions of years ago but not before plant types like them gave rise to the modern gymnosperms which include conifers such as pines, cedars, and spruces. Ferns also gave rise to the first primitive angiosperms.

Numerous species of ferns lived and died in great abundance for 70 million years during the tropical Carboniferous or "Coal Age." It is the remains of their decomposed bodies, compressed over eons of time, that created the great coal deposits of the world, allowing the rise of our modern civilization which is based on an oil and coal burning lifestyle.

Bracken ferns which grow farther up the gulch on the higher, drier slope beyond Botany Bay are of particular interest to Gabel. As a mycologist or fungal specialist, Gabel is particularly interested in fungal plant pathogens that cause diseases in plants.

Fungi are filamentous, spore-bearing organisms which lack chlorophyll and are unable to synthesize their own food. Some fungi may have evolved from algae (phytoplankton) that, after attaching themselves to other plants or animals for a long period of time, lost their ability to make chlorophyll. Finding it easier to parasitize other living organisms, they consequently became dependent on them for their sustenance.

Fungi live as saprobes obtaining their nourishment either from dead plants and animals, bringing about in turn their eventual decay. Fungi also function as parasites of living plants and animals causing disease. In Botany Bay many examples of fungi are apparent at all levels of life and death from mushrooms to tree shelf fungus. These particular fungi are breaking down dead cells. However, also apparent in the moist climate of Botany Bay are the parasitic fungal plant pathogens that appear as odd-colored spots on green leaves. These curious anomalies include Blisters, Smuts, and Rusts that are actively attacking living plant protoplasm.

Gabel is presently doing research on a fungus called *Cryptomycina pteridis* that attacks Bracken ferns in the United States. Bracken ferns are poisonous and carcinogenic to livestock. As a global species, Brackens are known to be attacked in most habitats by *C. pteridis*, except on the isles of Great Britain. In the moist climate of Great Britain with no apparent biological check, Brackens have taken over large areas of land, growing to heights of seven feet—in effect making it a serious plant nuisance that has become both difficult and expensive to deal with.

Presently Gabel is studying and working with this fungus that parasitizes Bracken Ferns in Botany Bay to learn more of its growth patterns and method of attack. Ultimately she hopes to determine if *C. pteridis* can be used as the perfect biological check on British Bracken Ferns. Perhaps the small enclave of Botany Bay in the northern Black Hills may provide the key in solving a serious problem on the other side of the world.

A bit farther up Robison Gulch, beyond the moist environs of Botany Bay, the hillside becomes much drier and more typical of the Black Hills environment. In this location some fine examples of 250- to 300-year-old ponderosa pines thrive. While this is about the average life span of this particular species, some may live to be almost twice that age.

These pines have been able to attain this great age because of the relatively steep, isolated, inaccessibility of the site. Ancient pines can be identified by their deep, pumpkin orange bark; their wide, straight trunks; and their high, flattened tree tops. There is no trail here and you must pick your way through the timber to get to them. Other examples of these old trees can be seen from the highway while driving up Spearfish Canyon.

Directions: To find Botany Bay and Robison Gulch drive six miles up Spearfish Canyon on U.S. 14A from the town of Spearfish. On the west (right) side of the canyon there is a small picnic area. Park here and proceed west up a steep trail for about a quarter of a mile until you get to the fern garden of Botany Bay.

THE ORCHIDS OF ENGLEWOOD SPRINGS

Not far above the old townsite of Englewood, South Dakota, high in the northern Black Hills, a strong artesian spring bubbles from the side of a steep hill. The water is clear and fresh and runs down a slope through thick stands of spruce to a small mountain park to become the headwaters of Whitewood Creek.

There is nothing to distinguish the gravel road that winds far below the spring except the faint sound of trickling water that flows in a culvert beneath the road. If you happen to stop there in late July and walk up the hillside below the spring, chances are good the tart, scarlet fruit of thimbleberries and raspberries will catch your eye and tantalize your palate.

Over ten years ago the "Orchid Lady" of the Black Hills, Myrtle Kravig and her husband Clarence happened to stop here one summer afternoon. Following the water up the hillside and knowing it held the promise of a mossy spring and perhaps rare flowers, the Kravigs climbed the hill. For their effort, they were rewarded along the way with the discovery of a host of rare and delicate orchids.

For nearly six decades the Kravigs conducted plant collecting expeditions throughout the Black Hills. Myrtle was an amateur botanist until 1958 when she went back to Black Hills State and earned a college degree in botany. After that she became one of the foremost authorities on wildflowers and plants in the Black Hills.

The story of the Orchid Lady begins in Lead, South Dakota, when Clarence, working for Homestake Mining Company as a geologist, met Myrtle in the early 1930s. Myrtle, a recent graduate of St. Cloud Teacher's College in Minnesota, had just started teaching music at the high school. They married in 1933 and theirs became a lifelong love affair with the rocks and flora of the Black Hills. As Clarence put it, "I liked rocks and she liked plants so it worked out well." Clarence did most of the photography amassing over one thousand color slides of Black Hills flora while Myrtle collected, pressed, and identified the plants.

In August of 1990, Myrtle passed away at the age of eighty-two. Shortly before her death, she and Clarence decided it was time to share the secret of the Englewood Springs orchids with other botanists in the state so that it might be recognized and conserved into the future. To that end, a handful of South Dakota botanists are now aware of the best collection of orchids in the Black Hills.

Orchids are pretty fussy plants. They require a cool, damp habitat to grow and produce the showy exotic flowers for which the family is justifiably famous. However, the casual visitor to Englewood Springs could easily overlook the particular orchid varieties that thrive in this humble, isolated setting.

Growing not far below the spring is the northern green orchid *(Habenaria)*. Its flowers are small, inconspicuous, and mostly green, alternating around a straight plant spike that never stands above two feet high. Commenting once to state botanist Dave Ode that there really was not much to get excited about regarding *Habenaria's* plain green flowers and small unassuming stature he replied somewhat defensively, "Not so, that flower oozes sexuality—you just have to see it through the eyes of a moth."

Another orchid species found near the springs, and considerably more glamorous, is the striped coralroot *(Corallorhiza)*. This small striking orchid consists of one delicate, rose-pink stalk less than twelve inches high with purple-striped flower parts arranged around the upper half of the stem. It is a true saprophyte, lacking green leaves and the capacity to make its own chlorophyll. It derives its nutrients from the dead remains of other plants and fungi in the soil.

Ode described another small orchid, the broad-lipped twayblade orchid *(Listera)* which grows near the water, barely attaining a foot in height, as simply the "ugliest orchid." Hardly more attractive than common plantain, I try to imagine a moth that finds it attractive. The twayblade derives its name from a pair of roundish broad leaves about the size of a glass coaster that grow along each side of the stem. Above the two leaves, intricate yellowish green flowers are arranged in a loose spike-like fashion. While it is common in New England and the Midwest, Englewood Springs in the northern Black Hills is the only site it is known to occur in the northern Great Plains area.

Another relatively uncommon plant in terms of numbers found at Englewood Springs is monk's hood. Like the orchids found at the Springs, it requires a special habitat that includes moisture, shade, and certain soil requirements. Monk's hood is well known by botanists for its beautiful purple flowers and its deadly poisonous seeds and root parts. Wherever they grow, they are relatively uncommon in terms of numbers. The flower has a highly arched, purple-colored sepal called the helmet. The opening of the flower is narrow and almost beak-like. Plants grow to heights of one to two feet tall with several deeply divided "crowfeet-like" leaves.

David Lewis, a biochemist from South Dakota State University, is presently conducting research on certain plant alkaloids that show promise as a new type of painkiller. He is researching monk's hood as a possible cure for pain. The seeds he is using to grow monk's hood for his research have come from the plants at this rare site.

In recent years the small mountain park below Englewood Springs, like many in the Black Hills, has become choked with thistle. Slowly and inexorably, thistle is moving up the slope and encroaching on the site. Besides the encroachment of thistle and leafy spurge, there is another danger from active logging which was being undertaken just a short distance away. Gabel and her husband, Mark, have written letters to the Forest Service informing them of the site's unique biodiversity and the need to afford it special conservation protection.

The site is so special and unique Gabel wishes it to remain unmarked; however, those interested in visiting and learning more about this rare orchid site should visit the Black Hills State University Herbarium or contact her or Dr. Mark Gabel at the college for more information on these regionally rare plants.

The Black Hills State University Herbarium in Spearfish contains the best collection of Black Hills plants in the world. It also houses the Myrtle Kravig Botanical Library which includes over one thousand color slides taken by her husband and over two hundred volumes of modern botanical literature dealing with the taxonomy, medicinal uses, food production, and ecology of plants.

BLACK FOX VALLEY

In 1892, Per Axel Rydberg took the train up to the booming Black Hills gold mining town of Rochford, South Dakota. Rydberg, a field agent for the United States Department of Agriculture, had been sent to compile an inventory of Black Hills flora. Wandering up the south fork of Rapid Creek, near its confluence with Rhoad's Fork, he found a rare plant growing in a tiny spruce swamp in the Black Fox valley. He called the herb sweet coltsfoot.

Botanists may be the only people who can truly get excited about finding a low, inconspicuous plant that grows about six inches above the earth, has one large green leaf that resembles the foot of a horse and prefers the climate of a moist, bug-infested swamp. However, it is areas exactly like Black Fox with its patchwork mosaic of spruce-element plant communities, that harbors the best potential for rare and unusual plants in the Black Hills.

Black Fox valley, at 6,800 feet, is a fine example of a northern Coniferous Forest Community dominated by white (Black Hills) spruce *(Picea glauca)*. The occurrence of white spruce in the Black Hills represents an isolated disjunct pocket of a boreal tree species that is separated by several hundred miles from its main range to the north.

Typically, extensive spruce forests in the Black Hills occur at higher elevations in cool canyons or in moist conditions on north-facing slopes. The headwater tributaries of Spearfish Canyon and Black Fox Canyon are particularly conducive to the growth of these dense spruce forests.

Black Fox valley proper begins a few miles above Rochford and stretches for about four miles up Rapid Creek's south fork to Rhoad's Fork. A closer inspection of the spruce community on Rhoads's Fork, just above its confluence with Rapid Creek, reveals the presence of some interesting and extreme botanical elements.

At the lower end of Black Fox valley there are a lot of "grass-like creatures" that inhabit the valley from the edge of the creek bank right up to, in some cases, where the spruce forest begins. "Grass-like" refers to plants that look like grasses but are in fact sedges or other grass look-alikes. Sedges are uniquely adapted for life in a wet environment. They have long hollow, slender stems with a fruiting spike at the end of each stem formed from an inconspicuous flower.

A preponderant share of the Black Fox valley is a wet sedge meadow containing some rare, unremarkable-looking plants like the delicate sedge and the gray sedge growing in the wettest areas. Above these wet meadows, scattered around the valley are a host of common woody shrubs that include elderberry, nannyberry, grouseberry, service-berry, and red-osier dogwood. These sedge meadow communities are the primary building blocks of this high mountain food-chain pyramid.

In the pre-white settlement days when wapiti (elk) were abundant, sedge meadows like Black Fox attracted small herds of them just after dusk to graze the sedge, browse the shrubs and water. Where there were wapiti in the food chain, there were mountain lions, wolves, and bears.

Sedge meadows of Black Fox are also important to a host of insects and small critters including voles, shrews, and small reptiles like the smooth green snake, the Black Hills redbelly snake, and the wandering garter snake. These animals form the next level of the food chain pyramid just above the plants.

The presence and abundance of these small creatures at Black Fox attracts a wide variety of forest raptors. Those present include the rarely seen and widely dispersed goshawk, as well as a variety of smaller broad-winged, buteo-type hawks. These raptors all nest in and around Black Fox valley feeding on the abundance of reptiles and small mammals that inhabit the swamp and meadow floor.

Up Rhoad's Fork and just across from the Black Fox campground, water seeps out of the base of a mountain creating one of the most extreme and bizarre habitats in the Black Hills—a moss barren. This barren (bare earth area) is the result of a concentration of iron so high that over the centuries it has created an impermeable, toxic substrate that inhibits the growth of most plants.

The only plant able to establish itself on this iron-rich stratum is moss, an ancient, primitive plant, which in some places has formed a series of two-foot-high hummocks. Normally rubber boots would be required to walk through the Black Fox moss barren, but at this time of the year (late summer) it is usually dry and easy to inspect the soft, lime green hummocks that act in some cases as a spongy support for struggling dwarf bog birches and spruce.

A bit farther up Rhoad's Fork, intergrading with the seasonally wet sedge meadows, are small spruce swamps. It was this type of spruce swamp where Rydberg found Sweet Coltsfoot and where it continues to grow today. The swamp fascinates botanists on the look-out for other rare species.

Having evolved in and occupying a wetter habitat, a Black Hills spruce community is usually immune to all but the hottest of forest fires. However, unlike pine, spruce with their low, tight whorl of branches are much more susceptible to fire and slower to regenerate an area.

Pure stands of spruce tend to grow tall and thickly together, creating a tight, dark canopy that literally shades out all other plant competitors. Henry Newton mentioned in his 1875 *Black Hills Resource Report* that the small, slender spruce trees were much sought after by the Indians who visited the Black Hills in the spring for the express purpose of procuring them for teepee lodge-poles.

In canyons where the soil is rich, white spruce can attain a height of one hundred feet and occasionally reach a diameter of two feet although eight to fifteen inches is the average. Regeneration in a dense spruce community occurs when an ancient spruce falls over, allowing sunlight to reach the forest floor. This spruce "tip-over" effect breaks the dark canopy and allows for the regeneration of small clearings that often harbor rare plants.

Ode compares a spruce swamp community, with its shallow-rooted plants, to a rain forest community where all the living and decomposing material is above the soil's surface. What is most significant about these spruce communities, he maintains, is the presence of permanent water in an essentially dry environment. These rare plants are not adapted to drought—if water for whatever reason should disappear, these plant communities would rapidly perish.

Another curious component, often associated with the spruce forest community and in evidence at Black Fox, is a stringy, bluish green growth that hangs in long drapes from the trees like Christmas tree tinsel. Commonly called "reindeer moss" or "old man's beard," *Usnea* is in fact a lichen. Lichens demonstrate a mutualistic relationship in which various species of fungi grow in partnership with simple cyanobacteria or green algae. The algae are contained in a network of fungal threads or hyphae. Food manufactured by the alga component is shared with the fungus, which furnishes the moisture-retaining habitat and structure necessary for the algae. Lichens, of which there are about fifteen varieties, are adaptable to the meagerest of environments including tree bark, rocks and bare soil.

Directions: The Black Fox valley covers approximately sixty-five acres in the Black Hills National Forest. The heart of this valley is at the confluence of the South Fork of Rapid Creek and Rhoad's Fork located seven miles west of Rochford on U.S.F.S. Road 231. It is at this point that the valley floor widens to about three hundred yards and supports a mosaic of spruce swamps, cattail ponds, and sedge meadows.

The United States Fish and Wildlife Service and the South Dakota Department of Game, Fish, and Parks have both respectively identified these streams as "highest priority" fishery resources and "high quality" trout streams. The spruce swamp and sedge meadow community types found in the Black Fox valley are considered very rare for South Dakota and occur only at a few sites in the Black Hills.

BOREAL REFUGIUM

It is slow-going, snaking through a maze of one-lane logging roads ten miles south of Beulah, Wyoming. Around a curve on one of the steep inclines, a loaded logging truck nearly pushes Hollis Marriott's Datsun pickup off the narrow lane. For a tense moment, we perch at the edge of a steep drop-off while the logger roars by in a cloud of dust.

After a series of tight hairpin turns and switchbacks, the gravel road eventually peters into a dirt track before finally ending at the brink of a steep cut-bank on Sand Creek known as the Sand Creek Crossing. The creek bed, which is about forty feet wide and bone dry, is clogged with round cobblestones the size of bowling balls. It is late August and the air temperature this afternoon, even at this elevation of nearly five thousand feet, will come close to hitting the century mark.

We clamber down the bank, cross the dry bed, and hike up into a small, unnamed side drainage that winds into the mountains in a southeasterly direction. The drainage is brushy and densely vegetated. There is no trail and we must bush whack our way around boulders and talus slides.

Scientifically speaking the "brush" is a young paper birch/hazelnut plant community that thrives in mesic (moderately wet) drainage bottoms and on steep, north-facing slopes in the northern Black Hills. This type of plant community is more typical of the boreal (northern) forests of the upper Great Lakes region and Canada. In the Black Hills it is a small, exotic community hundreds of miles removed from its great boreal parent to the northeast.

The Black Hills have long been famous as a botanical crossroads with elements of vegetation from four of the major biomes or vegetative complexes of North America. The four biomes that characterize the Black Hills include the Rocky Mountain coniferous forest which is dominated by the ponderosa pine; the northern Great Plains grassland complex; the deciduous forest complex represented by eastern hardwoods; and the northern coniferous or boreal forest complex dominated by the white (Black Hills) spruce.

Research on the species origins of over one thousand Black Hills plants conducted by biologists in the late 1920s revealed that 30 percent were Rocky Mountain species; 17 percent were Great Plains species; 9 percent were eastern deciduous forest types; 6 percent were of boreal origin; 4.5 percent characterize southwestern species with the remaining 33 percent representing widespread species and introduced forms. Only .5 percent were considered possible endemic forms.

In regard to the boreal plants, their arrival can only be guessed at, but their departure probably coincided with the end of the Ice Age. About ten thousand years before the present, the boreal forests of Canada, which had once extended as far south as Nebraska, had by this time retreated far to the north. The retreat followed in the wake of a climatic trend in the northern hemisphere characterized by warmer and drier weather conditions. In this climate, boreal plants gave way to species better adapted to periods of drought and heat. However, a handful of relic boreal plant populations managed to survive in suitable refuges such as the cool, moist gulches of the northern Black Hills. These survivors, now widely separated from their main ranges to the north, are referred to as boreal disjuncts.

Relic boreal plant populations are found where a suitable habitat exists. If the habitat is large enough, there may often be several different species of boreal holdovers that comprise a community of plants making their last stand in the Black Hills against the warming of the Holocene.

For botanists and biogeographers an interesting aspect of the northern Black Hills is this relic "boreal zone." The boreal zone is sharply defined by physical and biological attributes, the most important being an average of about twenty-four inches of annual precipitation and a relatively cool, microclimate.

This relatively wet zone (the average rainfall of the surrounding grasslands and foothills is about eighteen inches) occurs at Black Hills elevations ranging from about four thousand to seven thousand feet with soils and substrates that include limestone, shale, sandstone, igneous rocks, and alluvial (stream bottom) deposits. The higher elevations, which are also generally cooler, compensate for the temperatures you would otherwise normally find several hundred miles north.

Since rainfall in the Black Hills is always an uncertain factor, a variety of overlapping and interacting topographical features, including springs and natural landforms, also helps to create the cool, moist habitat necessary for a Black Hills "boreal refugium." Boreal refugia tend to be restricted to steep, north-facing, heavily shaded side drainages where direct exposure to sunlight is at a minimum, allowing life-sustaining moisture and snow to linger the longest. Often this is not enough for some of the rarest, primitive, water-loving plants that require a steady reliable source of moisture like a north slope seep or spring.

Within the small boreal refugium of upper Sand Creek, sheltered in the cool, dense green foliage of birch and hazelnut, are surprises that include the regionally rare and graceful sword fern or northern holly fern. Here also lingers a population of clubmoss known as ground cedar that is common in Canada, northwest Montana, and the Great Lakes region. This population is probably comprised of only one plant or clone (it spreads by means of root rhizomes and reproduces asexually) making it extremely rare for the Black Hills.

Up another side drainage on a north side slope, a tiny inconspicuous boreal plant called moschatel, grows on a lush, green moss mat that drips with water. Another small plant called mitrewort that prefers mossy rocks near shaded streamlets is also present. Sword fern, clubmoss, moschatel, and mitrewort are found along with six other rare plants in a series of small drainages on upper Sand Creek. These populations are very small ranging anywhere from one to two hundred individuals, making them regionally rare and extremely vulnerable to destruction.

While the stream bottom of Sand Creek has been heavily impacted and highly disturbed by over a century of mining, logging and grazing, the side drainage slopes which Marriott and I visited—because of their steep, rugged, inaccessibility—have remained pristine, providing habitat for a half score of rare plant species. It is this handful of isolated drainages on upper Sand Creek in the Wyoming area of the Black Hills, too rugged for timbering and grazing that Marriott periodically surveys for the Nature Conservancy. She, on behalf of the Nature Conservancy, has proposed this refugium for protection under the U.S. Forest Service's Special Botanical Area (SBA) designation.

Marriott believes it is important to conserve these relic boreal zone plants in the interest of preserving the biodiversity of the Black Hills. "We need to preserve this small gene pool," she explains, "as a clue to the past. These plants act as indicators of environmental change and as a clue to evolution, telling us how plants change after being isolated for over ten thousand years."

She stressed the fact that decisions made by the Nature Conservancy (TNC) in regard to the best natural areas for protection are based strictly on scientific information and data rather than scenic values or emotional appeal. "The primary goal of TNC," she said in regard to the Black Hills, "is to effectively protect the full range of biological and genetic diversity."

Marriott believes the Nature Conservancy has found an effective way for analyzing and protecting natural habitat diversity. She describes it as the filter factor. "There are two ways the conservancy screens an area," she said, "through a coarse filter and fine filter." She described the coarse filter as TNC going after relatively pristine examples of natural plant communities that protect entire ecosystems. These areas might end up as nature preserves. The fine filter is TNC's effort to preserve singular relatively small areas that harbor rare plants and animals that might be missed by the coarse filter like the upper drainage of Sand Creek.

As a society, Marriott feels we can afford to protect these small enclaves of rare plants, believing that "we are not so economically impoverished that these areas should be overlooked. It's like saving an old historic building or an archaeological site," she said, "when it's gone, it's gone."

CASCADE SPRINGS VALLEY

Watching the clear, pure water of Cascade Springs bubble up out of rock can be a primal, mesmerizing experience. Because water is one of the four elemental mediums necessary for life, warm springs like Cascade were often considered to have sacred significance by native peoples of the Black Hills who described them as "beneficent gifts of the Great Spirit."

Cascade Springs, located near the edge of the relatively dry, southern Black Hills, was undoubtedly once accorded such reverence. Here, in a quiet scenic gulch, two large artesian springs send a torrent of sparkling water down through a ghost town, over a waterfall, and eventually into the shallow Cheyenne River. The trip from well spring to river is a mere two miles.

A century ago a group of Chicago speculators founded the town of Cascade Springs at the mouth of Alabaugh Canyon just below the outlet of the main springs. The feature centerpiece for the town was to be an impressive mineral spa house made of stone to rival the Evans Hotel in nearby Hot Springs. In June of 1891, the boom kicked off with the sale of town lots. During the next three years a frenzy of promotion and construction produced twenty businesses and six hundred residents.

Three years later in 1894, the town went bust when the railroad stopped at Hot Springs. Most of the boomers picked up what they could carry and left the rest for the scavengers. Only a few scattered remnants of the town, located nine miles south of Hot Springs on South Dakota 71, remain as evidence of those short-lived glory days.

In 1898, Dr. Charles E. Bessey, one of the pre-eminent botanists of nineteenth-century America, and Dr. Frederic E. Clements, a notable Victorian ecologist, paid a visit to Cascade Springs to confirm the presence of a fern known as the southern maidenhair. Tipped off to its presence by a local plant enthusiast, the biologists were delighted to find the fern growing in great profusion and "adorning limestone crevices" along the banks of the stream.

The eminent botanists noted that the southern maidenhair ferns growing along Cascade Creek were hundreds of miles north of their normal range which encompassed the stream valleys of the desert Southwest and the lowlands of the southeastern United States.

Following in Bessey's footsteps thirty years later, Dr. Arthur C. McIntosh investigated the botanical marvels of Cascade Valley. McIntosh also noted that the ledges of the stream gorge just above Cascade Falls contained a peculiar rock formation composed of fossil stoneworts.

Stoneworts, also known as Charophyta or simply Chara, are primitive plants that bear an affinity to algae and mosses. They grow in extensive colonies below the surface of clear-water lakes and streams. This peculiar rock formation along Cascade Creek is composed of petrified stoneworts and other tube-like structures McIntosh speculated may represent fossilized worm burrows. McIntosh theorized that the water in Cascade Creek, which is richly charged with inorganic compounds including calcium salts, fossilized these plants.

The process may have developed something like this. In the distant past, Cascade Creek meandered over a wide area slowly building up a hard pan, non-porous, calcium substrate. Shallow wet sloughs were created as part of this process. The heavy load of mineral salts flowing through the sloughs eventually encased dead and decaying plants solidifying them into stone. As the Black Hills uplifted, Cascade Creek slowly cut down through the rock it had created, leaving the fossilized stoneworts exposed as a ledge now some twenty feet above the present stream grade.

This process is still in evidence today just above Cascade Falls. There a slough is being flooded in the same manner that must have occurred in the distant past. Everywhere you place your foot down in the tall grass it sinks into inches of water before it hits the hard substrate. At the edge where the slough borders the flowing stream, water pours uniformly off of it like spilled milk off a table. In the slough, dead grass stems and roots can be readily observed discoloring and hardening from the calcium-laden water. It is a rare instance where the process of fossilization occurs even as the observer looks on.

Other rare plants present around this unusual micro-habitat between the springs and the falls include the stream orchid, beaked spike rush, and the tulip gentian. Of these three, the former two plants along with the maidenhair fern are found only in the Cascade Valley and no where else in the Black Hills and northern Great Plains. The rest of their kind live hundreds of miles to the south, making them a rare, isolated group of southern disjuncts.

What allows these plants to thrive here is the relatively warm water. At a constant sixty-seven degrees Fahrenheit, Cascade Springs never freezes. Since it maintains a constant steady flow year round, it has created a unique stream corridor that serves as a winter haven for a handful of relatively unusual plants and possibly animals.

Dave Ode, South Dakota state botanist, refers to these rare southern disjuncts as "ecological clues" or tip-offs that this area may also be a unique habitat for a host of other species including small mammals and invertebrates. Invertebrates are animals without a backbone and include the vast spectrum of aquatic and terrestrial arthropods.

To test his theory, Ode set out a series of traps in 1984 along Cascade Creek below the springs to sample the invertebrate population. The results, however, proved inconclusive. The following morning a group of elementary kids on their annual field trip waded into the stream and collected all the traps before Ode could check them.

Nonetheless, noting that a lot more investigation and research of the flora and fauna needs to be done, Ode believes—like Bessey and Clements a century earlier—that the Cascade valley is a significant ecological site for floral and possibly faunal disjuncts.

The last chapter of the Cascade Springs story begins around 1910, when a businessman named J. H. Keith purchased the land that encompassed the old townsite, the main springs, and the falls. Following Keith's death, the property went to his daughter, Mrs. Edna Keith Florence, who, recognizing the beauty and significance of the springs and falls to a host of songbirds, wild animals, and humans, donated both sites to the U. S. Forest Service to be conserved in the name of her father.

One pleasant summer afternoon, sitting by the springs in J. H. Keith Park and reflecting on Edna Keith Florence's gift, Ode remarked that "for all practical purposes, she gave this land to all of us." We both understood without speaking that the "all of us" encompassed the host of creatures great and small, winged and legged, feathered and finned that draw sustenance and refreshment from that "beneficent gift."

8

Fire in the Forest

It is mid-May, the beginning of the fire season in the Black Hills. The weather pattern, which for the last few weeks has been wet and cool, has abruptly shifted to hot and dry. On Friday evening the first big thunderstorm of the season rumbled into the Hills from the northwest, creating a dazzling nighttime display of electrical energy.

The following Monday morning I drive up to the Black Hills Harney District Ranger Office outside of Hill City, South Dakota, to meet with District Ranger Glen McNitt and Dick Kessler, the Forest Timber sales group leader. Kessler, an eleven-year veteran of the Black Hills National Forest, is taking McNitt and me out on an afternoon orientation tour of the Bearhouse Project. McNitt is a recent transfer into the district from the Pike-San Isabel National Forest in southern Colorado. In his thirties, he is personable, straightforward, and seems open to suggestions and new ideas. He is like a lot of the new, young district rangers coming up through the ranks and understands the public's need and desire for more information on how national forest lands are being managed and used. He and Kessler have made every effort to accommodate me.

As McNitt makes his final preparations to depart with us for the day, the office radio starts to buzz. There is a fire, maybe two, somewhere in the district. One report has one burning near Keystone; another is reported to be near Hill City. Doug Alexander, a young forester, tells McNitt he is going out to check out the Hill City report. McNitt quickly decides to pack his fire fighting gear; if we can spot the fire on our way to the Bearhouse, we will swing by it.

We load up Kessler's mint green forest service jeep and head south for Hill City. Around the first curve into town, we get a clear view of a white plume of smoke rising to the west. The fact that the smoke is white indicates it to be a cool, slow-moving fire. Kessler believes it is up on the Newton Fork of Spring Creek, west of Hill City, and probably a direct result of Friday's lightning storm. He speculates it was started when lightning hit a tree or snag that dropped, then smoldered over the weekend in thick pine duff until conditions were hot, dry, and windy enough to give it a good start.

In Hill City Kessler turns west and heads up the Deerfield road a few miles before turning south onto U.S.F.S. Road 386. We have not seen the smoke plume since we left town. Driving up the bottom of gulches and small valleys limits and narrows your view of the sky.

Unfamiliar with the mountainous terrain here and the winding roads, my sense of direction quickly becomes confused. With the exception of the main highways, few roads follow anything that resembles a straight course. Most secondary roads in the Black Hills wind gently through small mountain parks, cross ridges, and then parallel meandering stream courses.

Pinpointing fires on the ground takes a combination of deductive and intuitive skills. It requires knowing your directions while in a valley or gulch, then guessing distance as the crow flies, and finally plotting a course to get there on the ground using a maze of old logging roads. You have to know the country and the rest is by feel.

Kessler turns south off the Deerfield road and drives a mile down gravel before he turns into a nameless gulch that opens up, giving us an unobstructed view of a mountainside to the west. Directly in front at a distance of a maybe a couple of miles, smoke is pulsing and billowing off a mountainside. For me there is an immediate adrenaline rush that comes with confronting a natural phenomena that is wild and potentially dangerous.

Again we loose sight of the smoke as Kessler threads the jeep up a one-lane track in the vicinity of where he believes the fire is burning. Unless you know them, it is difficult to anticipate where these old logging roads are going. The one we are following winds and twists west up a shallow gulch before it abruptly turns south and climbs along a mountain flank before moving into the timber.

Around a curve a forest service pickup is parked on the side of the trail ruts. It is the one driven by Alexander who left the ranger station just before us to scout the fire report. There is no one in sight. Everything is quiet. To the east there is a gentle slope into a grassy, dry gulch; to the west there is a steep rocky slope covered with thinned out ponderosa. Spread out under the pines is a thick layer of tinder-dry pine slash—the organic residue of the pine trees and branches that were thinned out many years ago.

Although I cannot see anything beyond the forest in this small gulch, the smell and taste of burning pitch is strong in the dry air. Crouching down and then craning my neck to look straight up the west slope I can see a line of red flames dancing under the trees. Now the fire is real and I get a rush again as I grab my camera and head up the slope.

Wildfire: destroyer and procreator; hated and loved; abused and praised. It has no respect for people or property. It is the dragon that consumes everything in its path and disgorges it blackened and twisted, not caring what you think or who you are—Nature's foremost leveler and progenitor. However you view it, fire always brings change and transformation.

After climbing the one hundred yards up the slope, I am within a dozen or so yards from the flames. At this distance I can hear it clearly snap and crackle as it calmly munches into the heavy slash. It is a cool, slow-moving blaze being fed oxygen by a mild, up-slope breeze. There are few flames higher than four feet eating the dry slash and licking up the slender sides of pine saplings.

Compared to the fearful Yellowstone fire in 1988 that burned for four months, charred over 1.5 million acres of timber, and involved 41,000 firefighters at a cost of over $112 million, the Battle Ax fire, as this one is soon named, is a gentle caterpillar, slowly and deliberately chewing its way through slash.

And yet there is danger, real danger. I can sense it in the anxious uneasiness of Doug Alexander who is standing twenty feet away from me with shovel in hand, watching it closely. There are no controls. All fire is wild and unpredictable. Now calm and gently banked into the wind, a wind shift from the north could in a matter of minutes pump in more oxygen, heat it up, and push it into the lower pine branches which are not much higher here than six or eight feet. From there it could spread to the crown, moving from the treetops in all directions. At that point a man can hardly move fast enough to get out.

Alexander is dressed in a yellow fire shirt, green forest service fatigues, and a red helmet. Talking into a hand-held two-way radio, he describes his position on the fire, its location, the slope of the terrain, the condition of the environment, wind velocity and direction, and the degree of the slash (thick). While he speaks, he never takes his eyes off the fire line as it moves leisurely down slope.

The earliest records of forest fires in the Black Hills are written in charcoal remnants buried underneath layers of earth and vegetable mold. Later ones can be deciphered by studying the growth rings of standing trees with healed fire scars. The oldest historic evidence of a major conflagration in the central Black Hills can be found near Rochford, Mystic, Custer, and in the Limestone Range. Dates derived from ancient fire scars on trees indicate that a great burn occurred sometime between 1730–1740. In this area there are numerous even-aged trees that are between 190 and 200 years old which probably started in the clearings made by the fire. These fire dates were fixed from a cross section of a 200-plus-year-old tree damaged in that fire with an entirely healed-over scar.

While the Black Hills were frequently burned during the next half century, no fire of so great an extent occurred again until about 1790. At that time evidence points to another great fire or series of fires burning over a large part of the Black Hills. The second-growth forest of the Limestone Range and northern Black Hills dates from that time. The scars from that fire are found on old trees throughout the Hills, and patches of forest 170 to 180 years old are relatively abundant.

Near Pactola, according to another early record, foresters traced a fire that swept through the woods about 1800. The fire originated near Deer Creek and traveled northeast. This information was again deduced from healed-over scars, tree-ring analysis, and groups of even-aged trees regenerated after that burn.

In 1842, Indians living near the Hills told stories of an old time when "the entire Black Hills were ablaze." Their information corresponds with trees and groups of trees in the northern Hills that are about 150 years old and probably had their origin sometime after this blaze.

In 1875, geologist Henry Newton observed that "the Black Hills have been subjected in the past to extensive forest fires, which have destroyed the timber over considerable areas. Around Custer Peak and along the limestone divide, in the central portion of the Hills, on the headwaters of the Boxelder and Rapid creeks scarcely a living tree is to be seen for miles. The timber, deadened by the fire, and the trees left standing, their decaying trunks stripped of bark by weather or prostrated by the wind, cover the ground, crossing each other at all angles, forming an impassable abattis."

In the days prior to the big Deadwood Gulch gold rush of 1876, the Black Hills was a forested haven of conifers and springs that supported big game animals including elk, deer, black and grizzly bears, mountain lions, wolves, and a vast array of smaller mammals, birds, and reptiles. While it held this vast and diverse biological wealth, few dared venture into the deep inner sanctum of the Black Hills. One of the reasons probably had to do with the difficulty of penetrating the interior of the Black Hills from the northeast and many of routes up the canyons and gulches were undoubtedly choked for long periods of time with dead, blown down timber that had either been bugged-killed or burned.

Another reason was superstition. Historic accounts relate how Indians, most notably the Sioux, who were the last native people to arrive and claim possession, told stories of great thunder and booming noises that emanated from them. Partly in response to this phenomena, they held the Black Hills to be *Wakan*, meaning holy or mysterious. *Wakan* also pertained to the powerful potency of the thunder and lightning storms that often formed over them in the spring and summer as the indirect result of super heated ground surface air rising quickly into cool mountain air then forming clouds, storms, and lightning—wildfire's trigger.

The relatively high, cool, forested Black Hills, situated as they are as an island in the middle of the hot, dry northern Great Plains grasslands can, if conditions are right, generate their own weather and literally create their own storms. It happens in this way: Air which is quickly and desultorily heated on the ground surface of the surrounding plains rises. A wind from the east or west pushes these heated air masses up against the Black Hills and creates an updraft known as an orographic lift. In this updraft, lighter, warmer air convects upward into the heavier, cooler air laying above the mountains.

Since the air masses are at different densities and temperatures, they do not readily mix and instead create convection cells. In these convection cells warm air rises, tops off, and eventually falls and dissipates into the surrounding cooler air. As the warm air rises, it also reaches the dewpoint at which it condenses its moisture into a white vapor forming a cumulus cloud. The bottom of cumulus clouds indicate at what altitude the air's moisture became cold enough to condense into vapor and visible droplets. The higher the cumulus, the drier the atmosphere and the less probability there will be of a rain shower.

If the atmosphere is relatively stable, cumulus clouds appear and dissipate. However, if the air is unstable, these cells continue to build into tall, darkening towers with cauliflower tops known as cumulonimbus. When the tremendous upward momentum of a cumulonimbus is deflected outward by the stable layer of the stratosphere it produces the classic flat, anvil-shaped thunderhead that usually spreads out in the direction of the storms path.

Thunderclouds occur most frequently in late spring and early summer when super-heated air is quickly thrown aloft into cold heights, creating violent updrafts. The updrafts in these thunderclouds create electrical charges that become scattered. Eventually, a mature thundercloud will gather a negative electric charge in its base and a positive charge in its top.

Because unlike charges in separate objects tend to attract each other, the ground beneath the cloud begins to gather a positive charge, resulting in the buildup of an electrically charged field between cloud and ground. When this electrically charged field exceeds 3 million volts per square meter, the air begins to conduct electricity. This attraction results in a powerful release or discharge of excess electrons we perceive as lightning.

Lightning in most cases starts as a relatively thin, stepped spidery leader stroke from the cloud to the ground. When the bolt approaches the earth, a very bright, heavy return stroke surges up to the cloud following the path of the stepped leader. A single lightning discharge may strike back and forth many times in a period of less than one-tenth of a second. While a lightning strike is of extremely short duration, it is incredibly potent, discharging up to 30 million volts of electricity at 100,000 amps. In terms of pure, raw power, it exceeds the discharge of an atomic bomb.

The crack of thunder, which always follows a lightning strike, results from the sudden expansion and contraction of the air as the lightning bolt heats it. It is similar to the bang of gun which is caused by the expansion and contraction of air at the gun muzzle when a bullet is discharged. The roll and rumble of thunder are the continuing echoes from the initial explosion which may last for a half-minute or more.

Clouds, lightning, and thunder are three ways the Earth redistributes energy across its magnetic field. The effects are physically experienced as wind, rain, and fire. These disturbances are critical in rejuvenating and recharging the atmosphere, the waters, and the earth itself.

Lightning storms and strikes are common, normal occurrences in the Rocky Mountain West. From 1972 to 1988, researchers in Yellowstone Park determined that of the hundreds of thousands of lightning strikes that hit the ground in the park in that sixteen-year interval, 140 turned into natural fires that burned an average of 250 acres before dying out. Statistically, 80 percent of all lightning-caused fires in Yellowstone went out by themselves and burned less than one acre. Statistics for lightning-caused fires in the Black Hills do not exist. However, with its lower average elevation of about five thousand feet compared to Yellowstone at seven thousand feet, it is generally hotter and drier at all seasons of the year. Early eyewitness evidence suggests that lightning-caused fires in the Black Hills were a common and frequent occurrence lasting for weeks and months at a time in the spring and summer seasons.

Biologists F. R. Gartner and W. W. Thompson wrote in a 1972 research article entitled "Fire in the Black Hills Forest-Grass Ecotone" that "early residents of the plains outside the Black Hills have mentioned the glow of flames in the sky over the Hills almost every night of the summer."

The September 21, 1883, issue of the *Black Hills Daily Times* published in Rapid City carried a detailed description of a fire that started on the south side of Terry Peak. The account described in three columns of impassioned prose how its "merciless flames, fanned by high winds," destroyed the small town of Centennial, the Centennial Prairie, and narrowly missed consuming Lead, Terry, and Deadwood.

One of the last big fires that occurred just prior to the turn of the century was known as the Iron Creek fire and started near Crow Peak in the summer of 1898. The Iron Creek fire burned over twenty thousand acres of timber between Crow Peak, Iron Creek, and Beaver Creek, an area roughly encompassed by Spearfish Canyon on the east, the Wyoming state line on the west, U.S. 85 on the south, and I-90 on the north.

According to the report the "fire swept through the forest blown by a gale of wind and was such a hot one that it killed nearly all of the standing timber within its path." The report went on to observe that "it was a very unusual fire in this respect, for usually a considerable amount of the larger timber is only badly scorched on the stump."

Over the ensuing decades studies began to show that natural fire in the Black Hills, contrary to being anomalous, was an important and integral aspect in the maintenance of a healthy, regenerating forest ecosystem. Furthermore, it was discovered that fire frequency also played a significant role in managing the size and types of vegetation on any given site.

Early forest managers perceived fire only as a devastating force that laid waste to the timber resource. A pillar of their forest management policy became the suppression of fire whenever and wherever it broke out. Few at the time realized or recognized the prominent role fire held in the natural scheme of ponderosa pine forest ecology. While it made sense economically to suppress fire, biologically it would prove to be a flirtation with disaster.

One of the first written government reports concerning the role of fire in a western mountain forest ecosystem was done by an army captain named G. H. Gale in 1894. Gale commanded the 4th U.S. Cavalry and was assigned to patrol the Yosemite National Park area in the Sierra Nevada Mountains of California. Gale, while not a biologist, was nonetheless a keen observer of the effect of cool burning wild fires in the Yosemite Valley. During his sojourn there he observed that annual fires removed the litter of fallen needles and toppled trees on the forest floor leaving the ground ready for the next year's new growth. "Enough younger trees," he reported, "escape the flames to replace the mature forest and the slight heat of the annual fires did not appreciably affect the growth nor the life of the well-grown healthy trees."

Gale also noted that if the forest litter of leaves, needles, and dead branches were allowed to accumulate year after year, they would increase the available forest floor fuel eventually resulting in a very hot fire.

Fire, he concluded, rather than the enemy of a mountain forest was in fact a presence crucial to the forest's well-being and survival. Unfortunately, Gale's report went unheeded probably for the same reasons fires are still fought today in national forests: They are dangerous to life and property when left out of control and destroy an important economic resource, timber.

Despite a few enlightened reports appearing at the end of the nineteenth century, fire suppression became the policy in all federal forests of the West. The result a century later is that overall western forest tree biomass has increased by as much as 50 percent mainly by the greater thickening of tree stands and at the expense of adjacent grass and meadowland. Conversely, old growth, mature forest stands which had once been open and accessible, have become choked with brush, dead forest litter, and young, thick stands of trees.

In 1967, the Leopold Committee, after thoroughly studying the hazardous fire situation on national park lands in the West reconfirmed in their report the necessity of fire in forest ecology. It was a crucial turning point against the "Smokey Bear" fire ethic and spurred more study and interest into the effects of fire on the mountain pine forest ecosystem.

A preliminary report from a study done in Wind Cave National Park in the southern Black Hills indicated that between 1820 and 1910, prior to intensive fire suppression, the fire interval for any given land area in Wind Cave was between 13 and 21 years. The report also pointed out that these natural fires were frequently surface fires of low intensity that primarily burned forest debris. Stated another way, if left to nature, any and every given stand of timber in the Black Hills could be expected to burn between five and six times in any given one-hundred-year span.

Other more recent studies have shown that fire frequency in the Black Hills before 1770 occurred on an average of every twenty-seven years. From 1770 to 1900 the occurrence was one fire every fourteen years burning the Black Hills forest mainly because of aboriginal peoples using fire to stimulate the growth and regeneration of berry-producing shrubs for their own use and to create the browse and grassland habitat favored by big game animals. After 1900, due to fire suppression, the average incidence of a major wild fire running its course throughout the entire Black Hills ecosystem plummeted to one every forty-two years.

Fire has the same effect in the Black Hills as Gale observed a century earlier in Yosemite of being a cleansing agent in removing dead and diseased trees and vegetation while stimulating the new growth of grass and shrubbery favored by deer and elk. In their turn these ruminants attracted larger carnivore predators on the top of the food chain—like mountain lions, wolves, and grizzly bears—that kept the herds trimmed and healthy.

Without fire, stands of pine "stagnate" while litter accumulates and young pine seedlings grow into impenetrable "dog hair" thickets, choking out browse (shrubbery deer rely on) and virtually creating what wildlife biologists often refer to as a biological desert. Berry shrubs, as well as grasses, rely on cool fires to clear away their dead stems and replenish the soil with ash nutrients. If you look at the forest like your home, you come to realize that it, too, must be cleansed and refreshed to maintain its vigor. Fire serves this purpose.

The Black Hills National Forest has been keeping track of acreage, cause, and location of forest fires since 1880, however their records are pretty spotty prior to 1910. As one might expect, the dry decade of the 1930s had some big blazes. The Rochford fire, one of the three biggest forest conflagrations in the last century, burned 21,640 acres in 1931. The forest service lists its cause as incendiary. A retired friend I know who has worked in the timber industry all his life believes the fire was intentionally set by twin brothers who were, as he put it, "hoping to get some work by helping put it out. Those were hard times, back then," he added as a disclaimer.

In the mid-1930s, the great drought in the northern Great Plains was at its peak, creating especially explosive fire conditions in the Black Hills. The *Spearfish Queen City Mail* set the tone of the weather for the spring and summer of 1936 observing the state of crops in the fertile and usually lush Spearfish Valley:

Drouth and Heat Make Heavy Crop Losses in County: No Hope Left for Seared Fields Except Corn Which Immediate Rain May Help

From 85 to 90 percent of Lawrence County rural residents will be in need of relief in the next 30 to 60 days, a survey asked by federal, state and county officials indicates.

Unprecedented drouth with both May and June practically devoid of any precipitation; an excessively hot summer and insect pests in dozens of varieties, by far the worst in this county's history, have combined to force on this comparatively favored county a tragic emergency.

A few weeks ago it was commonly believed that no matter how serious the drouth, this county could not be so adversely affected. Residents were repeatedly told by visitors that Spearfish was in a paradise. . . . Now it is apparent that in Lawrence County itself a total crop failure on dry lands can only be averted if heavy rains come immediately; and then only forage from the corn fields will be rescued. Estimates now are that there will be a 35 percent crop on irrigated lands.

That summer five forest fires ripped into the Black Hills. Two of them were major and occurred on the Wyoming side of the northern Black Hills.

Madison limestone, Bear Butte.

Harney Peak granite—crystalline core, Central Black Hills.

Native wildflowers on Castle Creek near McIntosh Fen.

Belle Fourche River cutting through the Spearfish formation near Devil's Tower.

Southern Black Hills scene, Wind Cave National Park.

Pronghorn doe, Wind Cave National Park.

Bison dust bath, Wind Cave National Park.

Prairie dogs, Wind Cave National Park.

Bear Butte, igneous laccolith and Sacred Mountain, northern Black Hills.

High Meadow Park, Black Hills limestone plateau.

Cathedral Spires, Black Hills.

Aspen beaver cuttings near Grizzly Creek, Norbeck Wilderness Preserve.

Spearfish Creek/Canyon, northern Black Hills.

The Sundance fire burned 8,361 acres of timber in the Bear Lodge Mountains just north and east of Sundance, Wyoming, in July of 1936. The story goes that it was accidentally started by a discarded burning cigarette. The official cause is listed only as "smoker." The following story on the fire is excerpted from the *Spearfish Queen City Mail* newspaper of Friday, July 10, 1936:

Bear Lodge Area Razed by Flames, Recruit Aid Here (Spearfish): Timber and Pasture Losses Uncalculated; Stock Feared Lost in Holocaust; Residents Ready to Move

Every available man from Spearfish early this week joined with Sundance and Crook County, Wyoming, residents in fighting a forest fire that by Thursday morning had burnt over 7,000 acres north of Sundance. The fire raced through the tops of trees making as much as two miles in five minutes and there was very little that 2,000 men cold do to fight it directly.

The fire started at 1 PM Monday just north of Sundance and was carried north by a strong wind. Its cause was not determined, but with a number of other fires in the west side of the Black Hills this week it is believed to have been man-caused in the extremely dry condition of the forests. . . . All residents in the path held themselves in readiness to move Monday, with household and farm goods packed and trucks available for transportation.

A month later the next big fire broke out near Moskee, Wyoming, just south of Sundance. The weekly issue of the *Spearfish Queen City Mail* reported it on Friday August 14, 1936, as follows:

Moskee Is Scene of 3-Day Inferno of Forest Blazes: One Hundred and Thirty Men from Spearfish Join Crews of Over 2,000 on Fighting Lines

The demon of fire loosed its fury 20 miles southwest of Spearfish for three days during the last week, laying waste 7,338 acres of the best standing timber in the Black Hills and threatening to wipe out the Homestake Mining Company camp at Moskee. During three smoky and sultry days, when Spearfish residents picked up charred bits of pine bark from streets and yards, tension and concern ran high and 130 Spearfish men were drafted to fight the flames.

About the middle of the afternoon, Saturday, what appeared to be white clouds began piling up over Cement Ridge. Spearfish residents soon got word of a forest fire in the Moskee area and the menacing cloud of smoke was watched with apprehension because it appeared to be just beyond the hill. Calls went out among the throngs in Deadwood during the final afternoon of the Days of '76 for all CCCs to report for duty. Before the evening was well advanced, volunteer civilians were being asked for by the forest service.

Another article relates a similar account:

Horizon Glows

With the oncoming dusk could be seen at the base of the southern smoke-clouded sky, a red glow which rose and fell. Sunday morning the entire Hills was talking about the big forest fire. Wild rumors flew of 100 CCC men trapped by the flames and a bulletin over Press Radio Monday morning told about the Wyoming Black Hills fire.

Dramatic scenes of the fire were those Sunday afternoon when the flames advanced on Moskee homes at eight miles an hour. There was desperation and fear in the town as the women and children gathered up their personal belongings to flee their endangered homes. Then at 4 p.m. the wind shifted; fire fighters on the long front redoubled their previous efforts to check a "topping" fire, and the town was saved.

During the fire, B. C. Yates, the sixty-six-year-old superintendent of the Homestake Mine in Lead who had just worked on fighting the fire, suffered a heart attack and died. Also, that same week in a curious climatological twist the paper reported that:

The air at Spearfish Wednesday was more heavily filled with smoke . . . than at any time during the Moskee fire. A steady wind (from the east) is believed to have carried the smoke here from Minnesota where 60 forest blazes were raging. Traveling over the prairies at some elevation the smoke hit the Hills' elevation and cast a thick blue haze over everything and made the outline of Crow Peak, five miles to the west (of Spearfish), a dim one in full daylight.

In the Black Hills the decade of the 1930s came to a fiery close with the McVey fire in 1939. McVey is officially listed as a lightning strike although there are still many who firmly believe it was intentionally set. McVey is considered to be the worst fire in recorded Black Hills history. The McVey fire started on July 8, 1939, and burned intensely for four days. At its peak on July 11, it was burning 29,000 acres an hour. On July 12 there were 1,755 men manning 47 miles of established fire lines.

The fire destroyed 12 million board feet of saw timber; 18,800 acres of young growth; burned 17 cabins and killed 100 head of cattle.

The forest service reported 22,000 acres of timber "destroyed," noting that for the next three years after the fire "damaging floods followed."

McVey is commonly referred to a half century later by forest service professionals like Al Braddock as the "daddy" of recent fires. Al Braddock, who is the fire management officer with the Black Hills National Forest, has spent most of the last half of his thirty-plus-year career studying the effects and setting fires in the Black Hills National Forest. He looks at the McVey burn as a boon for wildlife—it created a large winter grazing range in an area that was virtually vast unbroken forest.

Braddock is responsible for coordinating and leading an interdisciplinary team of biologists and foresters that plan and implement prescribed burns. He studies the forest and litter densities, moisture content, and terrain before determining how to create a fire and at what intensity. Since 1982 the forest service with Braddock as a coordinator has set prescribed burns over 50 percent of the former McVey forest fire area.

These prescribed burns are ignited using aerial ignition devices including "ping-pong balls" that are filled with special chemicals. While sitting in a flying helicopter, the firing boss injects the balls with glycol (anti-freeze) just prior to dropping them out the door above the forest area. Forty seconds later they burst into fire on the forest floor. Depending on how many balls are dropped, where, and at what rate, determines the intensity of the fire.

While it would seem that fire has finally achieved its recognized due as a necessary and important factor in forest ecology, many forest service professionals still view fire in the woods as a curse and, like many local residents, are quick to point out the recent burns prescribed or otherwise that got away or were ignited by other man-caused means. One fire of recent origin that was particularly frightening happened in 1959 and nearly destroyed the town of Deadwood.

Deadwood, situated as it is in a narrow gulch, has been plagued with fires throughout its history, going back to the first fire that completely destroyed the pioneer town in the late 1870s. The most recent Deadwood forest fire started in Deadwood Gulch just east of Central City on a Tuesday afternoon in early September 1959. The ambient air temperature that afternoon was over a hundred degrees and the relative humidity was a parched 15 percent. No rain had fallen for two months and the drought index had stood at "emergency" readings for weeks.

The official fire report of the 1959 Deadwood fire stated that an elderly resident who lived at the Hillcrest Home for the Aged went out to burn some papers in a twenty-five-gallon ventilated drum incinerator. The wind at the time was 40 mph, gusting to 60 mph from the southwest, when the man struck the match and lit the papers. Before he could put the lid back on the drum, a flaming piece of paper flew out. The wind picked it up, blew it into the dry grass where it ignited it and the nearby forest. It all happened in the space of a few minutes.

The following is an excerpted account of the fire from the September 9th, 1959, issue of the *Lead Daily Call* on the day after the blaze started.

Worst Holocaust in Northern Hills in 80 Years Is Believed Controlled

The most disastrous forest fire in the history of Deadwood was believed under control at noon today after burning 3,000 acres of timber land around the renowned mining town.

Howard Lee, U.S. Forest Supervisor at Custer, estimated that it might be 10 days to 2 weeks before all of the fires are controlled. . . .

As darkness came the hills surrounding the city looked like a myriad of lights formed by the dotted forest fires. The fire literally exploded northwest of Deadwood Tuesday afternoon audibly whipped from tree-top to treetop. It started at the Hillcrest Manor near the city limits from a trash burner at the rear of the home for the aged. Within 5 minutes the blaze had skipped up the wooded hillside and within 45 it had burned its way through the forest to the opposite end of the city.

Fanned by a fickle wind that tossed it from one side of the hills to the other, the fire jumped the Spearfish-Deadwood highway (U.S. 85, northeast of town). By 4 PM the fire had surrounded the historic city on 3 sides and escape from the flames was possible only by means of the highway leading to Lead through Pluma (U.S. 85).

When the first alarm was sounded residents were routed through lower Main Street towards Sturgis . . . however this means of escape was cut off shortly when the flames jumped the highway in that vicinity. Exit via U.S.385 was blocked when the flames jumped the highway there and downed power lines blocked 14A via Central City.

Within 45 minutes schools were dismissed and parents were asked to locate their children. Phone service was limited to emergency calls. Within the hour most businessmen had locked their stores and left town or went to assist with the fire fighting.

The fire followed the hill in back of Deadwood's Main Street, then hopscotched across the highway into the lower Main Street area and up

Spruce Gulch. It hit the Northwest Wood Preserving Company where flames exploded 4 large tanks of creosote and burned large piles of posts. For the entire evening gusty winds whipped burning wood chips into the air.

For several hours it was feared that the bulk fuel tanks across from the hospital would explode but the area miraculously escaped.

Deadwood resembled a war front as heavy equipment, bulldozers, tanks, and trucks rumbled through the dark smoke-laden streets. Street lights were out and only a few homes, housing the handful of residents who remained behind were illuminated. Firefighters complained that the smoke at times was so intense that they could not tell where the fire was located and often it was as much as a mile away.

It was during this fire that the new, innovative discovery of bentonite mud slurry bombing would be put to use for the first time. The slurry bombing proved successful in containing the blaze and has since become a standard tool for putting out large fires in the Black Hills and Rocky Mountain West. The following report is from the *Deadwood Pioneer Times* of September 11, 1959:

Bentonite Bombing Major Factor in Stopping Big Blaze

The white, extremely water absorbent clay has turned out to be a miracle worker in fighting forest fires. The bentonite slurry has the capacity to cool and smother the flames. Put to its first test in Deadwood, 50,000 gallons of bentonite slurry were dumped on the fire by bombers. The slurry, a combination of water and 55 tons of clay was mixed at the Spearfish airport.

The next big blaze of consequence came in 1964 and was located mainly in Wind Cave National Park in the southern Black Hills. The terrain at Wind Cave consists of gently rolling hills and draws with stands of pine and wide areas of grassland.

The first day the fire, pushed by a west wind, spread very quickly through the grass and traveled all the way from the park headquarters near U.S. 385 some eight miles east to South Dakota 79. Since it was more a grass fire than a forest fire, a few heavy equipment operators were caught in the fast moving fire lines.

In one instance a man who was in the process of making a U-turn in a pickup truck to escape the fast running blaze got caught but the fire moved so fast past him that his truck was not even singed.

In another instance a bulldozer operator who got caught in a fast moving blaze was not so lucky. An eyewitness at the scene said that after the fire passed the bulldozer, the operator held out his arms and had skin hanging from them all the way down to his waist. The operator's comment was simply, "I think I've been burned." The fire, which burned 15,000 acres, did relatively little damage to property and improved the range at Wind Cave.

In 1985, the Flint Hill fire and the nearby Seven Sisters fire burned a combined total of over 32,000 acres in the southern Hills. Both were lightning caused and got a good head start because of a manpower shortage. The day before those two southern Hills fires started there were five lightning-ignited fires going on near Whoop-up Canyon, south of Newcastle on the far western Wyoming side of the Black Hills. Al Braddock, who was on those fires, said that night you could see "lightning blasts all over the southern Hills."

The next day four fires were going, two went out while one eventually turned into the Seven Sisters fire located three miles south of Hot Springs on the Seven Sisters Range, and the other on the prehistoric Flint Hill Indian quarry site eight miles east of Edgemont.

Both fires ran hot—killing a lot of trees. The Flint Hill fire burned 25 percent of the 22,000 acres it consumed in the first day and the rest over the next eight days. The Seven Sisters fire went fast too, burning nearly 10,000 acres in less than a week.

Braddock admitted that these two fires, if they had been adequately fought, would not have burned so much timber. There simply was not enough manpower to cover them, he said, and they had to be allowed to burn for two days before adequate reinforcements were available to take control action. This response (or perceived lack of) as it was later interpreted, created a great deal of misunderstanding and animosity between local ranchers and forest service personnel at the time.

The biggest recent fire in the Black Hills, the Galena fire, took place in the scorching drought year of 1988—the same year as the Yellowstone fire. The Galena was a hot fire that started from lightning in a very rugged, inaccessible area of the park. Within four hours, Fire Command had three air tankers dropping slurry and then six tankers the next day. In spite of this quick action, the fire jumped U.S. 16A in the middle of the park and came very close to burning the historic Game Lodge which once hosted presidents Calvin Coolidge and

Dwight Eisenhower during their respective administrations. The final toll was 16,788 acres charred, most of it in the high mountainous confines of the 73,000 acres of Custer State Park. That same year the Westberry Trails fire just west of Rapid City burned 3,600 acres of timber and nearly a dozen houses. This was an intentionally set arson fire.

In 1990, the Cicero Peak fire burned 14,000 acres of forest just west of Custer State Park. It was started when a log skidder's brakes got hot and ignited some pine needles packed underneath it. Leaking hydraulic fluid from the skidder kept the blaze going and hot. Eventually the skidder's big rubber tires got hot enough, caught fire, and blew up, spreading flaming liquid rubber far into the forest.

Al Braddock has a series of graphs that depicts fire trends in the Black Hills National Forest for the last half century. The graphs clearly show that since 1985 the trend of Black Hills fires in terms of frequency, intensity, and size has dramatically risen.

"We have a completely different forest environment now (1992) than we did in the 1800s," said Braddock. "The forest then had an open, single-story canopy with a lot more aspens which tend to slow a fire down. There were also a lot less ladder fuels back then to allow fire to spread in the crown or treetops. If I lit a match one hundred years ago in that forest environment, there would be a big difference in the fire then as compared to today," Braddock continued. "The environment today is a totally different one; due primarily to our protection and enhancement of pine and the fact that fire is no longer taking its normal role in nature. We are now starting to reap the results of fire suppression beginning back in the 1920s."

Fire suppression over the last fifty years in the Black Hills has allowed large accumulations of forest litter to build up, allowing for the development of many more younger stands of even-aged trees. Younger, even-aged pines growing below an overstory of mature pine trees act as a "fuel ladder," permitting fire to climb into the canopy or overstory of the mature trees thereby creating a crown fire inferno of intense heat.

Braddock describes fire as a "fuel manager" that sweeps the forest floor and understory free of dead and naturally occurring debris. Without it the forest develops heavy ground litter and relatively dense mid- and upper-level canopies. Once a fire starts in these conditions, it burns intensively on the ground, climbs actively in the trees, and spreads at high rates of speed through the canopies causing hotter fires and increased acres burned. In the decade of the 1980s, the weather cycle in the Black Hills region had been very dry, making the fuels even more explosive and contributing to this trend of increasingly hotter fires.

Braddock believes that the abnormal accumulation of over a half century of forest litter and the profusion of dense mid-level tree stands has set the stage for fires of explosive proportion—fires where the heat can be so intense that it literally cooks all the life out of the soil, hard plating it to the point where water cannot penetrate or percolate through it, in effect creating another kind of biological desert devoid of life. These catastrophic fires, known as "stand replacement fires," devastate all vegetation sending the cycle back to stage one— bare mineral soil and rock.

On the positive side, fire suppression has dramatically increased the volume and amount of harvestable wood fiber. The challenge for foresters, said Braddock, is to try and find the mix where you get an optimum wood fiber output but have enough vegetative control so you do not create explosive fire conditions.

"However, since we have eliminated the natural role of fire over the last fifty years by suppressing it," said Braddock, "we have found that we are unable to keep up either by using physical or mechanical means to control that build-up. Eight years ago I would have told you prescribed burning was our panacea; the answer where timber harvesting could not be used to keep the forest stand in a properly stalked condition."

Braddock said that prescribed burning tends to simulate conditions of the past with its emphasis on frequent low-intensity burns. He gave a general breakdown overall of how Black Hills federal forest land is managed. Out of approximately 1,400,000 acres of national forest land, about 1,000,000 acres can be harvested for timber, leaving 400,000 acres of inaccessible canyons and mountains that need to be "treated."

Burning those inaccessible areas on a fifteen- to twenty-year rotation cycle means burning about 16,000 acres per year at a fire cost of $80 per acre. For a couple of years, Braddock said, the forest service was able to burn 4,000 acres a year; however, it soon became apparent that they were working at maximum potential, given their manpower and resources. The additional manpower and money was not available to achieve the forest service's original goal.

Another obstacle to this management plan arose in 1991 with the escape of a forest service prescribed burn on Horse Creek just north of Sheridan Lake. The ensuing negative public reaction and criticism resulted in more constraints put on the forest service's burn policy. The additional constraints doubled the cost per acre of doing a prescribed burn and effectively moved them farther away from any kind of habitation. "It's a Catch-22 now," said Braddock. "The wildland/ urban interface areas which are growing annually are the areas that need fuel hazard reduction the most." These are the places the forest service now has to move back from.

The negative perception of forest fires in the Black Hills has also caused a major reduction in prescribed burns the forest service will conduct—ultimately resulting in a continued fuel build-up on that 400,000 acres of inaccessible unmanaged forest service land. Braddock asserted that "nature will eventually burn those 400,000 acres and possibly a few dozen houses with it." He added, "In the final analysis, you just can't solve all your problems with a chain saw."

Remembering the strong smell of burned pitch in my nostrils and the anxious expression on Alexander's face while confronting the crackling flames of the Battle Axe fire, even though it turned out to be an insignificant blaze, made me wonder if those who chose to live surrounded by pines really understood the precarious nature of their existence in the forest.

9

A World Under the Bark

It is mid-March, just before the vernal equinox when the northern hemisphere shifts into spring. On this particular morning I have joined two foresters on a reconnaissance trip to the Bear Mountain basin south of Hill City, South Dakota, to review the damage of a mountain pine beetle infestation. Conrad Rupert works as a timber buyer for Continental Lumber Company in Hill City. His manner and dress is typical of the forestry professional of the Rocky Mountain West. He is tall, lean, and reserved. His dress is the standard foresters garb of worn blue denim jeans, plaid flannel shirt, wool jacket, and an insulated ball cap. He wears black leather, lace-up high top logging boots complete with heavy vibram cleated soles and kilty trash guards.

The trademark of logger dress is heavy cleated boots with the kilty. The kilty is an extra flap of leather, fringed on the end that covers the bottom six inches of the boots tongue and shoelace. In the old days when loggers limbed trees with an ax, the cut ends of the slashed limbs had a sharp oblique edge. With all the sharp pointed residue slash laying on the ground around a logging site, it was an easy matter to get one caught in your shoelaces while walking and have it stab through the boot tongue and into the insole. The kilty was a second layer of protection that covered the shoelace and the tongue. Today, most limbing is done with a chainsaw which leaves a flat even cut that is only dangerous when you trip over it, so the kilty trash guard on a pair of Red Wing boots is a vestigial remnant of the old logging days.

Tom Troxel, the second forester, spent a decade working in the forests of northern Idaho and Montana for the U.S. Forest Service. He is a timber industry promoter and acts as a liaison for the sawmills in their dealings with the forest service. These days he spends more time in a car and on the telephone than in the forest.

Our destination, Bear Mountain, is an ancient Precambrian granitic dome that was rafted upward in the Tertiary period about 60 million years ago when the northern Black Hills was experiencing the height of its igneous uplifting. Bear Mountain granite, however, is much older than the Tertiary and has been dated at 2.5 billion years old making it some of the oldest exposed rock in North America.

Geographically, Bear Mountain is also about as close as you can get to being in the exact center of the Black Hills. It lies a few miles southwest of Hill City and is approached by gravel roads via Reno Gulch and then over the drainage divide to Negro Creek, recently re-christened Medicine Creek.

The day is unseasonably warm as has been the entire winter of 1991-1992. As a result, the Reno Gulch road is firm and dry, however, as we turn and proceed up Medicine Creek, the road begins to fill with wet, heavy slush. As we gain elevation, Rupert's red chevy suburban plows through ever-deepening slush. In a matter of thirty minutes we reach the foot of an insignificant peak called Copper Mountain. Below Copper Mountain the road forks; the main road winds down Sixmile Draw to the west while a one-lane track filled with snow drops down Bobcat Gulch into the Bear Mountain basin.

Rupert pauses at the top of Bobcat Gulch to take a sip of coffee before shifting into four-wheel drive. "It's the point of no return," he remarks casually turning onto the snow-drifted track enroute to the heart of the beetle infestation. The road winds down along a small gulch drifted with snow like hundreds of others in the Black Hills. There are a few dark groves of spruce scattered along the creek while the upper slopes are thickly mantled with ponderosa.

About a third of the way down, the gulch opens up to reveal the profile of Bear Mountain to the south. The mountain is a long, high ridge cloaked in a dark green expanse of ponderosa. Upon closer examination the forest appears to be pock-marked with small, rusty orange "hot spots" of dead pine trees. It is the post-mortem indicator of a forest that has already been laid waste by an insect amazingly adept at destroying pines with an arsenal of biological weapons and stratagems.

Bear Mountain basin stretches out to the north of Bear Mountain and covers about twelve hundred acres of pine and meadow. The U.S.

Forest Service refers to it and another adjoining four thousand acres of thickly forested slopes as the Bearhouse Project Area. Because of two timber cutting contract defaults over the period of the last fourteen years, an unhealthy stalked condition has developed over a large segment of the project area. Most of the trees in the basin are medium in size with average diameters in excess of seven inches and are growing in moderate- to high-density stands. These conditions, as forest pest entomologist Bill Schaupp puts it, "set the table" for the beetle.

How to slow the beetle's progress and salvage standing timber is the concern both to the wood products industry people and the U.S. Forest Service. Beetle-killed pine quickly becomes punky and useless a year or so after it is dead. It also creates the hazard for an intense forest fire. It was the great stands of beetle-killed lodgepole pine that played such a big role in feeding the voracious appetite of the Yellowstone Fires in the summer of 1988.

Ecologically, the mountain pine beetle along with wildfire are the two biggest factors in the destruction and ultimate regeneration of pine forests in western North America. The mountain pine beetle is to the western pine forests of this continent what the Black Plague was to the human population of Europe; a reaper and a leveler. Like the plague virus that lived on a flea and destroyed one-third of the population of sixteenth-century Europe, the beetle can destroy a third of the living trees or more of any given western pine forest during a major epidemic outbreak.

Bill Schaupp, who works for the Rocky Mountain Regional Office of the forest service in Rapid City, provides technical assistance on forest insect and disease matters to land managers in Nebraska, South Dakota, and northern Wyoming. As an entomologist he specializes in forest health management and insect pests. He estimated that since 1989, over 80 percent of the trees growing in the Bear Mountain basin were either dead or dying. Visiting the basin with him the following week, he pointed out the fact that the red needled pines are an old story; the adult beetles have already left, and these trees are now dead. The trees currently infested, he said, look healthy and are green.

Armed with a hatchet to prove his point, Schaupp chopped out a section of bark from a green tree near the foot of Bear Mountain. Under the bark were numerous egg-laying galleries. Schaupp explained that if the bark was stripped around the entire tree, the tree's cambium would be covered with egg galleries, the cumulative effect of which girdles the tree.

Schaupp referred to the process as a kind of tree death by strangulation, starvation, and dehydration. It happens after beetle eggs, laid under the bark hatch and hundreds of larval insects start feeding on the living tree cambium, effectively depriving the living tree of nutrients and water. The end result shows up the following year as a lifeless, rusty orange needled tree.

The commercial impact of pine forest devastation can be serious. The Black Hills is by the far the biggest producer of timber and spin-off wood products in the Rocky Mountain West. In 1991, timber resources in the Black Hills National Forest generated over $66 million, harvesting 33,300 acres of timber. That figures out to be 140 million board feet of lumber with a total material value of $110 million, making the Black Hills National Forest one of the top timber-producing federal forests in the lower forty-eight states.

That being the case, the mountain pine beetle along with wildfire can quickly ruin everybody's illusion of what a perfect mountain pine forest should be from a commercial as well as an aesthetic perspective. But, like wildfire, when the beetles get revved-up, they are tough to stop.

Judy Pasek, entomologist supervisor with the Rocky Mountain regional office of the national forest system, has been studying the life cycle of the mountain pine beetle for years. At a public meeting a few weeks later held in the basement of the Harney Ranger District Headquarters in Hill City, she introduces this virulent insect pest to concerned citizens and appraises the status of the infestation. The small room is jammed mostly with representatives of the timber industry along with a handful of loggers, private land owners, environmentalists, and reporters. Pasek, who is the lead entomologist on the Bearhouse Project infestation, is caught up along with Schaupp in the battle against the beetle. Like Schaupp, she displays a passionate interest and a fascination in trying to understand all the variable biological dynamics that define and feed this insect.

Pasek introduces the beetle as *Dendroctonus ponderosae*, alias Black Hills beetle, alias mountain pine beetle. *Dendroctonus* was first noted in the Black Hills back in the 1890s when it received its first common name. Sometime later it was described in *Miscellaneous Publication #273* published by the U.S. Department of Agriculture as "the most aggressive and destructive insect enemy of ponderosa pine in the Rocky Mountain region." The publication further noted that it is "distributed from the Black Hills of South Dakota to eastern Montana and south through eastern Wyoming, Colorado, Utah, Arizona, and New Mexico."

At that time the Black Hills pine beetle was considered to be a slightly different species from the mountain pine beetle *Dendroctonus monticolae* which had been identified somewhat later and credited for the devastation of the high mountain pine forests of California, Oregon, Washington, western Nevada, Idaho, western Montana, northwestern Wyoming, and British Columbia. Today, however, they are recognized as the same insect. The early confusion may have resulted in the fact that the Far West member of the family showed no special preference in its diet for pine tree cambium attacking all pine species equally.

In many western forest areas the mountain pine beetle all but wiped out thousands of acres of lodgepole and western white pine as well as taking a heavy toll of sugar pine, white-bark pine, ponderosa, and many other pine species within its range. Even fir, spruce, and hemlock were considered vulnerable when in the vicinity of pines under an especially aggressive attack.

Under typical conditions in a healthy forest, pine beetles are comparatively rare and found only in weakened, decadent trees. However, for a variety of reasons based on a few significant variables, beetle populations can build and explode with an average epidemic cycle of eight to twelve years.

The first extensive epidemic of mountain pine beetles was reported in the Black Hills in 1894 and lasted until 1908. Five major outbreak areas accounted for a widespread mortality of ponderosa throughout the Black Hills. At that time it was estimated that 1 to 2 billion board feet of pine were lost and that 40 to 60 percent of the entire Black Hills pine forest was affected. Timber resource managers in 1992 estimated that at any given time there is approximately 5 billion board feet of timber standing in the Black Hills. Due mainly to a century of wild fire suppression, that total figure represents an increase of about 40 percent more timber standing now than a century ago.

Forest Health Management records show other beetle epidemics have taken place during the periods of 1931-1942, 1945-1955, 1957-1965, and 1969-1981 with peak tree mortality occurring in 1946, 1957, 1962, 1967, and 1974. A full-blown epidemic builds momentum slowly as small endemic beetle infestations spread over a few years always getting bigger until they eventually converge over a widespread area. For example, the last major epidemic prior to the current build-up started in 1969. By 1974, beetles had destroyed 200 million board feet of timber mainly in the more heavily timbered reaches of the northern Black Hills.

How exactly the beetles go about their business is fairly well understood by examining their distinct behavior modes. They are characterized by endemic behavior, killing a few trees that are weakened by lightning strikes or from fungi and other insect parasites. At this stage when their numbers are small, they attack only sick or stunted trees since they are the most vulnerable and easiest to overcome.

Many insects like pine beetle are also biologically programmed to attack a particular tree when certain sequential conditions occur. If the conditions are all favorable, the beetles will be successful. Like most insects, the pine beetle's general biological activity is probably stimulated by the weather, humidity, and possibly barometric pressure. However what triggers *Dendroctonus* to specific trees has to do with a number of other variables.

All living creatures, plant and animal, give off scents peculiar to their species for a variety of purposes and reasons. Pine trees emit a strong pleasant resinous odor. When pines are in a drought stress situation their odor seems strongest. The reason for this is due to the fact that the pine leaves (needles) are covered by a thin, filmy tissue that sheaths each needle like skin. This transparent sheathing waterproofs the needles and protects them.

In times of dryness or drought, these delicate, translucent sheaths contract and rupture, allowing the needles scent to escape and waft on the wind. This phenomena usually occurs at the driest time of the year which in the Black Hills is late July and August. During these dog days of summer, the air of a pine forest, if it is extremely dry, will often appear glittery or hazy, as bright sunlight highlights countless floating, diaphanous particles of ruptured sheathing. It is also at this time that the swarm flight of the pine beetles begins. While it may be only a coincidence, it seems plausible that the powerful scent of drying pine may be one of the factors that stimulates and calls the beetles to the trees. Their own biological system may tell them they need the resinous chemical in their system.

What calls the females to specific trees is as yet a mystery. Nonetheless, the female beetles hit the trees en masse and begin boring into them and ingesting the pine's chemical into their systems. They then produce a pheromone, possibly mixed with bore hole sawdust, which induces the males to follow. Pheromones are odors insects send to each other that are received by their antennae. Minute quantities of pheromones serve as guides and signals to beetles.

After egg fertilization, the females chew out a vertical brood gallery in the cambium up the tree. In this gallery she begins laying a succession of a half-dozen to two-dozen eggs in a run, alternating along each side of the chamber. Between six to thirty inches of egg gallery are constructed suggesting that the total output of eggs could be anywhere from 30 to 150 in any given gallery.

A combination of beetle pheromones probably calls a swarm to a certain tree until the beetles are either repulsed by the tree's defenses or have overwhelmed them. When the tree becomes fully occupied, beetles sense the presence of close neighbors by sounds and vibrations caused by their boring activity. This stimulates the production of an anti-aggregation pheromone that communicates to the other beetles that the tree is full.

In every attack it is a battle of insect numbers against the ability of the tree's immune system to flush them out. If the beetles win and occupy a tree, those coming later during a major swarm flight will usually attack the next closest tree.

Another aspect that makes an assault on a pine by pine beetles so lethal is related to the host of blue staining fungi *(Ceratocystis)* these insects carry on a specialized structure known as the mycangium on their body.

Blue staining fungi begins to work on the vascular system of a tree a few weeks after the beetles have made their initial penetration. Blue stain helps the beetle's assault by slowly growing into the tree's water conducting tissue and ultimately constricting the flow of the tree's life-sustaining moisture. A lack of moisture creates a more conducive environment for the beetles. Moisture becomes a critical survival factor for the pine both in the tree's survival and because the beetle's invasive boring stimulates the pine's resin ducts to produce a heavy sap flow in an effort to flush them out.

A tree that has struggled will usually be marked by the presence of numerous, hardened pitch tubes that appear as small, round, amber blobs of dried sap about the size of a quarter scattered around the circumference of the trunk. The more pitch tubes the greater the attack of beetles and the less likely the tree will survive. The more the tree resists attack, the fewer, larger, and more gooey the pitch tubes.

The rest of the pine beetle's life cycle is pretty basic. The insect eggs hatch later that summer season and the larvae start eating their way out radially from the brood gallery. During the winter larvae remain in a state of suspended animation until spring when they pupate into callow (immature) adults with soft brown shells.

The immature insects continue to feed on the pine's phloem layers (tree cambium) all during the next spring and summer until their shells harden and turn black. At this point they become sexually mature adults and emerge from behind the pine bark. The bark of an emergence tree is filled with holes about the size of #6 pellets and often resembles the blast pattern of a shotgun. In late July or early August, with the inauguration of the swarm flight, the nuptial and regenerative phases of the beetle's life cycle begins again. At this point the success of the beetles' "nuptial flight" depends on weather conditions. A strong wind velocity can send the beetles adrift for miles in search of appropriate host trees.

Mountain pine beetles are not, however, without their own predatory adversaries. Predatory insects like clerid beetles get excited by the beetles' pheromonal signals, but for entirely different reasons. Clerids are predatory insects that search out and eat mountain pine beetles. A species of fly *(Medetere aldrichii)* parasitizes adult beetles by laying their eggs on their back. The eggs eventually hatch larvae which feed on the living host beetle. There are also mites species that engage in phoresy—riding the beetles like hitch-hikers and reducing their vigor.

A wasp species *(Coeloides dendroctoni)* locates the mountain pine beetle larvae by "hearing" it chew under the bark. When the female wasp locates it, she deposits one of her eggs on it, again using the larva as a host for her own larva's meal. There is a species of nematode (microscopic round worm) that lives inside the mountain pine beetle as well as a host of parasitic fungi that attack it. Woodpeckers and other insect feeding birds kill large numbers of broods by hammering off large chunks of bark and eating the soft, succulent pupae and larvae. Pine beetles provide a veritable feast for a host of predators and parasites, but no amount of gorging can come close to naturally stopping an epidemic in full tilt.

The weather, particularly moisture, can be a factor in hindering an epidemic's progress. A hard rain in August at the right time can knock them out in the swarm flight and dilute the pheromones in the air, in the bore dust, and in the pitch tubes. Even so, only extended periods of severe cold temperatures, especially unseasonably early in the fall, can seriously cause high mortalities of mountain pine beetle larvae.

Schaupp's brood mortality estimates, which includes all the stages from egg to adult within a host tree for the Bearhouse project area for 1991-1992 from August through February, was a surprising 96 percent. He described this as a high figure. Other figures reported from different infestation sites range from 53 to 89 percent brood mortality for October through April varying with infestation intensity.

Nonetheless, while high, a brood mortality rate of 97 percent can actually signify an increasing population trend while mortality rate of 99 percent can signify a decreasing trend. This may seem large, but even after a 90 percent mortality rate for an entire generation populations can dramatically increase if the most important variable is available—adequate food. When it comes to insects, nature is extremely lavish with their capacity for regeneration and production.

There are numerous other insects in the Black Hills that live under the bark of pine trees with pine beetles that are described as inquiline (guest) insects. "They are nest mates," said Schaupp. "They are not necessarily eating or parasitizing the tree or [the beetles], they are just there and we don't know the reason why. Maybe they are just spectators," Schaupp noted. "What goes on under the bark of the pine is another whole universe."

10

"To Gather Stone"

To the east the sun has cleared the top of the Black Buttes. As I pull the last barbed-wire gate shut, I become aware of how unusually still the morning is. Although early, the prairie is silent—not a whisper of wind or even a bird song. A small herd of pronghorn, always wary, graze a few hundred yards away on a slope near the top of a white gypsum dome. Below them a pair of yearling mule deer forage in a buckbrush depression. Calmly, the deer flick their black-tipped tails against unseen insects, turning their heads occasionally to give me a sideways glance.

While it all looks natural and peaceful, there is for me an odd sense of tension—an anxiety that I experience in the pit of my stomach whenever I approach Inyan Kara. I have always sensed, in some unknowing way, that this is a timeless place steeped in power and mystery.

A mile or so down the rough one-lane track over the "red beds" that leads to the north side of the mountain, I leave the prairie and turn up a shallow draw. In a small clearing at the edge of the pines, a small group of people, mostly professional and amateur archaeologists, are gathered around the white ash remnants of the previous night's campfire. Like me, they are here to probe the prehistoric legacy of the ancient peoples who camped on Inyan Kara.

Tim Cowan, North Zone archaeologist for the Black Hills National Forest, steps out of a camper and greets me. Cowan is responsible for all the archaeological work in the Bear Lodge, Spearfish, and Nemo districts on the national forest. Inyan Kara lays in the Bear Lodge ranger district which encompasses most of the

Wyoming portion of the Black Hills National Forest. The mountain proper covers about 2.5 sections or about sixteen hundred acres of high, rugged topography which the forest service has neatly drawn a boundary around. It lies in the middle of the Red Valley, about fifteen miles south of Sundance, Wyoming.

Cowan, who is somewhere in his forties, dresses like most field archaeologists—for comfort without regard to style. He wears a royal blue T-shirt and a pair of gray sweatpants with a wide, white military stripe down each side. He completes the ensemble with an old pair of green, Vietnam vintage combat boots. From previous discussions on other occasions I have come to regard him as a professional, dedicated archaeologist who takes his work seriously.

Inyan Kara is an outlying basalt peak on the west side of the Black Hills that pokes up into the middle of the Red Valley. Geologists refer to it as a pluton—an igneous rock body which was forced up as volcanic magma into the surrounding subsurface of sedimentary rock. It is a molten intrusion that never erupted, becoming a plug that slowly cooled to form a laccolith. Once buried in the surrounding country rock, it has, over the last 60 million years, been uplifted and eroded to the point where it now stands twelve hundred feet above the surrounding red clay prairie.

From a distance, looking at it from the north, its pine-covered slopes and towering basalt columns lend it a dark, brooding appearance. Singularly unique and conspicuous, it was an object of awe to the early natives and a point of curiosity to the early military explorers, notably Lieutenant Governeur Kemble Warren and General George A. Custer.

In 1857, Lieutenant Warren, a young surveyor with the U.S. Army Topographical Engineers, was ordered to locate the big Sioux military road that would connect Fort Laramie and the South Pass road with Fort Snelling. A keen observer and conscientious officer, his report provides a window into what was occurring in the Red Valley around the northern perimeter of Inyan Kara in the late summer of 1857.

Warren's party consisted of a military escort of thirty men and included the well-regarded explorer and geologist, Ferdinand V. Hayden. They embarked from Fort Laramie some 150 miles to the south in early September, proceeding north to the Black Hills via Rawhide Butte and Old Woman Creek. Upon reaching the vicinity of the southern Black Hills they skirted the west side following the Beaver

Creek drainage. A good part of their journey parallels U.S. 85 where it runs from Lusk to Newcastle, Wyoming, over the eastern edge of a huge short-grass plain known as the Thunder Basin.

Near the head of the Beaver's drainage, somewhere in the vicinity of present Four Corners, Wyoming, Warren entered the "Red Valley" of the Black Hills, veered northwest, and struck Inyan Kara Mountain. He described the mountain as "a remarkable, high, basaltic peak, one of the highest of these mountains, and so far to the north that we had a full view of the prairie beyond (i.e., to the west)."

Near the foot of the mountain Warren encountered a contingent of Sioux buffalo hunters who were waiting patiently to slaughter a large herd of meandering bison. The situation was tense as he recorded his thoughts and impressions that September over 130 years ago:

> Here (Inyan Kara) we were met by a very large force of the Dakotas who made such earnest remonstrations and threats against our proceeding into their country that I did not think it prudent for us as a scientific expedition to venture further in this direction (north).
>
> Some of them (Sioux) were for attacking us immediately as their numbers would have insured success but the lesson taught them by General Harney (at the battle of Ash Hollow, Nebraska) in 1855 made them fear they would meet with retribution and this I endeavored to impress upon them.
>
> We were at the time almost in sight of the place where these Indians had plundered Sir George Gore in 1856 for endeavoring to proceed through their country, and one of them was actually mounted on one of his best horses taken at the time. (Sir St. George Gore was a wealthy Irish nobleman who funded an elaborately equipped, three-year expedition on to the great plains that was to set the standard for frontier luxury and wild animal slaughter for years to come. By the time his outfit disbanded in the spring of 1857 his reckless slaughter had brought down two thousand bison.)
>
> The grounds of their objections to our traversing this region were very sensible and of sufficient weight I think to have justified them in their own minds in resisting . . . our passage. They (their objections) are of sufficient importance to be repeated here. . . .
>
> In the first place they were encamped near large herds of buffalo whose hair [was not] sufficiently grown to make robes. The Indians were, it may be said, actually herding the animals. No one was permitted to kill any in the large bands for fear of stampeding the others and only such were killed as straggled away from the main herds.

The whole range of buffalo was stopped so that they could not proceed south which was the point to which they were traveling. The intention of the Indians was to retain the buffalo in their neighborhood till their skins would answer for robes, then to kill the animals by surrounding one band at a time and completely destroying each member of it. In this way no alarm is communicated to the neighboring bands which often remain quiet, almost in sight of the scene of slaughter.

For us to continue on then would have been an act for which certain death would have been inflicted on a like number of their own tribe had they done it, for we might have deflected the whole range of buffalo fifty to one hundred miles to the west and prevented the Indians from laying in their winter stock of provisions and skins on which their comfort if not even their lives depended.

Their feelings towards us under the circumstances were not unlike what we should feel toward a person who should insist upon setting fire to our barns. The most violent of them were for immediate resistance when I told them of my intentions. Those who were most friendly and in greatest fear of the power of the United States begged that I "take pity" on them and not proceed. I felt that aside from it being an unnecessary risk to subject my party and the interests of the expedition to, it was almost cruelty to the Indians to drive them to commit any desperate act which would call for chastisement from the Government.

But this was not the only reason they urged against our proceeding. They said that the treaty with General Harney gave to the whites the privilege of traveling on the Platte (river road) and along the White River between Forts Pierre and Laramie and to make roads there and to travel up and down the Missouri in boats but that it guaranteed to them that no white people should travel elsewhere in their country and thus frighten away the buffalo by their careless manner of hunting them.

And finally that my party was there examining the country to ascertain if it was of value to the whites and to discover roads through it and places for military posts and that having already given up all the country to the whites that they could spare, these Black Hills must be left wholly to themselves. Moreover, if none of these things should occur, our passing through the country would give us a knowledge of its character and the proper way to traverse it in the event of another war between themselves and the troops. I was necessarily compelled to admit to myself the truth and the force of these objections.

The Indians whom I first met were the Minikanyes (Minneconjou Sioux) to the number of forty lodges near whom, as they were very friendly, we encamped. They were soon joined by the warriors of a large camp of Unkpapas (Sioux) and Sihasapas (Blackfoot Sioux) and our position, which was sufficiently unpleasant in the presence of such a numerous party of half-avowed enemies, was rendered doubly so by a storm of sleet and snow which lasted two days and two nights and against which we had but little protection.

A young Indian, who had accompanied us from Fort Laramie, considered the danger to us so imminent, that he forsook our camps and joined his friends, the Minikanyes. Under these embarrassing circumstances my associates evinced the most resolute bravery and determination to abide the result like true men.

I consented to wait three days without advancing in order to meet their great warrior, Bear's Rib, appointed first chief by General Harney's treaty. [During this time I] merely changed our position to one offering greater facilities for defense.

At the expiration of the time, Bear's Rib [having] not made his appearance, we broke up camp and traveling back on our route about forty miles, struck off to the eastward through the southern part of these mountains (Black Hills.) The point where we turned back is well marked by Inyan Kara Peak whose position was fixed by us.

Seventeen years later, thirty-four-year-old Brevet General George Custer with his expeditionary force of twelve hundred troopers, along with a civilian compliment of scientists, engineers, Indian guides, and newspaper correspondents, entered the Red Valley from the north. Armed with a three-inch mountain howitzer and three Gatling guns, his orders where to reconnoiter and ascertain the resources of the Black Hills with recommendations for the best strategic locations for military outposts in the region.

On July 22nd, 1874, Colonel Ludlow made this entry into his report on the northern Red Valley near Inyan Kara:

The course led southward up the Redwater valley, which is from four to ten miles in width, and bounded by high hills heavily timbered with pine. The gypsum appeared in enormous quantities. One of the guides took me off to the right to see a huge mass of it, crystallized and shining beautifully in the sun. The Indians, for generations, have, in passing, split off pieces for ornaments, and by degrees cut a shoulder several feet deep on it at the level of the ground. Inyan Kara was in sight all day to the southward, approaching which the trail turned to the left (east) around two igneous-looking peaks (Sundance and Green Mountain) and reached camp on Inyan Kara Creek, so called from flowing west past the foot of that peak. A heavy well-marked pony and lodge trail led up the Redwater Valley southeasterly to the Red Cloud and Spotted Tail agencies.

The command camped five miles to the northeast of the mountain. It was an inauspicious camp. That morning two privates quarreled over the cross hobbling of a horse with the result that one was shot to death. The day before another private had succumbed to dysentery. Both were buried on the hillside near the camp in full view of the mountain.

The next day, July 23rd, Custer, his staff, the scientific corps, and the reporters were escorted to the foot of the mountain by two companies of cavalry to view the surrounding countryside. It was hoped that a pass or route into the interior of the Black Hills proper to the east could be ascertained from the summit.

The two cavalry companies were left at the foot of the mountain while the remainder of the party split into two groups for the ascent. One group approached the peak from the south, the other from the northeast.

Upon gaining the summit, Ludlow made these observations:

It resembles a lunar mountain, having a rim in shape of a horseshoe, one and a half miles across, with an elevated peak rising sharply from the center. The rim, 1,142 feet in height above the exterior base, has a sharp edge at the summit, and falls steeply on both sides. The central peak, towering 170 feet above the rim and resembling a formation of basaltic columns, was gained by means of a narrow spur projecting from it to the southwest. A small spring flowed from the foot of the peak out northward through the opening in the horseshoe rim. The inner space between peak and rim was heavily wooded with pine and clumps of aspen. In open places were found in abundance strawberries, raspberries, black and red currants, Juneberries, and a small whortleberry. From the summit an extensive view might have been obtained, but the Sioux had fired the prairie to the south and west. After two hours of waiting, the smoke having only grown denser, we returned to camp.

Newspaper correspondent Knappen reported:

Colonel Ludlow, with much difficulty, reached the highest point of the mountain, leading his horse . . . [there], high on its flinty side he (Ludlow) cut the following name and character, viz.: "Custer, 74."

William E. Curtis of the Chicago *Inter-Ocean* wrote:

Inyan Kara . . . is by far the most imposing and beautiful [mountain] of any we have seen. Today General Custer remained in camp in order to give it a thorough exploration. . . . Colonel Ludlow by the barometer finds its height to be 6,600 feet above sea level and 1,600 feet above its surroundings. . . .

Samuel J. Barrows of the *New York Tribune* wrote:

> This range is called by the Indians Heeng-ya-kara (Inyan Kara). We had seen this landmark for several days and used it to steer by. It is one of the most prominent landmarks in the Black Hills, though not by any means the highest. Seen 40 or 50 miles away from the angle at which we approached it (from the northeast), it resembles in shape the cover of a soup tureen and we called it "Cover Butte," a name which we rejected on identifying it with the Heeng-ya-kara. . . .
>
> The mountain as before noticed is shaped like a tureen cover with a heavy knob on top. This knob is very steep, being inclined at an angle of 48 degrees, and is surrounded at its base by a sharp ridge of horseshoe shape, separated from the knob by a deep ravine. . . . The mountain is about two miles long and a mile wide . . . and is evidently the result of an upheaval. . . .
>
> On the top of the ridge (summit), small pieces of white quartz were found. As they had no geological business to be there, they were no doubt left there by the Indians who are fond of making offerings to their gods from these lofty altars. Strawberries, raspberries, gooseberries and Juneberries were found growing plentifully on the mountain side. Our miners prospected for gold but found none.

The following year, 1875, the Newton-Jenney scientific expedition probed Inyan Kara. Henry Newton wrote in his *Report on the Geology and Resources of the Black Hills of Dakota*:

> Inyan Kara is the most prominent peak on the west side of the Black Hills. It is situated in the Red Valley, west of the limestone plateau. . . . The summit of the peak is 6,600 feet above the sea, and has an elevation of 1,300 feet above the bed of Inyan Kara Creek nearby. The igneous mass of the peak occupies the center of what in form resembles a crater, for separated from it by an annular valley there is an encircling ridge or rim whose top is 500 feet below the summit of the peak. This rim . . . completely [encircles] the peak except at a narrow break on the northeast side where the drainage escapes. The limestone wraps around the outer slope of the peak like a cloak. . . . The upper red clays of the Red Beds lap up against this limestone, which appears as a breakwater raised against the turbulence of the billowy sea of the Red Valley. On the inside of the rim is the annular valley, surrounding the igneous nucleus and having a width, from rim to center of peak, of from one-half to three-fourths of a mile. It has evidently been formed by the denudating of the easily eroded strata beneath the limestone.
>
> From the midst of this crater-like depression the peak rises so abruptly that there is but one side with an easy slope for climbing. The summit is a

broad but very irregular area, whose larger dimension has a bearing about 30 degrees west of north and upon which the rock is well exposed.

After Custer's and Newton's brief visits, the mountain slid back into obscurity, probed only occasionally in the following century by cowboys, homesteaders, and, most recently, archaeologists, the latest being Cowan and his crew who are interested in gaining information regarding aboriginal use of the mountain. Cowan hopes to gain enough information regarding its significance to have the entire mountain placed on the National Register of Historic Places. As it stands now, only forty acres of the summit in the vicinity of Custer's name is listed.

After a brief meeting with the other archaeologists, Cowan invites me to join his small group which includes two young women; the first, Casey Sugarman, is a marine biology student from Connecticut, the other is a British archaeologist named Bridgit McGill from Canterbury, England. Both are volunteers on vacation.

Following a short drive to the northwest flank of the mountain, we stop on a low saddle ridge that juts out perpendicular from the base of Inyan Kara. The ridge extends a few hundred feet north up to a small knob before ending abruptly with a cut-bank and dropping into the Red Valley. Opposite the knob on the south end of the saddle, Inyan Kara rises steeply into the pines. Scattered here at random intervals about the base of Inyan Kara are piles of large, chipped stone flakes, mostly of red quartzite.

The center of the saddle just below the mountain's slope, however, appears to have been the focal point of knapping activity. This small vicinity, covering perhaps thirty square yards, is strewn with stone chips and flakes in such great profusion and abundance that Cowan believes this was a primary lithic workshop area for possibly ten or eleven thousand years.

There is some evidence in the form of large split rocks on the hillside above the saddle that suggests stone knappers built fires under the quartzite outcrops creating hot spots to spall the rock. They then probably brought the best pieces down to the relatively level area of the saddle to knap them into tools or projectile points.

From a small pile of jagged rock flakes, Cowan picks up a discarded piece and points out its characteristics which include the ridge, the striking platform, and the resultant bulb of percussion. "When struck properly the force of the blow fractures the molecular structure of the stone, producing a flake or chip," he explained. Production of a good point involved knowledge of a particular type of stone's fracturing characteristics and a fine sense of touch in placing and controlling the knapping impact.

"Look around," he adds, "if you find a nice spot out of the wind, either up on the hillside, down here in the saddle, or up on that knob, it's a good bet you'll find evidence of someone working on stone there. On a pleasant day, when the wind was calm, the native stone knappers would find a nice piece of stone to work and then settle on a promontory to keep on eye on the valley below them while they worked."

The view from the top of the knob is a wide sweep of the Red Valley which stretches out for a dozen miles to the north before it runs up against Sundance Mountain and the Bear Lodge Range. In the middle distance, there are grassy clay ridges, irregular white domes of soft gypsum, and a handful of small, pine-studded buttes. With its varied soft shades of yellow and vermilion, along with its crags, crevices, and curves, it is a landscape wonderfully rich for the eye to linger over.

Winding throughout this landscape are numerous ephemeral side drainages that fissure down and around the ridges and buttes, deeply carving the topography. These dry arroyos or draws eventually gather into the center of the valley to join the dry meandering loops of Inyan Kara Creek, which flows to the northwest. Except for a couple of faint, one-lane vehicle tracks worn into the prairie sod by ranch vehicles, the wide vista is but little changed from the one enjoyed by Warren, Custer, and countless aboriginal people. It lacks only the great scattered herds of bison Warren recounted over a century earlier.

Most of the side drainages coming away from the mountain support a thin green ribbon of even-aged cottonwoods and boxelders. One drainage even has a small aspen grove—a curious, disjunct population to be located so close to the parched plains. These deciduous groves are sure signs of water either in a seep or just under the ground. A few of the draws have artesian springs, that run a trickle of cold water into stock tanks. The shade, the springs, and the grass would have made an attractive combination to bison who like to water at least once a day early in the morning. It is fine country for bison. For the stone knappers and hunters who years ago perched on this outlook, there is little that could move undetected along those dry creeks and draws.

Bridgit McGill is involved in mapping a stone circle about twenty feet in diameter with a small rock cairn in the center. Placing a thin metal stake near the center of the circle, she measures the position of all the stones relative to the stake and draws them as such on a piece of graph paper. All the stones are deeply set in the sod, suggesting it to be a relatively old archaeological feature. Generally, depending on the site, the longer stone features lay on the prairie, the deeper they tend to be covered by Aolian (wind) deposits, giving them the appearance of settling into the sod. The top of the knoll, in and around the circle, is like the saddle, littered with cultural stone flakes.

Fred Chapman, an archaeologist from the Wyoming State Historic Preservation Office who is also out here observing the dig, refers to these stone circles and cairns as "problematic stone piles." It is an euphemistic way of saying he is not sure what their function was.

Stone circles were once relatively common across the entire Great Plains. A cluster of stone circles generally indicated the site where a group of teepees once stood since large stones, when available, were often placed around the outside perimeter to hold the inner hide lining down against the wind.

However, a single stone circle on top of a knoll or ridge suggests a different story. A single stone circle in these locations that incorporate bedrock boulder features into their outline may have served a completely different function. These single circles are often inconspicuous and, in many instances, difficult to discern from natural aggregations of field stone.

Some of these solitary ridge circles may have possibly served as trail markers or guides. From time to time native peoples, for reasons including game availability, drought, and the approach of enemies, have had to travel great distances across the plains; knowing the trail and the location of water holes and springs saved precious time, resources, and energy. This becomes of paramount importance when being pursued by hostile invaders.

Stone circle trail markers, as well as other types of guide devices, had to resemble natural phenomena in order not to be of use to enemies unfamiliar with the country but who were otherwise nonetheless expert in reading subtle nuances of "sign" and movement over the landscape. As such, scouts could only alter the shape of the natural object slightly by arranging a few stones differently, breaking a tree branch or incising a mark in a rock to indicate the best and easiest direction of travel.

A stone circle may have functioned as a directory that would orient a scout as to the direction of another trail marker. This mark might be a series of parallel gashes on tree bark, resembling the claw marks of a bear that point in the direction of travel; the next sign might be a cross incised into a sandstone cliff; the next, the broken limb of a tree pointing in the desired direction of travel; the next, a stone outline of a pointing arrow on a ridge, and so forth—all leading the followers to an intended known destination. Since these routes may be used infrequently, scouts moving through the country would have to know the sequence of the signs.

There were other implications connected with stone circles that included metaphysical considerations relating to the natural power of the Earth. Rocks piled up on top of each other in the center of a stone circle was a sign that the physical and the spiritual were in balance here, creating a concentration of power and energy. Ancients all over the planet believed that this energy could be drawn upon to restore one's body from fatigue, to heal, or perhaps to call in or divine animal spirits, each depending on what your power might be.

Literally and symbolically, the circle was a powerful and ubiquitous concept that appeared in many facets of aboriginal North America and served a host of functions. The context in which a stone circle appeared told the individual how it was to be interpreted and used. In the aboriginal scheme of life, everything existed within a context.

Philosophically, the circle for the Indian was an all-encompassing symbol that had many meanings of a cyclical nature. As a "medicine wheel" it represented the myriad cycles of life while emphasizing the importance of renewal and balance. It exemplified the turning of the seasons and the journey of plants, animals, and man as a series of movements, events, and transformations. Inherent in transformations were opportunities for personal growth as well as the passing on and sharing of energy and power.

Since all creatures possessed their own energy and shared the life essence, none was considered greater or less, only different. All living creatures were mutable expressions of the Oneness, the Great Mystery, at different points of the cycle or wheel. It was, therefore, imperative to regard all living creatures with respect, acknowledging their place on the wheel and remembering, after taking their lives, to thank and release their spirits; the continuance of life always meant the inevitability of death for other creatures. They would understand that in all things they should behave as relatives, which essentially meant the gift of life was to be shared. What you took and the spirit in which you accepted it became part of the personal essence of who you were and what you were becoming. To break the circle out of greed or self-ishness was to invite disharmony, sickness, and disaster.

When McGill finishes mapping the solitary stone circle on the knolls crest, she asks if I would care to help her map another one on a small outcrop just below this one. The second circle is smaller and barely discernible. Perhaps it is older than the one higher up or bison, cows, and nature have taken their toll over the intervening years, knocking the stones out of order. Perhaps, too, it is just a natural aggregate of rolling stone. This one is difficult to "read."

While we are plotting this circle, Cowan and Sugarman have started digging a forty-centimeter-diameter test pit midway in the saddle. Next to them they have erected a scaffold with a screen sift-ing box swinging from it. Everything that comes out of the test pit will be sifted, screened, and sorted through the box. All cultural and organic material will be bagged and tagged with reference to the cen-timeter level it came from. Every bit of cultural and organic debris unearthed from the hole is treated by Cowan as significant and per-ceived as one more piece of the archaeological puzzle here.

As the dig progresses, Cowan's test pit proves to be incredibly pro-lific in cultural flakes supporting what he suspects: that the accumula-tion of cultural materials on this site covers a long period of time dating perhaps as far back as the first big game hunters who came out onto the Great Plains in pursuit of bison and elephants eleven thou-sand years ago. Cowan is anxious to find a projectile point that would serve as a time and cultural group diagnostic indicator.

The top ten centimeters of debris from the hole is made up almost entirely of deep, vermilion-colored quartzite flakes with some chert. The flakes unearthed come in all sizes. Many are primary flakes still having some of the original outside cortex attached to them. These flakes are considered to represent the initial reduction stage of the raw material while others are secondary flakes.

Secondary flakes, as opposed to primary flakes, are generally non-cortical and result from the further reduction of the raw core or nod-ule. At this point, secondary flakes are still considered blanks from which the stone knapper, taking into consideration size and quality of the material, will decide to either shape as a bifacial or a flake tool.

Bifacial reduction is a technique that produces one tool from a large core, while flake tools are produced by preparing a core to make many blade flakes. Blade flakes are then further knapped and shaped into specific tools. Flake technology is far more economical in using the raw lithic material than bifacial technology and is generally considered to have developed over the course of prehistory out of bifacial technology.

Also present in the test pit are tertiary reduction flakes which generally are the size of fingernails. These flakes, often referred to as thinning flakes, are a byproduct of the final shaping process. The last type of flake present in the pit are micro-flakes. Micro-flakes are very tiny, about the size of a tie tac, and are often considered to be the result of the reshaping of a tool due for a different use as opposed to initial tool manufacture.

At the level of the second ten centimeters, Cowan finds the cultural lithic material even denser than the top ten. He fills six plastic pint bags with fire-broken rock shards. Most are quartzite and have right-angle fractures, indicating that the parent rock was heated and then rapidly cooled. Cowan speculates that these pieces may have been used to heat cold water in a bison paunch. He is still looking for a projectile point to get some kind of time diagnostic.

Most projectile points, often erroneously referred to as "arrowheads," are in fact atlatl dart points. The atlatl dart system was developed in Ice Age Europe thirty thousand years ago and spread from there across Asia. At the time of the conquest of Mexico in the sixteenth century, the Spanish faced atlatl darts employed by the Aztecs. Deadly against mammoths and other prehistoric big game animals, atlatl darts were the weapon most feared by the ruthless conquistadors. A well-thrown obsidian-tipped dart, having the penetrating force of a sixty-pound compound bow, could penetrate the armor breast plate of a conquistador at a distance of thirty yards while a musket ball of that period would be deflected. While the atlatl dart system was primitive, in the hands of an adept thrower it was, nonetheless, deadly.

The bow and arrow system is a relatively recent phenomena on the northern Great Plains, dating back to about 1,700 years BP (AD 300). It replaced the atlatl dart system which had been in use on the Plains for the preceding ten thousand years of human occupation. True arrowheads are smaller than atlatl dart points and are the ones collectors often refer to as "bird points." Most "arrowhead" collections, according to Cowan, are about 80 percent atlatl dart points.

Sometime after noon we all break for lunch. We have been fortunate in regard to the weather; the morning, which was partly cloudy, will probably help forestall the projected high temperature today, predicted to be in the high nineties. The sun, however, is now out and, at our elevation of 5,300 feet, the afternoon rays are bright, direct, and intense.

Back at the test pit in the twenty- to twenty-two-centimeter level Cowan finds some exotic material: micro flakes of obsidian, chert, and white quartzite. Flakes from rocks of this type had to have been imported in from a good distance and suggest older stone weapons were being repaired or reshaped here.

Cowan looks closely for evidence of fetal animal bones to get an indication of what time of the year this level of deposit may have been laid down. Knowing the type of fetal animal gives a gestation period and produces a good indication of seasonality. In archaeology the context of everything discovered with and around cultural materials is of enormous importance because they give clues to time and period.

While Cowan digs and Sugarman sifts and sorts, we talk about the *Indiana Jones* movie phenomena where archaeology is synonymous with glamour and exotic adventure and the archaeologist is a handsome, dashing, treasure hunting hero. The contrast between real archaeology and Hollywood's depiction is vivid for me as I notice how sweaty and smeared with dust both Cowan and Sugarman have become. Field archaeology is basically hot, dirty, tedious work, and it has always been that way.

The origin of archaeology begins with nineteenth-century grave robbers in the Middle East. The plundering of ancient necropolis at that time was endemic and constituted a way of survival, while the object of the buyers was simply to amass the greatest treasure collection of objects that could be dated back to antiquity. By the early twentieth century, archaeology was slowly becoming a systematic science with an interest in gaining more cultural information. Starting about 1950 with the invention of radiocarbon dating, samples of earth, lithic flakes, and opal phytoliths became important in constructing a total picture of what life was like in ancient times. Artifacts became just another aspect to the overall collection of information from which inferences regarding human behavior and lifestyle could be made.

Today archaeology is not an end in itself but a servant to anthropology where the goal is the study and understanding of primitive cultures and technology. "It was a big step from treasure hunting to knowledge," Cowan said. Also, it explains why professional archaeologists become so irate with looters of antiquity who, during their hasty removal of artifacts, destroy the surrounding context of materials and knowledge it represents.

Between centimeter level twenty-two and thirty-four the cultural material, while still present, begins to thin out. Between level thirty-four and forty-four, Cowan finds a broken projectile point that is culturally unidentifiable. The point, however, is associated with a piece of charcoal that, when radiocarbon dated later, produces a time frame around 4,850 years before the present. Cowan goes down another ten centimeters before he quits at the fifty-four-centimeter level.

"This was just going to be a thirty-centimeter-deep shovel test pit," he says looking at me, his face smudged with dirt and sweat, "but the richness of the cultural debris is phenomenal, just phenomenal." He speculates further that the cultural flakes may well continue on down for many more feet.

While backfilling the pit, Cowan mentions that if this where a complete dig, soil samples would have been taken back to the lab to be viewed microscopically to determine the soils opal phytolith. Opal phytoliths are the microscopic structural remnants of grass plants that remain behind in the soil after the plant has died.

Typically, growing plants absorb water containing dissolved silica from the soil. Microscopic silica bodies are then formed by the partial or complete silification of plant cells, cell walls, and intercellular spaces. The resulting silica bodies, which help give rigidity to the plant, have characteristic shapes called opal phytoliths (phyto meaning plants, lithos meaning stone). Opal is the common name for amorphous, hydrated silica dioxide.

Phytoliths form in most plants and are produced in a multitude of shapes and sizes. They act as an identifiable diagnostic "signature" when their shapes and/or sizes are specific to a particular plant taxon. Many phytoliths are resistant to weathering and are preserved in most soils and sediments for long periods of time. An analysis of opal phytoliths can determine the species and presence of plants growing at a much earlier soil level. Identified plant species can then be used as indicators of climatic conditions.

For example, on the plains purple gayfeather is usually found in the same context with fringed sage, goldenrod, black Sampson, and little bluestem grass. All are good indicators of a dry, prairie plant community. However, analyzing soil samples for opal phytoliths can be an expensive proposition.

Back at camp Fred Chapman has offered to lead the way up to the summit of Inyan Kara before the sun sets. It is about a thousand-foot climb from where we are camped. Since there is no marked trail that leads all the way to the summit, I am interested to see how he gets up there. Cowan and Sugarman also decide to make the climb. Cowan has scouted around most of the mountain's perimeter and should know the best routes.

Chapman takes the route that begins at a good spring on the northeast side of the mountain, probably the same place most of the earlier expeditions started from. He follows a trail up a narrow gulch that winds around the east side of the mountain. The going on this trail is relatively easy and along the way I pause to sample some Oregon grape growing in profusion on the forest floor. As the trail climbs, we encounter many small openings in the forest canopy due to talus slides or places where mountain pine beetles have killed small stands of timber and the trees have fallen. Around these edges grow small ripe, tasty raspberries and currents. Oregon grape, which grows only a few inches high in on the shaded forest floor, is by far the most abundant berry now in mid-August and although its dark purple fruit appears inviting, its taste is pulpy and tart.

About three-quarters of the way up to the summit, Chapman decides to take a short-cut to the top of the ridge. It involves climbing over bare rock and boulders. In this east-facing micro-habitat, the dominant tree species changes from ponderosa to Rocky Mountain juniper, which thrives on this barren rocky slope away from fire and competition from other taller, faster growing tree species. Many of the trees we encounter, although no taller than eight or ten feet, may be centuries old. In their grizzled, gnarled appearance they resemble smaller versions of the ancient bristlecone pines of the Great Basin.

This sparsely vegetated rocky slope allows us an excellent view of an outcrop of long, vertical, hexagonal basalt columns. This type of formation is perhaps best exemplified by the Devil's Tower laccolith some forty miles to the north. Climbing up this barren slope proves most challenging to Sugarman who has on flat-soled athletic shoes and lacks any kind of experience in rock climbing. The most difficult part for all of us is maintaining footing between the rocks that, in many cases, are deeply buried under a duff of slick, dry pine needles.

Finally gaining the top of the ridge, we all stop to catch our breath. Like the slope we just climbed, this ridge is characterized by stunted pines and junipers growing out of rock crevices. The view is expansive east and west while the true summit, a few hundred yards away, blocks the best view to the north. We pick our way down a rocky saddle and climb to the summit over a slide of loose boulders. On the summit, the north wind, now blowing unobstructed at 6,368 feet, hammers us full on. The red, rocky outcrop of the summit's ridge is composed of eroded basalt and has sharp angles and edges which have been softened in appearance by its luxuriant covering of mint green and orange crustose lichens.

The middle of the summit's ridge is marked by a two-foot-high rock cairn that contains a rusty can, inside which are scraps of paper with the comments and the names of those who have reached the summit before us. Perhaps none is more famous than the one Chapman is about to bring to light. Slowly he removes a small pile of flat stones laying on the bedrock to reveal faint letters that are barely discernible in the late afternoon light. Even in the fading light there is no mistaking the chiseled inscription of "G. A. Custer" with the date "'74" on the upper right above the name just as Knappen reported it 138 years ago.

Cowan and Chapman squat down in front of the inscription and discuss how best to preserve this famous etching for posterity. Cowan warns Chapman that if he hides it under the stone pile, water will accumulate under it and hasten the erosion process. Chapman counters that if he leaves it open and unprotected, visitors, whose first natural impulse is to finger those historic grooves, will hasten its obliteration by depositing acid on it from their hands. Cowan, who worked as a residential construction contractor in Pennsylvania for a dozen years before becoming an archaeologist, finally advises Chapman somewhat facetiously to dump resin on it as a preservative.

It is a thorny question that, for archaeologists, poses a serious dilemma concerning the preservation of many types of cultural "rock art." A couple of hundred miles to the northwest, near present Billings, Montana, the famous explorer William Clark carved his name and the date 1805 in the soft, yellow sandstone of Pompey's Pillar on the Yellowstone River. It is the only record carved in stone commemorating the famous explorer's expedition to the Pacific and is now protected from vandals under a steel frame and Plexiglas. Next to Clark's name a host of other signatures and initials left by later unremarkable visitors has all but defaced the surrounding smooth sandstone.

In the context of Pompey's Pillar, Clark's signature is easily accessible and clearly needed protection. Custer's name, however, is not accessible and some might argue in the context of this time and this wild summit, might best be left for nature to erase.

The ferocity of the north wind howling over the peak makes the topic academic and it seems prudent to get off that point, both literally and figuratively. We all drop down behind a large outcrop and climb over to the southeast corner of the summit and out of the wind.

On a rough, bare, rocky ledge, Chapman points out a faintly discernible rectangular outline about six feet long and three feet wide that has been delineated with sharp, angular stones. Next to this outlined box is a cache pile of the same type of stones. In the middle of the box is one stone Chapman calls an offering stone.

Chapman refers to this rock box as a "fasting area," or more commonly known as a "vision quest" site. He speculates, based on historic ethnographic data and contemporary information from his Wyoming Indian informants, that it could be a prehistoric site where a man spent three days and nights fasting and waiting for a sign or a vision. These quests are still undertaken by native peoples to learn from the spirits what their place or power in this life is to be. Just above this outline, Chapman points out another, less well-defined, stone box a few yards away. While the first one had some protection from the north wind, this one is wind blasted.

I decide to depart the group for a moment and wander a short distance to the very eastern edge of the summit. Ancient ground junipers with fantastically gnarled roots and trunks cling here to rock crevices and ledges that overhang a sheer drop of seventy or eighty feet. I am intrigued at how such a difficult and hostile environment has created such graceful and elegant plant shapes. It leads me to consider the effect of fasting in such a difficult environment.

The idea of fasting on mountains in isolation is common to both American Indian and certain western religious ascetic orders. The object is to remove distraction and expose the body to the elements for purposes of purification. The intent is to clear the mind and shift perception in order to collapse the world of forms and experience the metaphysical reality of life. Those who would be visionaries sought these places of isolation and exposure to see beyond the doors of perception into the mystic realm. This exercise of the spirit was not for the faint of heart and often nothing of consequence was revealed.

However, for some, isolation and long exposure to the elements taught humility and perseverance. Watching natural relationships unfold can be healing in restoring an essential sense of faith in the inherent order and beneficence of nature and the universe.

The cold wind pushes me back to the group and away from the brink of the precipice to the sheltering outcrops. Standing again near the second, higher rectangular box I can see the silhouette of Mato Tipi (the Bear's Lodge) or Devil's Tower to the northwest. Up close the tower, with its basaltic columnar structure, appears as a wide, inaccessible obelisk. From this vantage point it resembles a wolf's cuspid with the tip worn down. Just beyond the tower on the farthest horizon and looking like three small, mis-shaped lumps of clay are the Little Missouri Buttes. The three buttes appear to occupy the angles of a triangle and are said to be called by the Indians "the buttes which look at each other." Though prominent landmarks, they rise only between four or five hundred feet above their base.

Due north is Warren Peak, barely discernible as a tiny blip at the center of the long, dark blue, Bear Lodge Range horizon. Warren Peak or "Peaks" as Henry Newton referred to them in 1875 are named for G. K. Warren, mentioned earlier in this chapter. Newton called them the crowning points of the Bear Lodge Range which he described as "an elevated, plateau between the Redwater Valley and the Belle Fourche."

The "peaks" consist of a cluster of two or three high, rounded, grass-covered hills, with little or no timber. While the summit of Warren Peak is unremarkable and easily accessible by car, it is a landscape of serene beauty in the spring when parts of it are carpeted by hosts of purple pasqueflowers.

Below Warren Peak, crouched like sentinals at the foot of the Bear Lodge Range, are the dark shapes of Sundance and Green Mountain. To the east are the low conically shaped Black Buttes, handsomely cloaked in dark, ponderosa pine. Twenty miles beyond them, high on the horizon of the Black Hills proper is the Cement Ridge fire tower standing out as a tiny, white square in the sunlight. Constructed of native stone and wood in 1940, the Cement Ridge tower was the last project undertaken in the Black Hills by the Civilian Conservation Corps (CCC's). Following the line of the ridge far to the southeast there is the lone, singular shape of Harney Peak.

From this vantage, Harney Peak appears as a small, curvilinear bump of deep purple, floating solitary above a wide, dark sea of coniferous forest. At 7,242 feet, it sits near the center of the Black Hills and is its highest point. Additionally, Harney Peak is the highest point west of the Mississippi and east of the main chain of the Big Horn Mountains. Black Elk, the famous Ogallala Lakota medicine man, often referred to it as the center of the world. As the crow flies it is about forty-five miles distant from here.

Inhabiting the top of Inyan Kara, in shallow depressions where a thin layer of soil has accumulated over the centuries, are the same dryland plants that grow on its flanks—ponderosa pine, at least three species of juniper, prickly pear, currant, bluebells, yarrow, goldenrod, Junegrass, Oregon grape, gayfeather, pussytoes. The plants seem to make no distinction between the top or the foot of the mountain.

"Inyan" is a corruption of "Heeng-ya" and in the Lakota language means "rock or stone"; "ka-ga" is the action word, meaning "to make or gather." A literal translation means "to gather stone," an apt name for a mountain that for millennia has been a focal point for the procurement of stone material for a host of purposes. Undoubtedly the mountain's function and name were passed down to the Sioux who became the last aboriginal peoples to use its now silent quarries.

The people of the plains have many traditions associated with Inyan Kara. In one, the mountain serves as the beginning and the end of the big race around the Paha Sapa (Black Hills). According to this tradition, the race is run by the four-legged and the winged to determine the fate of the two-legged (humans). The act of racing, it is said, wore a ring around the Black Hills, causing them to uplift to their present elevation. The race track became bloody from the contest and is marked today in appearance as the Red Valley.

Another tradition the Lakota hold has to do with the taking of three stones from Inyan Kara to be used in the seasonal sun dance ceremony often held near Matotipila Paha or "Bear Lodge Hill" (Devil's Tower). If these stones survive the sun dance ceremony intact, they are returned with gifts of thanks to Inyan Kara and replaced in the exact location from whence they were gathered.

Like Bear Butte, another prominent laccolith on the northeast edge of the Black Hills, Inyan Kara is also recognized as a place where "all the four colors of the stone can be gathered." The four colors of stone that were crushed and used by Plains people in their various ceremonies were red, yellow, white, and black. The mountain also figures prominently in the Lakota's first movement of the stone legend which is part of their metaphysical acknowledgment of the act of creation and the existence of the Great Spirit. The stone nation people go back to the beginning when the Earth was molten fire; the stone nation has witnessed all that has been. Their movement renews a sense of contact and being with all the movement that is and was life.

As evening begins to settle upon us, Chapman leads the way down off the summit by way of the northwest face. For the first one hundred yards we move down cautiously over a talus slide of smooth, flat igneous stones. There is no trail and the talus is treacherously unstable and prone to slide out from under foot. At the edge of the talus, we cross a saddle and enter a grove of tall, spindly pines. Over the next ridge we drop down into an old growth ponderosa forest. It is a magnificent stand of thick, orange-and-black, bark-scaled trunks, many bearing the wounds of fire scars centuries old, arranged in random uniformity across a long, gentle east-facing slope. It may be the largest grove of old growth pine forest left in the Black Hills; stretching as far as I can see are huge, straight trees with an unbroken canopy so high I have to strain my neck upwards to view it.

As we continue to walk down the slope, Cowan points out an aboriginal stone quarry pit situated under the great pine canopy. The quarry is littered with primary cultural flakes of brownish gray chert, some of it with white, wavy striations running horizontally through it.

Further down the slope, following the backbone of the ridge, are more quarries and fire hearths. As we continue our descent, Cowan speculates that this is the route natives traveled to quarry their stone and ultimately reach the summit of Inyan Kara. The presence of those ancient peoples begins to feel almost palpable in light of all the stone quarries and hearths left open and undisturbed as if those who worked them would soon be returning.

Except for a few random clusters of arrowhead balsam root, with its long oblate leaves and tall, dried flower stalks, the entire forest floor is free of ground vegetation. As we walk under the high canopy of pines, the evening light streams down through the tree trunks in golden streaks, imparting the sense of passing through the nave of a great cathedral.

At the edge of the old growth pine forest we reach a wet bog, which in prehistoric times probably had a good flowing spring. Near the bog is evidence of old campsites and hearths. Below it a series of adjoining quarry pits follow the brow of a low ridge. Laying around the pits are stone blanks of all sizes along with a profusion of agatized chert flakes.

Farther down the slope, as we near the base of the mountain, the chert plays out and the outcrops become gravelly and of no value in regard to workable stone. On one of the knolls I startle a nighthawk which jumps up and flies off into the evening. Just below the nighthawk's roost, Carol Agard, the chief forest service archaeologist, has tied a tobacco offering around a wooden pole along with long strips of cloth that comprise the four sacred colors used by the Lakota. She did this at the beginning of the dig earlier in the week. The old ones, some of whom still watch here in spirit, would understand that the guardians of the mountain must be thought of and offerings made to them before any work is undertaken. It shows respect for all that was and is here.

The offering links us with the host of peoples that also camped and labored here: Mandan, Ree, Kiowa, Apache, Crow, Shoshone, Arapahoe, Cheyenne, Lakota, and others—many, many others—more ancient, unknown, and now forgotten, but here in essence. Inyan Kara was the place to gather stone in the name of the hunt, the kill, and the mystical. For the old ones it was all the same power seamlessly woven together and ultimately focused into the stone's movement.

Their legacy of stone circles, quarries, and now the hanging colored cloths poignantly reminds me of their struggles and endeavors; their hopes and beliefs. It is there I forge a bond with them and begin to appreciate the power and the mystery that imbues Inyan Kara—impending, primal, and immanent; it is a feeling like something long ago and yet to come.

11

Black Hills Wapiti

The Shawnee Indians of southern Ohio called them wapiti or "white deer," probably in reference to their white rump and tail. The white deer was a powerful life spirit that exemplified strength, grace, and nobility, providing the people with meat, clothing, tools, and healing potions. Wapiti, more commonly known as elk, have come to symbolize the high, remote sanctuaries of the Rocky Mountain West. Their bugling, which can carry for miles in the crisp air of early autumn, evokes primal emotions that seem to embody the essence of wilderness and the melancholy of fall. Their wilderness mystique, so closely associated with the high country, ironically belongs to the deciduous forests of the East and the Great Plains, their original primary habitat.

Three centuries ago wapiti, the largest of the grazing grassland deer, inhabited the prairie and forest ecotones of the East and Midwest along with the vast grasslands of western North America. Their combined continental population was estimated at 10 million animals. By the beginning of the nineteenth century, settlers had exterminated wapiti east of the Mississippi.

In the spring of 1803, Lewis and Clark, following the serpentine course of the Missouri north from St. Louis, first encountered them in profusion in what is now northeastern Kansas. They described seeing these regal animals in small groups along with herds of deer and small packs of wolves wandering over a great expanse of prairie dotted with small copses of trees.

Following their extirpation in the East, the Great Plains, stretching south from central Alberta to Texas and then east for hundreds of miles, became the favored habitat of the wapiti. Here millions of them mingled with the vast herds of bison, pronghorn, and deer in what has been described as one of the most protein-rich ecosystems anywhere on earth.

In the seven decades following the commercial opening of the West by Lewis and Clark, elk were completely annihilated by settlers and market hunters on the tall grass prairies east of the Missouri. Most of the elk in the plains states west of the Missouri were slaughtered in the following decade from 1870 to 1880.

In the Black Hills, George Grinnell, zoologist with the 1874 Custer expedition reported the following:

> Although but few elk were seen during the trip, we found in the Black Hills every indication of their recent presence in large numbers. During a single day's march eleven pairs of horns, attached to the skull, were picked up by members of the expedition. Horns that had been shed were very abundant, and it was by no means an unusual thing to see fifteen or twenty single antlers in a morning's ride.
>
> On Elkhorn Prairie we came upon a collection of horns gathered together by the Indians. Three lodge-poles had been set in the ground so as to form a tripod, and supported by these was a pile of horns 8 to 10 feet high. The horns had all been shed, and had apparently been collected from the surrounding prairie and heaped up here by the Indians. There is much variation in the horns of this species, most of which I imagine to be due to injuries to the horns while young and soft. Many of the specimens examined this summer were much flattened near the extremities, so much so in one or two cases as to be from 6 to 7 inches wide. In two instances the basal prong of the horn, instead of projecting forward and downward in the usual manner, turned outward and downward, and then curving inward and up again, brought the point of the snag immediately under the animal's throat.

When the expedition crossed Windy Flats east of Custer Peak in the northern Black Hills on August 9th, 1874, Grinnell reported evidence of large numbers of elk also living in this vicinity. He also reported evidence of other cervids (deer) on this high, wind-swept meadow park, noting that his men killed one hundred deer there, mainly white tail. He estimated that during the brief time the expedition actually spent in the Black Hills, one thousand cervids (mostly deer) were slaughtered.

The discovery of gold by Custer's miners and the following gold rush in 1876 brought an estimated influx of ten thousand people into the Black Hills in the span of a few years. The result was that in slightly over a decade, market hunters swept the Black Hills and surrounding northern plains area clean of elk along with the pronghorn, deer, and the American bison.

While bison were probably never abundant in the Black Hills, they certainly wandered into them on occasion off the plains—most notably choosing to graze the more open southern Hills areas, gaining easy access therein via Buffalo Gap and Pleasant Valley. Even before the 1876 gold rush and the subsequent slaughter of wild animals for food, bison, however, were becoming scarce, as Grinnell later reported:

> No buffalo where seen during the trip (from Fort Lincoln to the Black Hills), nor do I know that any exist at present in the region traversed, but one or two circumstances lead me to infer that there may still be found a few individuals in this section of the country.
>
> In Prospect Valley I found the skull of an old bull, with the part of the hide still clinging to it. Also, on French Creek, not far from the Big Cheyenne, I noticed the lower jaw of a cow, with the priosteum still on it.
>
> It is but a few years since the country through which we passed was the favorite feeding ground of the buffalo, and their white skulls dot the prairie in all directions. Sometimes these are collected by the Indians, and arranged on the ground in fantastic patterns. In one of these collections which I noticed, the skulls had been painted red and blue in stripes and circles, and were arranged in five parallel rows of twelve each, all the skulls facing the east.

In the early 1880s the remnants of the northern plains bison herd was concentrated on the Yellowstone-Missouri River divide in east central Montana. During the year of 1881, the Northern Pacific extended their track into Glendive and Miles City, Montana. The extension of the line stimulated bison hunting and in 1882 five thousand hunters and skinners had laid out a cordon of camps along the entire length of the western upper Missouri. This battle line completely blocked migratory bison from reaching their northern ranges on the Milk, the Musselshell, and the Yellowstone—in effect rendering it impossible for scarcely a single bison to escape to the north.

The next hunting season of 1883, a reported herd of fifty to eighty thousand buffalo crossed the Yellowstone south of Miles City, headed for their northern grazing ranges. They were reportedly met by a "hail of lead." By the end of the season, all had disappeared. No one believed the slaughter could be so complete for, as recent as only two years earlier, 250,000 hides had been shipped from Miles City to Minneapolis. The abrupt extermination of the northern plains herd in 1883 and 1884 resulted in six hundred deaths from starvation among the Montana Blackfeet.

That same year, 1884, the last free-roaming bison native to the Black Hills was killed in Pleasant Valley in the southern Hills. In 1886, William Hornaday, chief taxidermist for the National Museum in Washington, managed to find and shoot twenty-five bison in Montana for a museum display. When D. G. Elliot came to Montana to hunt and collect bison hides the following year of 1887 for the American Museum of Natural History, he could not locate a single, wild buffalo on the northern plains after a three-month search. The failure of this expedition came as a shock to both naturalists and hunters. Hornaday at the time estimated that only eighty-five free-ranging bison remained with another two hundred in Yellowstone.

The following year, 1888, the last free-roaming wild elk *(Cervus elephus manitobensis)*, a northern plains subspecies native to the Black Hills, was killed. The slaughter of the last bison and the last elk in the Black Hills marked the end of an era. The vast herds of ruminant plains animals that had dominated life on the Great Plains of North America for most of the 10 millennia following the end of the Ice Age, disappeared in the short span of a century. Figures vary on the slaughter from 30 to 60 million bison, and perhaps half that many combined total of pronghorn, deer, and plains elk.

Included in that elk population were a half-dozen subspecies uniquely evolved to the idiosyncrasies of their specific environments from coast to coast. After the slaughter was over, two subspecies, the Merriam and eastern elk were completely wiped out while four subspecies, including the coastal range elk *(C.e. roosevelti)*, the tule elk of California *(C.e. nannodes)*, the Manitoban elk *(C.e. manitobensis)* located in Manitoba and Saskatchwan, and the Rocky Mountain elk *(C.e. nelsoni)*, had somehow managed to survive.

In 1881, some four hundred Rocky Mountain elk lived in the high, remote enclaves of the Greater Yellowstone ecosystem. The creation of Yellowstone National Park near the end of the nineteenth century in large measure was the critical factor that saved these elk, along with the American plains bison and probably the pronghorn, from extinction.

In 1901, protected in the 2.2 million-acre vastness of Yellowstone National Park, the Rocky Mountain elk had increased to twenty-five thousand head. The next year five thousand died of starvation. By 1914 records show that in spite of some major winter die-offs from starvation, there were an estimated thirty-five thousand elk living in Yellowstone Park. These elk would become the genetic nucleus for their re-introduction and recovery in the Rocky Mountain West.

Early unpublished records in the files of the South Dakota Department of Game, Fish, and Parks indicate that the initial re-introduction of elk into the Black Hills from the Yellowstone herd took place around 1911. At that time approximately one hundred head of elk were released in a joint effort by state conservation agencies of both Wyoming and South Dakota. In 1912 and 1913 an additional forty-two elk from Yellowstone were released on the Wyoming border (west side) of the Black Hills. Subsequent releases were made in 1915 and 1919 so that by 1920 a total of some two hundred elk had been transplanted into the Black Hills ecosystem.

Eight years later, in 1928, the Black Hills herds were now firmly established and had grown to an estimated one thousand animals. Complaints from farmers and ranchers of elk depredation to agricultural crops, however, prompted the opening of the first elk hunting season that same year with a management objective of killing all the free-roaming elk outside of Custer State Park and Wind Cave National Park. This unenlightened management objective was eventually abandoned in the 1950s in favor of increasing elk numbers and dispersing them more evenly throughout the entire Black Hills area.

Bob Hauk is a big game wildlife biologist with the South Dakota Department of Game, Fish, and Parks. He is also an admirer of elk. Hauk is the primary resource person in charge of monitoring and managing elk for the state in the Black Hills. In early June of 1992, he spent a day showing me how he does part of his job by taking me up to the Sheridan Lake area to monitor the whereabouts of two cow elk about to calf. During the short drive up from his office in Rapid City we discussed his past experience and the state's elk management goals and objectives for the Black Hills.

In 1992 he estimated that there were approximately one thousand head of elk in the combined herds of Custer and Wind Cave parks, and another twelve to fifteen hundred head living outside the parks at large in the greater Black Hills ecosystem. Hauk wants to see their total numbers increased outside of the wildlife parks to four thousand free-roaming animals by the end of this century.

While Hauk's first love is the outdoors and elk management, he also acts in the capacity of assistant West (Missouri) River regional manager responsible for all the big game management in the Black Hills, as well as most of the entire West River area of South Dakota. His responsibilities include managing wild big game animal populations in seventeen South Dakota counties. For this he relies on fourteen conservation officers to survey and handle all types of resource problems. They are, as he puts it, his "eyes and ears."

Based on the information he receives from his line conservation officers, he recommends the number of hunting permits for big game animals along with the length of the hunting seasons. This information is passed on to the South Dakota Game, Fish, and Parks Commission which either modifies, rejects, or approves it.

Hauk, a Rapid City native, has been with the department for twenty years. In 1983, he helped start the state's Turn In Poachers (TIPs) program in the Black Hills after two elk were wantonly shot and left to rot on the first weekend of the 1983 Black Hills deer season.

Hauk said the program was started by a group of local Rapid City businessmen who were so upset by the senseless slaughter of two magnificent bulls that they decided to take action. It was done informally, he said, over coffee one morning that winter. The group offered a $3,000 reward for information leading to the arrest and conviction of the poachers. Two informants, who were unconnected to each other, soon came forward with information that convicted the poachers. The following year a citizen's wildlife protection group was organized and incorporated to continue the work started by the Rapid City businessmen and TIPs (Turn In Poachers) was born. That next fall five hundred tips on poachers were called in resulting in one hundred cases. In 1986 TIPs went statewide.

Driving up Sheridan Lake Road along Spring Creek from Rapid City, I watched the country change from an urbanized clutter of houses, cars, and dogs to a quiet environment of dark schist outcrops and meticulously thinned ponderosa groves. Looking out his cab window at the neatly trimmed stands of pine, Hauk commented on the fact that the Black Hills, to a large extent, is managed as an urban forest environment, explaining that it lacked the rugged back hills country prominent in other national forests of the West. It is, he added, also surrounded by a relatively large human population that uses the forest for many different recreational and commercial purposes.

As a mountainous region the Black Hills are easily accessible and contain many private inholdings within the national forest boundaries that are being residentially and commercially developed. These competing interests complicate many forest and wildlife resource management issues.

Reaching the head of Spring Creek near Sheridan Lake, Hauk pointed out an area where foresters were managing the pine forest for timber production. The trees were all even aged and had been selectively thinned, creating a monotonous park-like setting. Hauk, considering the needs of elk, did not like it.

"Elk prefer habitat created by forest fires," he said. "Burn areas rejuvenate into a patchwork mosaic of different kinds of timber and brush." In this regard he is often at odds with foresters who generally prefer to manage timber in even-aged stands without the benefit and the destructive threat of fire. Surveying the thinned-out tree stands again, Hauk went on to point out that "elk do not use an area like this that has been selectively thinned and opened up from ridge line to ridge line."

On the other side of Sheridan Lake we stopped at Horse Creek Inn to pick up Rick Halseth. Halseth, another wildlife biologist, joined us with a radio monitor and antenna to track down the whereabouts of cow elk #28 and #135. After two and half years, cows #28 and #135 were the last two out of six transplanted elk that still had on a radio collar. Hauk and Halseth were monitoring them closely to discover their movements and preferences for calving areas in a part of the Black Hills that had not been inhabited by elk for many years.

During the winter of 1990, cows #28 and #135 were rounded up by helicopter in Wind Cave National Park along with 268 other elk of random age and sex for transplanting to various reserves in the area. Since hunting is not allowed in Wind Cave, elk must be rounded up and culled periodically to keep the herd within the carrying capacity of the park's grazing and habitat resources.

The South Dakota Wildlife Division acquired and tagged fifty-eight head of elk from this roundup. They transplanted half of this herd (twenty-nine) on Red Hill and the other half on Veterans Peak. Both peaks are roughly located opposite each other across Vanocker Canyon in a high, rugged area in the northeastern part of the Black Hills just west of Sturgis, South Dakota. Those fifty-eight head of elk joined a small resident herd of ten which, according to Hauk, had remained stable at this number for many years. The management objective here was simply to increase the herd size.

Hauk had six radio collars to work with; of those he placed five on cows and one on a ten-year-old bull. Before the winter was over the bull elk was found dead of natural causes just a few miles from the release site near the Black Hills National Cemetery. The following spring the next collar turned up mysteriously buried a couple of feet down in a mud hole wallow in Virkula Gulch, also relatively close to the release site. Hauk is still baffled by this curious situation since neither the elk nor any sign of it was ever found. The third collar was retrieved from a cow poached in November of 1990 near Dalton Lake. The cow had given birth that spring to a calf before it had been shot.

Another cow turned up in the Custer State Park herd, completing its migration all the way back to the vicinity from which it had originated. That left only cows #28 and #135 still free roaming in the vicinity of Sheridan Lake, Horse Creek, and Victoria Creek.

If you track the progress of the six radio-collared elk on a forest service map it turns out to be a clear progression of animals intent on migrating south back "home." This is not unusual since most herd animals, by instinct, tend to return to their home range country. Hauk estimated that 25 to 30 percent of the elk transplanted around Vanocker Canyon will eventually end up back in the Wind Cave herd.

He cited a couple of reasons for this. One being the country above Vanocker Canyon is very rugged and forested, much more so than the easy open slopes of the southern Black Hills. Secondly, the winters in the northern Hills, as a rule, are generally colder with more snow than the southern Hills. Whenever possible elk like to wander out of the rough country and the deep snow. There is also the instinctual pull of the home range where the animal is intimately familiar with the location of the water holes, grazing areas, and sheltered rest areas. These imprinted memories of the routines associated with the home range exert a very strong attraction.

Looking at all the factors, it is easy to understand why the highest percentage of free-roaming elk prefer the southern Black Hills, just west of the two great wildlife parks of Custer and Wind Cave.

The southern elk herd, which takes in the whole area south of U.S. 16, has about five hundred to seven hundred animals as of this writing. Many of these animals cross back and forth regularly between the adjacent wildlife parks and the national forest in spite of the high woven wire fences in place to discourage them.

The central herd covers the largest area ranging over the central limestone plateau north of U.S. 16, west of U.S. 385 and south of U.S. 85. The number in this unit fluctuates with some seasonal migration from elk moving into this area from the north, south and west. About 500 elk live here with the potential for more.

The northern Hills herd ranges north of U.S. 85 up to Interstate 90 and west of Spearfish Canyon (U.S. 14A). This herd numbers about two hundred animals, but there is a good deal of seasonal migration in the winter west out of South Dakota and into the open areas of the Wyoming Black Hills foothills when the snow depths in the higher elevations (i.e., six thousand feet) reach the two-foot level.

The Norbeck Wildlife Preserve, which includes Harney Peak, the Needles, and the Black Elk Wilderness, comprises some of the highest, most rugged country in the Black Hills. While picturesque, it is a tough place to survive much less flourish and elk numbers here are small, consisting mainly of seasonal migrants from the Custer State Park herd.

The last unit is located in the northeastern part of the Black Hills and is bounded by U.S. 14A on the north, U.S. 385 on the west, I-90 on the east and South Dakota 44 on the south. It is a large area with a sparse population of elk, numbering some seventy-five individuals scattered out singly or in small herds. It is the area where Hauk released the fifty-eight tagged transplants in 1990 and where the two cows Hauk and Halseth are "beeping" have just wandered out of.

Searching for the two cows with a radio antenna is a relatively uncomplicated business. That particular June morning Hauk stopped his jeep on a logging road west of Sheridan Lake on the south edge of the Horse Creek Burn Area to "beep" them. We got out to stretch and look over the country while Halseth put on his head phones and pointed his radio antenna northwest in the direction he believed the elk were located. When Halseth is accurate in pointing his antenna in the elk's direction the beeping gets more intense and louder, the opposite being the case when he moves away from the radio-collared animal. The numbers 28 and 135 that are given to the elk refer to the wave frequency their radio transmitters are set at. That morning #135 came in faintly which meant she could have been far away (some three miles) or behind a mountain in a gulch. Number 28's signal came in stronger.

Halseth decided to move a bit farther north and we climbed back into the jeep, drove around a mountain, and proceeded up Horse Creek a few miles until the road ended at the head of gulch. Here Halseth got a very strong signal from #28 when he pointed his antenna west towards a mountain with dense pine cover.

"She's probably up on that high ridge," Hauk said looking at the mountain. The habitat for elk was good; there was an open area at the foot of the mountain with some grass and a growth of young aspen that offered the elk grazing and browse.

Hauk noted that elk prefer a good mix of vegetation and favor a variety of habitats that include open grassy areas at the bottom of gulches, a little water, aspens, and then some high rugged ridges to rest, ruminate, and keep an eye out for danger. Elk will range several miles for food while deer may stay in the same square mile their whole life if they have all they require in regards to food and habitat. An elk's daily routine in the Black Hills generally consists of moving down from the high, rugged ridges in the evening towards the bottom of the gulches to graze and water. The bulls also like a wet place where they can wallow in soft mud when they are in the rut.

As the night proceeds, elk will slowly graze and progress from the bottom of the gulch up the mountain. As first light comes up, they will move back into the deep timber and situate themselves in the highest rugged slopes for cover and shelter. Often elk will graze up the south side of a mountain where the grass and browse tend to be the most abundant, then walk over the ridge and settle down just over the top on the north slope of the mountain to ruminate during the long daylight hours.

The north side of a Black Hills mountain is the ideal choice in the summer, since it is shaded most of the day and is therefore cooler. Since the snow stays here longer in the winter, the timber is usually thicker providing a low, dense "jack pine" cover. Hauk believes that this is a learned survival behavior adapted by Black Hills elk noting historically that elk were diurnal grazers of the open country. "If you want to know where the elk are, look around 360 degrees," he said, "and find the highest, roughest, remotest peaks in the area. That's where they will be. Also," he added, "in the fall look for a wallow—a mud hole."

While we came close to finding #28, Hauk did not go after her since she was close to calving and he did not want to disturb her. It was enough to know her general vicinity at this time of the year.

Before heading back to the regional headquarters in Rapid City, Hauk drove south through Custer and then fifteen miles down the Pleasant Valley Road to show me Paulsen's Ranch which had recently been purchased by the Rocky Mountain Elk Foundation. Pleasant Valley is a wide valley bounded by low, pine-clad ridges. It trends in a general north-south direction. For millennia this valley served as a natural access route from the plains into the interior of the central Black Hills. Bison used it extensively as did the Indians who hunted them. Custer, who followed the Pleasant Valley route south to reach the edge of the southern Black Hills in the summer of 1874, reported finding an old, well-used Indian trail which his command followed for fourteen or fifteen miles.

Paulsen's Ranch consists mainly of 423 acres of bottomland planted into rye, alfalfa, and oats. It was regarded as an area where elk were causing major agricultural depredation. In large numbers elk can do extensive damage to standing agricultural crops and haystacks as well as fences which they tear down by jumping over them.

Paulsen's Ranch, which lays a dozen miles due west of Wind Cave as the crow flies, is basically nothing more than an old oat field in the middle of a dry, open valley. It is, however, heavily used by elk at all times of the year and is one of their favorite places to congregate in large numbers at night to graze and water. Rather than decimate their numbers, the Rocky Mountain Elk Foundation purchased the property to serve primarily as an undisturbed feeding oasis for the wild, free-roaming southern Hills elk herd. While the ranch's primary focus is to serve as a haven for elk, Hauk also sees its potential as habitat for a host of other game and non-game animals—including raccoons, rabbits, raptors, and songbirds.

On the way back to Rapid City, Hauk talked about how elk tend to graze more than the smaller whitetail and mule deer species which tend more to browse. He also mentioned how cattle, when moved into a specific area of the Black Hills will push the elk away. "As a general rule," he said, "elk will not mix with cattle."

About halfway back up Pleasant Valley Road from the elk refuge to Custer he stopped his jeep to point out a bronze plaque set in a large boulder on the west side of the road. It had the name of the three men who at this site in 1884 killed the last wild bison in the Black Hills.

Hauk wondered aloud why anyone would want to be commemorated a century later for such a senseless act. Times, of course, were different then. Pioneers subsisted on wildlife and the Black Hills and prairies were abundant with it. Newspapers like the *Black Hills Journal* were constantly running stories like the item in the April 5, 1884, edition that read: "Beckett and Foote brought in hides and furs Thursday. They had 1,000 deer and antelope, 400 coyotes, and 200 buffalo."

The philosophy of over a century ago in the West was one of nearly complete freedom; both land and wild game were free and thought to be inexhaustible. Every man was a law unto himself having to answer to no one in particular. This was the subliminal message proclaimed between the lines in articles of the *Black Hills Journal* that attracted so many men West. The other message for anyone who cared to read it was that an era was dying and hundreds of plains men like Beckett and Foote were killing it.

From the relative comfort of the late twentieth century, it is easy to speculate on the right and wrong of the actions taken by our predecessors. Unlike us, however, very few had the time or the luxury to cultivate the fine sensibilities and ease of security their work has enabled us to enjoy. Perhaps on some larger cosmic level, the slaughter of the last native Black Hills bison, elk, pronghorn, and wolf had to be accomplished to finally end the old unenlightened order of hunting and plunder. An entire generation had to pass away and the next become more settled and civilized before they could reclaim and rebuild an even older pattern of awareness that included respect and appreciation of wild animals in their own right and for their own intrinsic beauty and value.

12

Night Flight

For a few brief minutes, evening casts her soft, rosy blush on a low, remote, jagged outcrop of white limestone on the east edge of the Black Hills. Gradually, night shadows fall and deepen. To the east, the outcrop ridge tapers down a thousand feet into the darkness of the Red Valley; to the west the orange afterglow of late summer dramatically backlights the pine forest.

I am part of a small group of volunteers gathered on the south side of the ridge at the foot of the outcrop. Located just above us is a long, horizontal crevice that dips down under the foot of the outcrop opening up into a low, cavernous room. The room, known as Gordon's Cave, is forty feet wide, about five feet high and extends back approximately one hundred feet. It appears to have received only minimal human disturbance.

Joel Tigner and Bill Aney, biologists with the Black Hills National Forest, supervise the volunteers as they string up a series of bird mist nets in front of the cave opening. This evening the two biologists plan to survey the sex, age and species of bats using this cave as a roost.

Tigner, who lived in England for a few years, began to read about and study bats while working in the Zoology Library at Oxford University. In England all bats and their roosts are protected by law. Anytime, anyone becomes aware of bat activity it must be reported and then monitored by government biologists. "The English," he said, "have a greater awareness and interest in their wildlife because theirs is so much closer to the edge (of extinction)." He added, "We (Americans) take ours (wildlife) for granted because there is still so much of it left, relatively speaking."

Tigner received "hands on training" by working with English bat biologists who monitored the calls on bats that came in. In the spring of 1992 he began to survey and evaluate potential roosting sites for bats by examining mine sites and natural caves in the northern Black Hills. His primary survey goals were to determine the locations of key roosting habitats along with the bat species associated with each site as well as site usage.

In the Black Hills eleven species of bats have been identified; eight of these species roost in caves, while the other three tend to be associated more with trees, preferring to roost in arboreal cavities or crevices. The bat species that prefer trees are difficult, if not impossible, to monitor since they are much harder to find and catch.

Cave bats in the Black Hills seasonally use different types of roosts for hibernation, maternity, nursery, and daytime resting. Like many birds and other mammals, bats also have roosting requirements that change seasonally with temperature and food availability. One factor common to all eight species of bats that roost in caves is the requirement of a relatively cool, constant roost temperature in their hibernaculum where they spend the long, cold Black Hills winter season in a state of suspended animation. Fluctuations in environmental temperature will trigger arousals which raise the metabolic rate and deplete the bat's vital stores of body fat critical for the completion of hibernation.

The successful completion of the hibernation is related to two important variables, animal body mass and the duration of hibernation season. Differentials between the bat's body temperature and the hibernating environment is generally within 2 degrees Celsius (with differentials increasing only when the environmental temperature approaches freezing). If conditions change too drastically, bats will rouse themselves from their torpid state and move, depending on the situation.

High levels of disturbance during hibernation, when coupled with an unusually cold or long winter, can result in high levels of bat mortality. Disturbances need not be drastic or severe; increased ambient temperature derived from radiant body heat of persons inside the hibernaculum has been shown to cause arousals.

Within a hibernaculum like Jewel Cave in the southern Black Hills, if the air temperature gets colder, bats will cluster together for more warmth. If the temperature gets too warm, the opposite will occur and they will spread out three to four feet apart. In a situation where a roost gets too cold and crowding together is not enough to keep them at their optimum body temperature (which varies according to species), a flock of bats may actually depart their hibernaculum during the winter and fly to another warmer roost. Tigner described this as a last resort scenario, and noted that more often they will either mover deeper or come closer to the mouth of the cavern as their temperature requirements dictate. The only other reason they arouse themselves from their torpid winter state is to excrete body wastes.

In the spring, as the outside ambient air temperatures begin to rise, the caverns in the Black Hills begin "to breathe." The breathing process, which amounts to air either rushing in or out of a deep cave, occurs when underground caverns equalize their barometric pressure and air temperature with that of the outside. Wind Cave is a classic example of that process and, in fact, was named for the cool wind that was discovered one very hot, dry summer afternoon as it was "exhaling" a large, constant flow of cold air.

The constant rise in outside air temperature, the increase in the level and length of light, and the depletion of stored fat reserves are all signals for the bats to once again fully arouse themselves for another season of night flight and procreation.

Following spring arousal, the sexes segregate with the females congregating together in maternity roosts to bear their young. As might be expected, maternity roosts are chosen for their warmth and, as such, are warmer than hibernation roosts. Fluctuations in maternity roost temperature are more acceptable at this time of year due to the bats' physical mobility and the availability of food.

The actual mating of the species, however, occurs earlier during the previous autumn just prior to hibernation. At that time the female receives the male's sperm and waits for the optimal time to implant her egg and begin gestation, usually delaying fertilization of the egg until spring. Even after implantation she is able to slow the growth of her fetus down if conditions take a turn for the worse.

The ability of the pregnant female to adapt to the vicissitudes of spring is one of the highest achievements in the realm of mammalian survival instinct. While the survival plan for many creatures in nature, most notably insects, small rodents, and rabbits, is to produce large numbers of offspring to perpetuate the species, bats appear to have moved in the other direction by enhancing their survival through an instinctively precise regulation of their ovum and reproduction cycle.

Given the great variability each female bat possesses in her reproduction cycle, all bat pups in the Black Hills are, nonetheless, usually born within a few days of each other—either in late May or early June, depending on the spring.

Following the birth of their pups, the females may then move again, coming together from a wide area to form a nursery roost. Nursery roosts are located near high insect-density areas like a pond or marsh. Besides the availability of food, levels of disturbance also play a major role in nursery site selection, as well as maternity roost site selection. Bats tolerate only a minimal amount of intrusion and disturbance within the maternity/nursery roost. Embryo reabsorption, premature birth, abandonment of young, or abandonment of roost are all common responses to high levels of disturbance. These factors, coupled with the bat's low reproductive rate which generally is one pup per year, can quickly and significantly impact species population size.

For the first couple of weeks the tiny bat babies cling to their mothers fur where they absorb the intricacies of night flight and insect hunting. Later they will learn to hang by themselves upside down at the roost until they are able to fly. The whole process from birth to solo flight takes four to five weeks. Some species of bats can reach sexual maturity as early as the following spring while others take another year.

One of the many curious aspects of these amazing creatures is their ability to perch upside down and then hang indefinitely. Whether from a tree branch or the ceiling of a cave, bats perch by flying up to the perch nose first. They then perform a quick mid-air spin maneuver grasping onto bark or rock crevices with their tiny, delicately clawed feet, and hang on.

Bat feet have a reflexive action that works like a pair of tongs. As they let their weight drop, their feet reflexively tighten their grip on the crevice without exerting any muscles. The bat then folds and wraps its wings around its small, furry body and comes to a complete rest.

As for predation, their two biggest adversaries are the pack or wood rats, who inhabit limestone cave crevices, and owls. Neither is very serious when compared to the damage a man can do by building a small fire in a cave roost and covering the rough walls with soot.

Both biologists, Tigner and Aney, are excited about coming to Gordon's Cave. This is the first time it has been surveyed for bat activity and both have high hopes that this evening's catch will yield a high diversity of species. When Tigner first inspected the cave in March, he found numerous scattered droppings and feeding perches, indicating that the site was receiving high use. He speculated that Gordon's Cave is being used mainly as a night roost since it lacks the depth and protection of inaccessible crevices bats prefer as day roosts. Gordon's Cave, he believes, is more of a social place where bats gather to rest and groom themselves at night high in the mountains. By nature bats are gregarious animals and many different species will often share the same roosts whether it's a cavern or a mine shaft.

By early nightfall the volunteers have strung two mist nets, each of which is about five feet high and fifty feet long, in front of the main cavern entrance. They have also partially blocked off a small entrance to the west. One of the mist nets is strung across the mouth of the cavern at its greatest width and stretches for about forty feet. In this net, Tigner hopes to catch all the bats leaving the cave.

Just above this net, a bit higher up and some ten feet away, a second, longer mist net is stretched. This one is designed to catch the incoming bats. Six people, who will extricate ensnared bats from the nets and place them in holding cages, are each issued a pair of leather gloves, the others, including myself, will be handling flashlights to illuminate the operation.

Aney stations himself up by the nets to supervise the capture while Tigner moves a few yards down the steep rocky slope and sets up his field laboratory. The laboratory consists of a small battery-powered fluorescent light hung from a pine tree branch that shines on a white oil cloth spread out on the ground as a table. On the cloth there is a metal centimeter rule, a weight sack with a weight scale in grams attached to it, and a small pair of pliers. Throughout the evening Tigner will identify captured bats as to species, sex, and relative age, as well as weigh and measure their forearm or wing bone. Before releasing them he will attach a tiny metal clip with a number to the bat's right forearm for future reference and identification.

After finishing setting up, Tigner checks the tension of the mist nets. They must be loose and hang in limp folds so that the bats will get hung up in them. If the nets are too taut, the bats have a tendency to bounce off of them as if they were trampolines. His last instructions to those new to capturing and removing bats from the mist nets are to remember that bat wings are their hands and that stretched between their fingers is a fine, thin membrane of skin that is their wing. This membrane connects all the fingers with the arm, sides of the body, legs, and tail and is extremely delicate. He asks them to exercise great care in extricating them from the net and to go first for the ones that are struggling the hardest since they will be the animals most stressed. If the bat gets tangled up in the net for too long, he instructs them to cut them out of the net. For Tigner, the animal's well-being is of paramount concern.

With the assembly line set up, the bat crew settles down to wait in the deepening darkness. Most bats begin their flight within a half hour on either side of sunset. There is a little activity around sunrise, but the evening and night flight is the most important. Bats are primarily crepuscular and nocturnal. Their activity peak is right after sundown, matching the time of greatest insect activity.

Normally the peak of the bat's insect hunting lasts for a few hours after sundown and then lulls. In the spring, when the insects are at their densest and the bats at their hungriest, females will hit several peaks of activity—coming out to feed, then returning to nurse many times throughout the evening and night.

After a wait of ten minutes, a bat appears. It flitters overhead above the cave entrance in the late twilight sky and manages to avoid the net. "He was an incoming one," says Tigner, "and could probably see the net." In effect, exploding the myth, "blind as a bat."

Bats, in fact, have tiny eyes that actually see very well in low-light situations. However, it is their remarkable ability to navigate and catch flying insects in pitch darkness that makes them truly amazing. It is this aspect of their life that we rarely ever "see." They accomplish this feat of flying in the dark and catching prey by echolocation. Echolocation is a way of locating relative position to other objects, either moving or stationary, by bouncing sound waves off of them. It employs the same principle of sonar which uses sound waves to detect objects submerged in water.

Bats use their vocal cords to generate high-pitched squeaks, inaudible to the range of human hearing. These squeaks bounce back and are picked up by the bat's tragus. The tragus is an extremely delicate sound wave reception organ in the bat's ear that can receive echoes that bounce off of a flying insect or a stationary object as fast as fifty per second. The closer a bat comes to its prey or stationary object, the faster the sound bounces back.

Bat sound vibrations can be picked up and heard on an ultra-sonic bat detector which is basically a small battery-operated receiver that looks and sounds like a Geiger counter. It brings the bat squeaks into the human range of hearing by converting them to a lower frequency.

After awhile Aney's bat detector begins to pick up a slow hum that soon quickens into what he describes as a "feeding buzz." In a matter of moments another bat flies over the net. But before anyone has time to get disappointed about the two that got away, the net bounces with an ensnared bat. It turns out to be a big brown female. Big brown bats *(Eptesicus fuscus pallidus)* are common and widespread, occurring in all the counties of the Black Hills. Big browns inhabit most of North America and are found in the Black Hills from elevations ranging between 3,500 and 6,200 feet.

At dusk, big browns like to forage over grassy, conifer-bordered meadows or over ponds and water courses. The big brown caught in the mist net weighs a whopping twenty grams (thirty-one grams equals one troy ounce). Both Tigner and Aney express incredulity at her weight and, before Tigner lets her go after recording her measurements, he weighs her a third time. At twenty grams, this juvenile big brown female will outweigh anything else that hits the net tonight by four times.

This big brown female will also be the only bat that seriously tries to bite Tigner as he takes her from the holding cage. Tigner, like Aney, prefers to handle the bats without gloves. They are so tiny and delicate it would be difficult to grasp them and sense how they are responding to handling. "It is unusual," says Tigner, "for bats to bite if handled properly by a trained expert."

However, big browns are capable of giving a painful bite. Even though only a very tiny percentage of bats carry rabies, about one-half of one percent (0.5 percent), as a precaution both men have taken the preliminary three rabies shots in the event of a serious bite.

Throughout the evening Tigner personally handles each captive bat with great care and gentleness, talking softly to them as he examines them and takes his scientific measurements. When he was working in England he kept and handled a menagerie of bats who were disabled in some way. These he would take with him when asked to do school presentations. "They all have individual personalities of their own," he said, noting that "some species tend to be more aggressive than others."

Tigner currently takes care of a crippled big brown which he described as a "bat ambassador" for use during school presentations in the Black Hills area. Tigner's bat ambassador can never be returned to the wild, having had what he describes as "an unfortunate run-in with a ceiling fan that permanently damaged his left wing." In captivity big browns have lived a maximum of thirty-five years, but that's the record. In the wild six to eight years is the reality. "Bats, by the way," noted Tigner, "make poor pets."

While Tigner takes his measurements, he tries to ascertain if the bat is an adult or a juvenile. This can usually be done by shining a flashlight under the wing and looking closely at where the forearm bones meet and join. If the joint is ossified, it is an adult; if there is a small translucent bubble, it means the bone is still growing and is indicative of a juvenile.

Then next captive is a northern male bat *(Myotis septentrionalis)* that weighs in at four grams, a little below the average weight. (The genus Latin term *myotis* means "mouse-eared.") The northern myotis is one of the smaller bats in the area with an average weight of about five or six grams. This will be the average weight of most of the twenty-two bats that will be caught and banded this evening. At Gordon's Cave, Tigner will encounter six of the possible eight species that use cave habitats in the Black Hills. The six encountered and banded include the little brown myotis *(Myotis lucifugus carissima)*, the small-footed myotis *(Myotis leifii ciliolabrum)*, the northern myotis, *(Myotis septentrionalis)*, the big brown bat *(Eptesicus fuscus pallidus)*, Townsend's big-eared bat *(Plecotus townsendii pallenscenes)*, and the fringed-tailed myotis *(Myotis thysanodes pahapsapensis)*, the latter is listed by the U.S. Fish and Wildlife Service as a candidate for threatened or endangered status. The two native bats not encountered were the long-legged myotis *(Myotis volans)* and the long-eared myotis *(Myotis evotis)*.

After taking all the measurements, Tigner bands the northern myotis' left forearm. Male bats are banded on the left forearm; females on the right forearm. The third captive is a female little brown myotis. Little browns consume about six hundred mosquito-size insects in an hour. When a flashlight is shined under her wing, it reveals that she is a juvenile as well as a carrier of a couple of parasites that look like tiny, red mites. These parasites are feeding on the dead cells of the membrane skin.

Bats, like all mammals, are plagued by flies and a host of non-specific parasites and insects which include mites, chiggers, and ticks that seek out all warm-blooded mammals. They also host species-specific parasites that have evolved with them and are unique to them only.

A survey done on 304 of Townsend's big-eared bats examined in the Jewel Cave hibernacula in 1967 revealed that 67 percent were parasitized by bat flies and that a large proportion of the population were hosting sarcoptid mites. Females in this survey displayed a higher incidence of parasitism than males.

When the net bounces again it contains a Townsend's big-eared bat. The Townsend's big-eared is distributed through most of western North America and is found in all counties of the Black Hills. It was first reported in the Black Hills in 1916. Since then many have been banded in Jewel Cave where an estimated two thousand Townsend's big-eared bats hibernate in winter along with big brown bats, little brown myotis, small-footed myotis, and long-legged myotis, which are considered to be the most common and widely distributed species of the genus myotis in the Black Hills.

The four above bat species are common in the Black Hills and routinely hibernate together in Jewel Cave. In the late spring they vacate this great limestone hibernaculum as well as other large caves and disperse throughout the entire Black Hills, segregating according to sex, with the females congregating in maternity colonies located in warm sandstone caves or attics of buildings where heat is at a maximum. At this time the males tend to remain solitary. By mid-July the females will have relocated again to their traditional nursery colonies that will range in elevation from 3,400 to 6,200 feet in the Black Hills.

The Townsend's big-eared creates a great deal of interest among the biologists because of its large outside ears which are twice the size of the other common bat ears mentioned above. Inside the outside ear of the Townsend's big-eared is a relatively large tragus which looks like a smaller second ear inside the first. In spite of its very sensitive and relatively large tragus, the Townsend's big-eared does not rely on it's use of echolocation as much as other bat species do. They prefer, instead, to use their incredibly acute sense of hearing. Tigner noted that "they seem to be more adept at avoiding objects and finding prey than the other bat species." They are, in fact, so adept at locating prey that they can shut their echolocation off and catch insects by passive listening. "They can hear things like a moth beating its wings," Tigner said.

To counter the Townsend's big-eared hyper-hearing sensitivity, some moths, when they sense they are in danger, will instinctively stop flapping their wings and drop to the ground like a stone. In most instances, in regard to mammals and the art of the hunt, the prey is usually first located by smell and later identified by movement. With Townsend's big-eared and other bats, the location of the prey and the chase is accomplished entirely by sound and vibration.

Whether in caves or mine shafts, the Townsend's big-eared is the most commonly encountered species of bat in the Black Hills. This may be due to the fact that it is hardy and can tolerate a relatively greater variation in ambient air temperature than other bat species. For this reason they are better able to exploit mine drifts as shallow as ten feet with winter ambient temperatures approaching freezing.

Townsend's big-eared bat populations and habits have probably been studied more than any other bat in the Black Hills. In late November of 1967, Jewel Cave was visited by a field party from the American Museum of Natural History. The party found approximately 600 Townsend's big-eared bats wintering there at the time and examined 304 of them. Of the first 200 examined, 131 were males and 69 were females. This group was distributed in clusters containing from 2 to 33 bats while the remaining 104 individuals, comprised of 64 males and 40 females, were solitary.

The ambient cave temperature of Jewel Cave ranged from 5.0 to 6.4 degrees Celsius (41 to 44 degrees Fahrenheit) while the average body temperatures of the bats measured rectally ranged from 3.6 to 6.2 degrees Celsius (38 to 43 degrees Fahrenheit). For all practical purposes the bats were hibernating very close to ambient cave temperature. Statistics from that survey also revealed that individual Townsend's big-eared bats from the larger clusters tended to have body temperatures 1 to 2 degrees lower than the solitary individuals or those in the smaller clusters, suggesting that those with lower body temperatures sought to share the ambient heat of other bats.

The scientific party also discovered that most of the Townsend's big-eared females had a plug that completely filled their vaginal orifice. These plugs were not reported in the Townsend's big-eared bats hibernating in California. A smear sampling of these plugs, which were later examined under a phase microscope, proved to be agglutinated clumps of sperm in semen suspension.

Between December 1959 and December 1963, 2,165 Townsend's big-eared bats were banded at Jewel Cave by the National Park Service. Eight years later, nine of the original group banded were recaptured. Of those nine, four were taken thirty miles south and east of Jewel Cave during the summer while the other five were recaptured in the cave itself. One male banded in December 1959 was recaptured in Jewel Cave in July of 1968.

Gently holding the captured Townsend's big-eared in his left hand, Tigner remarked how it can fly through the tight, tangled branches of a dense stand of pine trees; how it can hear an insect moving under the bottom a leaf and pick it off; how it can do all this in the absence of light under the pitch dark cover of night instinctively in an instant.

With this kind of sensory perception I wonder aloud to Tigner how they can get caught in something as relatively unsophisticated as the mist net strung out in front of Gordon's Cave. "They just aren't expecting it to be here at the mouth of the cavern," he said. "They are familiar with this cavern and are used to accessing it freely. While they can pick it (the net) up; they just don't expect it—it's new—it's different for them."

Already on my knees, I lean over the hard rocks and broken sticks that litter the site to pet the fur on the tiny head of this amazing creature Tigner holds in his hand. His tiny beady eyes reflect the bright light from my flashlight. When I place my index finger on the fur of his head, I receive no sensation. The head, which is about the size of a marble, is so small and the texture of the fur so fine and soft, that my sensation of touch is too coarse to feel it.

While watching the Townsend's big-eared, Tigner mentions the fact that some bats are in the process of being reclassified taxonomically, due in large part to the fact that their teeth and skulls have been found to be so similar to those of early monkeys as to suggest a common ancestor for both bats and primates. The reclassification will more closely relate them to man or, depending on your perspective, more closely relate us to them. It is difficult not to envy a mammal that has such a sensitively tuned physical system which, over the course of millennia, has managed to evolve in a light-weight body possessing the most incredible sense of hearing and echolocation imaginable.

It is late in the evening as Tigner, having finished his measurements, slowly raises his left hand with the Townsend's big-eared in it. Relaxing his grasp on the tiny creature, he offers the bat its freedom once again. "Have a nice night," he says softly, watching it for a moment before it flutters from his hand into the sweet coolness of silent darkness.

13

At the Beaver Ponds

Starting in the spring and lasting through the summer and into mid-fall, beaver in the Black Hills become active in the sense that they begin dispersing. Two-year-old sub-adults are forced from their natal colonies to search out a new stream habitat to colonize. It is this dispersal activity and its effects that often puts them into conflict with landowners and people like Blair Waite, an extension trapper for the South Dakota Department of Game, Fish, and Parks. Waite is in charge of handling nuisance and predator animal problems in the southwestern corner of South Dakota, which includes the southern half of the Black Hills. His area covers three-and-a-half counties, over which he drives about forty thousand miles annually trapping and answering calls concerning all types of wild and feral animal problems.

The early October morning I catch up with him, he is busy checking on beavers working the streams in the Hill City/Keystone area of the Black Hills. This area is a hot spot for beaver activity and he comes here routinely in the fall to check out landowner complaints. Over the last twelve years, since becoming a state trapper, he has trapped over 700 beavers in the southern half of the Black Hills, and of those, successfully transplanted 650 of them to other suitable sites.

His first stop this morning is on Spring Creek, about a mile east of Hill City. A neat, low dam made of mud and woven willow is in place across the small mountain stream and has already backed up a pool about ten feet wide and a couple of feet deep. There is a healthy abundance of sapling willow in the stream channel making it prime beaver habitat.

Laying on the pool side of the dam, partially submerged, is the Hancock live-trap Waite set a few days ago. The trap is made of heavy gage wire woven together in the fashion of a slack chain-link fence. In size it resembles a propped open valise with its sides collapsed. Situated in the middle lid of the trap is a metal lever pad. When the beaver hits the pad with his body, the trap snaps shut around him, capturing him alive and unharmed.

The Hancock trap is an ingenious design invented around 1930 by a trapper from Martin, South Dakota, named Charles Lynn Hancock. He invented and designed it specifically to live-trap muskrats out of the LaCreek National Wildlife Refuge south of Martin. Hancock's trap performed so well, two game wardens asked him if he could enlarge his design to catch beavers with it. Again it proved successful. Hancock modified his design once more to live-trap otters. Waite believes it is the only trap of its kind that does not harm or drown any of the animals it is designed to capture.

Following the advice of the two wardens, Hancock patented his design in 1932. When he retired a few years ago, Waite and a partner acquired Hancock's patent and took over his business. "Any state with beavers uses the Hancock trap," said Waite, who added that "most trapping these days is all done live. We try to take the problem animals (beavers) and transplant them to another location where they have a chance to thrive."

Recently, Waite had occasion to ship eighteen Hancock otter traps over to Portugal where the government is involved in an effort to save the European otter. The otter is an endangered species there and Waite takes a certain amount of pride in playing a part in that conservation effort.

Waite, who is in his early middle age, in no way resembles the grizzled, hard-bitten trappers of the old days. He is trim, of medium build, and has a shock of blond hair and blue eyes. His grandfather started him trapping when he was eight around Sioux Falls where he grew up. He has been trapping ever since. As for the beavers, he speaks of them with admiration and a certain fondness, describing them as gentle creatures.

After inspecting the trap he had set on the dam for any recent beaver sign (there is none), he walks down the stream a few yards to cut a few fresh sprigs of willow which he attaches to the top of the trap above the water for "eye appeal." Then with a twig, he digs into his jar of castoreum and spreads a dab onto the willow sprigs.

Castoreum, or simply castor, is a brownish, unctuous substance beavers secrete from glands located in their groin area near the base of their tail. It has a strong, sweet pleasant odor and was formerly held in high regard as a medicinal substance as well as an ingredient in perfumery.

The smell of each beaver's castoreum is unique to them as an individual and serves as a sign or territorial scent marker. The scent informs other traveling males of their presence and also acts as an attraction for female beavers. Castoreum is one device nature employs to help beavers of different genders find each other over great distances for the purpose of procreation.

"Usually the scent of a strange, male beaver's castoreum will attract the resident beaver to the trap to see the intruder," said Waite contemplating the empty trap, "but none has showed up." As another incentive to get the beaver to the trap, Waite breaches the small dam. A beaver, if it is still in the area, will invariably return to fix the dam. These instinctual and predictable aspects of their behavior made these large aquatic rodents an easy prey to the "beaver men" who took them in vast numbers during the early half of the nineteenth century.

Beavers, which commonly weigh around sixty pounds, are most active at night and in the half light of dawn and dusk. Rarely do they stray far from water or their dam pools. They feed almost exclusively on the inner green cambium of aspen, willow, cottonwood, and birch trees. With all the evidence of dams, pools, and fallen trees, a beaver "sign" is hard to ignore and easy to recognize.

A few days have already passed since Waite set this trap and since there is no sign of activity or interest here, Waite speculates that the beaver at this site was a traveling sub-adult recently dispersed out from the family colony. "Sub-adults are not very territorial yet," he said, "and as a result do not always come to castor. If they are still around, I usually catch them the next day."

If castor is unsuccessful in attracting them, Waite will switch scents and try to lure them with apple extract, anise oil or spearmint extract. "This one may have been caught once already and had his toes pinched in the trap," he added. "He could be trap shy."

Along both sides of Spring Creek grows a thin, ribbon thicket of willow bordered by a low cut-bank. Above the banks on both sides of the creek are groomed bluegrass lawns. On the east side of the creek is a front lawn of a private home, on the west, the back lawn of a motel that fronts U.S. 16. Neither landowner wants the beaver around their suburbanized landscape, knowing that their dam pool will eventually flood their lawns and that their nearby shade and ornamental trees are at risk from gnawing.

Gnawing trees, building dams, and plugging up road culverts that eventually cause water to back up over roadways is what gets the beaver into the most trouble with suburban man. Most people generally like the idea of having wildlife around as long as it does not infringe on their trees and lawns.

What also makes the beaver unwelcome is his predilection for not only dropping big trees but then having the audacity to ignore them once they have fallen. Gnawing down big trees for beaver is often just a way to wear his teeth down and has nothing to do with the procurement of food, although he may eventually nibble on the tender upper shoots.

A beaver's two upper and lower incisors grow constantly throughout their lifetime and must always be used and honed down, regardless of their need for vegetable protein. Old beavers, unable to keep their teeth honed, often die of starvation when their incisors get so big they cannot move their jaws any longer.

Waite believes beavers are the reason there are few big softwood trees along the creeks of the Black Hills; the other reason he believes there is a dearth of riparian trees has to do with the suppression of wildfire. Fire encourages aspen, willow, and birch, the beavers preferred diet, to spread, sucker, and sprout. Without fire, natural tree regeneration is slow to non-existent. In the pre-white settlement days prior to 1874 when the Black Hills burned off regularly, there was more water and more of the fire-transitional softwood types of trees beavers prefer to eat.

Habitat degradation, however, was just one of the factors that once threatened beaver populations. The return of Lewis and Clark to St. Louis in 1805 with their wealth of information and maps concerning the Great Plains and Rocky Mountains set off a stampede of traders and fur trappers for the Northwest. One of the first documented American trapper parties to actually travel through the Black Hills was made up of a dozen men led by Jedediah Smith in October 1823. James Clyman, secretary of the party, kept a diary in which he describes their coming west from the Missouri via the White River, crossing the Cheyenne River near Buffalo Gap, and thence proceeding through the southern Black Hills. Premium prices were being paid for beaver pelts which were in fashion for hats in Europe and the American East Coast, and trappers started moving in early to work the streams that drained the Black Hills.

While beavers were abundant in the Black Hills at this time, Waite believes, based on his research of old trapper journals, that few were inclined to trap inside the Hills proper because of what he describes as the "Indian problem." The Indian problem had to do with the fact that the Black Hills were being jealously guarded by warlike Sioux who, as the nineteenth century progressed, became less and less tolerant of white incursions into what they had come to regard as their private Paha Sapa domain. What this meant, in effect, was that any trapper would be forced to assume an inordinate risk of life and limb to enter their sanctuary for beaver.

The result was that all the later military expeditions that penetrated the Black Hills in the mid 1870s, including Custer in 1874, Newton-Jenney in 1875, and Dodge in 1876, reported a great abundance of beaver. Grinnell with the Custer Expedition gives this account of beaver:

> This species was common on all the large streams which we crossed on our way to the Black Hills (from Fort Lincoln) and in many places having by means of their dams retained a plentiful supply of water when the creek both above and below was dry. They were also numerous in the Hills, as their dams and houses in many of the streams bore witness.

Beavers had once been so plentiful on the plains of western South Dakota and in the Black Hills that a trapper, working out of Fort Pierre, South Dakota, in 1862, noted that when they became particularly overstocked, they could be seen migrating down the Missouri River with the spring rise.

Following the 1876 gold rush to the Black Hills, beaver numbers, along with all game species of wildlife, quickly declined as a result of unrestricted market hunting and trapping. By 1887, after years of intensive trapping in the Black Hills, only a few could be found in places far back from settlements. The North American population of beavers, which had once been estimated to number 60 million, had been for the most part systematically exterminated east of the Mississippi by the early 1900s. In western South Dakota they had been nearly completely eradicated from all the prairie streams and rivers where they had once flourished in abundance.

Beginning in 1914, in an effort to bring beavers back into the Black Hills, a pair were moved from Yellowstone National Park into Custer State Park and planted along Grace Coolidge Creek. Two years later, another family was added.

During the 1930s and early 1940s, a total of three hundred beavers were restocked in the Black Hills from healthy populations that were again thriving along the James, Vermillion, and Big Sioux rivers in southeastern South Dakota. This restocking action was also successful, in part, due to the introduction of responsible management practices that included the enforcement of wild game and trapping limits. In a gesture of invitation, early game managers of that time actually constructed artificial dams and lodges on streams in the northern Black Hills to entice the released beaver to stay.

By 1953 a viable reproducing beaver population had been successfully re-established in the Black Hills National Forest and was estimated at the time to number between three and four thousand individuals. In October 1957 the *South Dakota Conservation Digest* reported that beavers, in recent years, were causing "extensive damage" to white birch, aspen, poplar, willow, and cottonwood trees along many drainage systems. For beaver in the Black Hills, life had gotten back to normal again.

The pendulum had now swung full circle. Conservationists were delighted by the news while foresters, whose primary directive revolved around the growth and production of salable timber, became nervous. Unfortunately the forest service over-reacted to the growth of the beaver population and embarked on a misguided resource management program to reduce and eradicate beavers, as well as aspen, from the forest ecosystem. Old-time wildlife advocates and conservationists still refer to those unenlightened attitudes that created intolerant forestry practices, in regard to wildlife, as the Black Hills "pine tree farm" mentality.

After leaving the first beaver complaint area, Waite visited the next one located about a half mile or so farther down Spring Creek. This one is also a complaint of beaver activity just below a residence. Again the creek meanders through a small willow thicket near a private residence surrounded by large trees and a well-groomed yard. Just above the area in question, the creek rolls up against massive, fractured cliffs of dark schist forty feet high. A large tall grass meadow on the opposite side of the creek completes this handsome Black Hills setting.

Flocks of juncos and chickadees are active along the streamside, flitting back and forth between the willows and the nearby pine forest while a red tail hawk cuts and wheels on the updrafts a few hundred feet over the meadow. The day, which started out cloudy and windy with a threat of rain or snow in Spearfish, is bright, clear, and calm here, near the center of the Hills. It is not an unusual phenomena. Weather in the Black Hills can be extraordinarily variable from one locality to another.

Often the northern Black Hills (Deadwood), which averages twenty-nine inches of precipitation a year, might be "blizzarded" in while the southern Black Hills (Custer), which averages nineteen inches of annual precipitation, might never receive more than a few skiffs of snow all winter.

About 75 percent of all the precipitation that falls in the Black Hills comes down in the form of rain during thunder showers between April and September. Nonetheless, winter snowfall can also be significant— averaging more than one hundred inches over the higher six-thousand-foot elevations of the Black Hills. This stands in marked contrast to the surrounding plains with a snowfall average of twenty to thirty inches and an annual precipitation average of about sixteen inches.

Temperature inversions can also play funny tricks in the late fall and winter when arctic air masses roll down the front ranges of the northern Rockies. Due to the relatively heavy, shallow, frigid nature of these arctic fronts, they are often unable to penetrate the interior higher elevations of the Black Hills so places like Hill City at 4,900 feet and Custer at 5,300 feet occasionally enjoy winter temperatures twenty degrees warmer than lower foothill elevation areas like Rapid City at 3,500 feet and Spearfish at 3,600 feet that have to shiver in sub-zero readings.

Extreme seasonal temperatures and weather fluctuations are relatively common in the Black Hills. The highest temperature on record is 112 degrees Fahrenheit recorded both at Belle Fourche, South Dakota, and at Hot Springs, South Dakota, while the lowest absolute temperatures at those two locations has hit the bottom of the thermometer at -42 and -41 degrees Fahrenheit, respectively.

Waite and I walk a few hundred yards up and down the creek, but there is no sign of a beaver except for a small insignificant dam constructed of a few twigs and stream flotsam. "If he was here," Waite says, "he was just passing through."

One of the most rapid temperature fluctuations to occur in the Black Hills was recorded in Rapid City on January 12, 1911, when the thermometer dropped from 40 degrees Fahrenheit to -13 degrees Fahrenheit over a two-hour period. However, the world's greatest variance in temperature fluctuation, documented in the *Guinness Book of World Records,* took place in Spearfish on January 22, 1943. It was an amazing see-sawing of temperatures that began at 7:30 AM when a "blast of hot air" raised the morning temperature from -4 degrees Fahrenheit to 49 degrees Fahrenheit in less than two minutes. After the thermometer climbed to 55 degrees Fahrenheit, it suddenly plummeted to -5 degrees Fahrenheit. Fifteen minutes later it went back up to 55 degrees again. About 9:30 AM   the thermometer dropped back down to 0 only to rise again to 55 and stay there until 4 PM   when it sank back down to 10 degrees and stayed there.

This "snow eater" or Chinook caused quite a bit of commotion and raised havoc in downtown Spearfish. Following the first meteoric warm-up, car windshields immediately iced-up and drivers had to stop in the middle of the street because they could not see. Downtown buildings were also almost immediately covered by a thick coating of white frost.

The same Chinook swept over Lead, South Dakota (elevation 5,200 feet), fifteen miles to the southeast. While the Chinook raised the temperature of Lead to 52 degrees Fahrenheit, it ignored the town of Deadwood (elevation 4,500)—stuck down in the bottom of Deadwood gulch less than three miles away—which remained at a bone-chilling -16 degrees Fahrenheit all day.

In Rapid City the Chinook warmed up the Canyon Lake area and part of the downtown to a salubrious 55 degrees while leaving other parts of the city in sub-zero temperatures. The most bizarre example of the Chinook's fickleness occurred at the downtown Alex Johnson Hotel. Eyewitnesses at the scene reported that about 11 AM the east side of the hotel (front entrance) shivered in biting cold while just around the corner on the south side, less than fifty feet away, it was a pleasant spring day. While Chinooks are not unusual in the Black Hills, this one was truly one for the record books.

Our next stop is Battle Creek which flows through the tourist town of Keystone, South Dakota. This is a complaint about a beaver-cut tree laying on the highway. "Its from a woman," Waite explains, "who recently lost a lot of big willows to beaver activity near her home."

Below Keystone we walk up and down Battle creek for a few hundred yards through waist-high thickets of red-barked willow. Most of these shrubby willows are the result of sprouting from old, previously gnawed tree stumps the thickness of a man's arm. There is evidence of one good size dam but no tree on the highway.

"It's the same situation," says Waite, "we are just below an urbanized stretch of valley and the landowners want all the beavers out because they are taking their beautiful trees. I have taken seven or eight beavers out of here already this year," he adds somewhat irritated. "Besides, this is government land here below the bridge—they have a right to stay if they are not causing any damage to private property."

Above the bridge Waite points to some stumps along the creek near a home where beavers have recently gnawed down some half-dozen twenty-foot-high willows. The three surviving willow trunks have chicken wire strung around them. "I try to educate the people on how to live with the beaver and protect their trees with wire," he tells me. "They won't gnaw through the wire."

Back in his pickup Waite talks about how he has taken hundreds of beavers out of the Battle Creek valley between Keystone and Hermosa, South Dakota. It is a rich area for beaver but not as impressive, he tells me, as the populations concentrated on two nearby tributary drainages to Battle Creek known as Grizzly Bear and Grizzly/Iron Creek. These tributaries drain most of the Norbeck Wildlife Preserve and the Black Elk Wilderness. It will be our next stop.

From Battle Creek we head south, climbing a low divide before dropping over into the Iron Creek drainage. Around a bend of the creek Waite pauses in the middle of the road to look at a high ridge that bristles with black snags, remnants of the 1988 Galena fire that burned nearly seventeen thousand acres in Custer State Park.

"I was parked here with a Conservation officer the night the fire came over that ridge. It was awesome. It rolled over the ridge thirty feet above the tree tops and had a roar of biblical proportion. The fire was so hot and needed so much oxygen, it created a wind that I felt here, a mile away, sucking me in."

Over the next divide we drop into the Spokane Creek drainage. The creek heads in the far east end of the Norbeck Preserve and borders the north edge of the Galena burn. Following a gravel road up Spokane Creek we cross into Custer State Park and drop over another ridge into the Coolidge Creek drainage.

"I transplanted a pair of beaver in here in 1986. They dispersed upstream and built a series of dams over about three miles. I think there are about a dozen (beaver) in here now." After considering the beaver here for a few minutes, Waite adds that most of the new beavers that move into this area come out of the Cheyenne River and then migrate up either Battle or Coolidge Creek into the Black Hills.

Driving a few miles up Coolidge, we turn back north via the Remington Camp Road, cross into the Norbeck Wildlife Preserve, and re-enter the Iron Creek drainage at a higher elevation. Waite stops next to a big dam overgrown with high grass that has backed up an acre of water near the Iron Creek Horse Camp. The dam is abandoned and the area has been denuded of all deciduous trees.

"All the wildlife in the area come down here to drink," he explains. "Four years ago I planted beaver in here and it looks like they left after they depleted their food resource. They'll be back after the vegetation recovers." At this point the recovery cycle of this old beaver pond will go something like this: Eventually the dam will breach and the pond will drain. A meadow consisting of forbs and grasses will quickly establish itself over the old silt bed. Willow and aspen groves, in a few years, will re-establish themselves on the meadow, attracting beavers, and the cycle will begin again.

Not far below the abandoned dam on Iron Creek, Waite unlocks a paddle-locked gate and we follow a one-lane track up a narrow tributary gulch of Iron Creek, eventually crossing over a low rocky divide into Grizzly Creek. Waite stops his pickup on the incline to afford me a better look at the drainage. The stream here meanders in an easterly direction and all I can see at this inclination is that an extensive area of the Grizzly Creek valley floor has been inundated by a enormous pool of water. We both get out of the truck for a closer look.

When I clear the pines and get down to the pond I am amazed by the sight of a great dam that stretches across the creek. Starting at the north edge of the pond, at a width of four to five feet, it snakes its way south across Grizzly Creek like a sleeping serpent. The south end of the dam is anchored to a large outcrop of Harney Peak granite, while the north end curves into the stream bank. Above the dam a pool of cinnamon brown water covers three or four acres to a maximum depth of seven or eight feet. It is a marvel of daub and wattle engineering. In 1947, five white beavers were reportedly observed in Grizzly Creek, which gives this site a somewhat mystical connotation. Historically, many plains Indian tribes considered any albino creature to be holy or mysterious.

Waite describes the Grizzly Creek drainage as a high-density beaver area. "This dam has been here for a least forty years," he tells me, "and it is still active." He points out the fact that there is fresh mud on the dam, which indicates they are keeping it chinked up. There is no vegetation growing in the pond water, another good indication of beaver presence since they actively weed all of it out and use it as a mud binder.

Waite suggests we climb a high granite outcrop that overlooks the dam and the valley to get a better view of the entire project. On the way up we cross a beaver canal coming down a small side tributary into the main pool. Beaver prefer to stay in or as near as possible to the security of water were they have an advantage over terrestrial predators. In long-established colonies like this one, where they are extending their territory, beavers are continually building small check dams up tributaries, excavating water canals, and daubing mud slides which they use to slide quickly up and down and, when necessary, out of a predator's way. On this little tributary there is a small check dam and a muddy slide path or runway that leads to a canal into the main pond.

Just above this check dam are two good-size aspens standing no more than two feet apart. Each bears evidence of having recently been deeply gnawed into. The gnawing on the left tree trunk is six or eight inches higher than the gnawing on the right tree trunk. "You can tell the age of a colony," says Waite looking at the two tree trunks, "by the height of the chew marks. If all the heights are the same you have a colony of adults and sub-adults. If you have a couple of lower heights it means growing kits are present which makes it an established, reproducing colony."

Climbing to the top of the granite outcrop some sixty feet or so above the beaver pond, the entire scope of this engineering marvel becomes apparent. The dam is perfectly arched into the main stream flow and then gracefully curves at various intervals to further contain the deflected water.

The pond water is dark and filled with suspended sediment, the sign that they are actively scooping mud up from the bottom of the pool and chinking it against the dam. By moving the silt up from the pool bottom, they also keep the springs, if there are any, open and clean. A big pool of water like this holds silt and run-off while providing habitat for ducks, fish, and a host of insects, amphibians, reptiles, and small mammals. Waite describes this beaver pond as "an ecosystem at its best."

After climbing down from the outcrop we start walking up Grizzly Creek. At an average interval of about 150 to 200 feet along the way, there occurs a beaver dam and a pool. Some of the dam ponds retain clear pools of water, indicating abandonment, while others show fresh signs of activity.

"It goes on like this for a couple of miles," says Waite, "colony after colony, lodge after lodge. If you drop over into the next drainage it's the same way; no stream, just dam pool after dam pool."

A series of dams like this represents decades and generations of beavers constantly moving upstream and modifying the environment. Six or seven years ago Waite traveled horseback all the way up Grizzly Creek and counted twenty-three established beaver colonies. This is what the mountain men must have seen back in the 1830s throughout the Black Hills and the Rocky Mountain West, every stream stepped and dammed for miles.

After walking about a mile up from the big dam on the Grizzly, we come to a dam just recently constructed. It uses a site where vehicles once forded the stream. The dam is about eighty feet long. On the north edge of the pool, an old aspen has recently been toppled and stripped of all its succulent branches and most of its bark.

Beavers, Waite explained, are the only animals that can create their own habitat and inadvertently encourage the growth of the food they prefer. When an old, live aspen tree like that comes down, the roots will sucker and a new grove will begin just as if the tree had been burned. If the tree dies standing from old age, the root stock will also die. By gnawing it down before it dies, the beaver keeps the root stock alive and stimulates it to grow, creating a food source for the next generation to live on.

On the south edge of the pool, a small pile of long twigs lays woven together half submerged and anchored in the pool. The limbs and branches in the pile are those stripped from the old, downed aspen and mark the site of a winter food cache.

Walking over the top and along the foot of the dam I get a good feel for the structure which is about five feet high and four feet wide, comprised of a tightly woven mass of sticks, mud, and grass. Even the tramping of cows weighing six to eight hundred pounds that have sunk in up to their knees along its side has not breached its integrity.

In the middle of the dam, a slicked-down, muddy slide comes up out of the pool, runs over the top, and then down into a canal that leads to the next pool. "Here's the spot," said Waite, pointing at an area on the runaway just below the dam, "where the old trappers would set their jaw traps for the beaver. There really was not much of a challenge to catching them."

At this point we turn and head back to the truck. Waite talks about how he used to make a living back in Sioux Falls in the 1970s working construction in the warm months and running a two-hundred-mile-long trap line in the winter. He worked from first light till dark, from mid-October until March.

Waite spent sixteen hours a day driving his trap line by daylight and skinning hides at night. He got $60 for a fox skin, $50 dollars for raccoon, and $80 to $100 for a coyote. "But those days are over, he said. "Pelt prices are way down because of a tendency today for short-hair pelts and the anti-fur movement. There is very little commercial fur trapping going on these days in the Black Hills."

After reaching the truck, we drive back into Custer State Park, drop back into the Coolidge drainage and follow the creek, taking American Center Road to check a road culvert that beavers have been habitually plugging. Beavers are quick to recognize elevated road grades with culverts as opportune man-made places to construct a dam. After plugging the colverts, these areas quickly flood and undermine the road grade.

Along the creek, above and below American Center Road, are average-size beaver dams of twenty to thirty feet length. This particular road grade rises about four feet above the water and by means of a culvert spans the stream course. It is, from an aquatic rodent's viewpoint, the perfect location for another dam—especially since all the mudwork construction has already been completed. All that needs to be done is the plugging of a small metal opening which the beaver quickly accomplished.

"I didn't want to trap the beaver here since they are in Custer State Park," said Waite who has a real empathy for these creatures. "This is a wildlife park so rather than remove them I conducted a little experiment to discourage their building a dam again in front of the culvert's mouth."

Waite's experiment might be described as beaver electro-shock therapy. A few weeks before our visit, he drove three metal fence posts into the bottom of the pond around the newly constructed beaver dam's perimeter where it had blocked the culvert's mouth. He then breached the dam and strung bare wire around the three posts were the dam had been and attached the wire to a six volt battery.

"They must have got a couple of good shocks when they hit the wire," said Waite with a smile, "because they haven't rebuilt their dam or touched it since the last time I was here. They persisted in trying to build a dam farther away from the wire for awhile," Waite commented, "but he kept raking it apart and moving the stakes farther out. Last week I removed the battery; I think I have them trained."

While watching Waite clear some leftover debris from the front of the culvert, I asked him why the road is called American Center. After World War II, he explained, then U.S. Senator Karl Mundt of South Dakota proposed having the new United Nations Center built here in Custer State Park. His reasoning was that since the Black Hills were in the center of the country, this would be an ideal place for the United Nations Center.

After cleaning the mouth of the culvert, we drive farther up Grace Coolidge Creek. Originally Grace Coolidge Creek was called Squaw Creek. It was renamed in honor of President Coolidge's wife on the occasion of the first couple's summer vacation here in Custer State Park in 1927.

During the time the Coolidges stayed here, check dams where constructed over the creek and trout, as one story goes, were clandestinely stocked on a regular basis at night to keep Coolidge occupied and pleased with his prowess as a fly fisherman. The goal, according to one historian, was to keep Coolidge in the Black Hills as long as possible in order to persuade him to support the construction of Mount Rushmore.

As we follow the gentle meanders of Coolidge Creek, which soon turns into an ephemeral watercourse, Waite points out the remnants of very old beaver dams that resemble low, earthen levees covered with sod laying perpendicular across the creek bed. Above these old dams are small, flat meadows thick with grasses.

Four years ago Waite introduced a pair of beavers back into lower Grace Coolidge. They built a series of low dams which started retaining water and raising the underground water table all the way up the drainage. The subtle changes in the flora are already evident. With the rise of the water table, clones of three-foot-high sapling aspens are establishing themselves on the edge of what was formerly a deep, rich pool of sediment.

At the head of Grace Coolidge we leave the park and drive into Custer, South Dakota, for lunch. During the drive Waite talks about the nature of his job and the problem of dealing with ever increasing numbers of coyotes.

"I perform two types of control work," he said. "The first is corrective in nature where I go in after the fact of an animal disturbance or predation to remedy the situation or remove the predator." The second he described as "preventative" where he suggests ways to protect livestock and vegetation from wildlife depredation.

Waite estimated that he spends about 20 percent of his time working on beavers he describes as "nuisance animals." In that category of nuisance he also lumps in skunks, raccoons, foxes, along with larger predators including bobcats and mountain lions. While these predators, on occasion, will take unprotected domestic livestock, they only account for about 5 percent of Waite's working time. The largest portion of his time, about 75 percent, is spent in trapping and shooting coyotes, mostly on the fringes of the southern Black Hills and south across the rolling plains country to the Nebraska state line.

It is not that the interior Black Hills are without coyotes, they are loaded with them. Prior to 1972 all the grazing allotments in the Black Hills National Forest were for sheep. That same year President Nixon, feeling pressure from the environmental community, banned 1080 (sodium monofluoracetate), a particularly nasty poison that not only killed coyotes slowly and painfully by attacking their nervous system and knotting up their guts but also a host of other, untargeted wild creatures unfortunate enough to scavenge the same poisoned carcasses the coyotes did.

Initially developed during World War II, 1080 was planned as a possible method of poisoning the Japanese civilian population by dumping it into their water supplies. Ken Rost, who grew up on a ranch in western South Dakota back in the 1950s and 1960s and whose father-in-law was a government trapper all his life, described for me one afternoon how 1080 was deployed against coyotes.

First they found a couple of wild range horses and shot them. They then hacked the horse carcasses apart with meat axes and tossed the pieces in the back of a pick-up truck. The following day they set the pieces out on the prairie after injecting them, using needles and syringes, with 1080. In a day or so they would go back and check "the kill."

Checking the kill meant circling the carcass. Within a quarter mile radius of the poisoned horse meat they would usually find the dead coyotes. However, the circle of death did not end there. Farther out they would often find dead skunks, foxes, bobcats, eagles, magpies, and crows; virtually every creature that ate the tainted meat lay in 1080s circle of death.

Coyote predation on sheep and lambs, which was always a tough problem, could not be controlled in the Black Hills without 1080. New sheep allotments were canceled in 1972 while all the old ones were allowed to expire. With the discontinuation of sheep grazing in the Black Hills, coyotes no longer posed a serious economic threat to livestock.

"All the allotments today are for cows," said Waite, adding that "coyotes get a few calves in the spring but not enough to make them a major problem." Since a lot of coyote control is accomplished by hunting them out of small airplanes, they are virtually out of sight and reach in the heavily forested Black Hills.

Every coyote trapper I know in South Dakota has a great, if grudging respect for the canny intelligence of the trickster, as the Indians called him. However, unlike the portrayal he receives in "Road Runner" cartoons as the hapless Wiley E. Coyote, the coyote *(Canis latrans)* is always on the move, exercising calculated, cunning boldness and cautious persistence everywhere along his way.

Coyotes are members of the family canidae which also includes wolves and foxes. In the Black Hills, coyote dogs and bitches pair up in January and whelp their pups in late March and April. For the most part coyotes prey on rabbits, hares, small rodents, and fawns. Like all wild canines, they have the ability to control their population through litter sizes which fluctuate in accordance with the abundance of prey species.

Coyotes naturally evolved as small dogs in the wide openness of the Great Plains and the high deserts of the American West. George Bird Grinnell, a young zoologist who accompanied Custer on his expedition to the Black Hills in the summer of 1874, reported that:

> The coyote was found in considerable numbers on the plains, and was especially abundant among the elevated table-lands (of northwestern South Dakota) that were crossed just before reaching the Black Hills. After penetrating into the Black Hills proper, however, I did not see a

single specimen until I left them (Black Hills) for the Cheyenne River (at the edge of the southern Hills) when I again noticed coyotes in numbers. In the Black Hills this species would seem to be replaced by the gray wolf.

I found the gray wolf one of the most common animals in the Black Hills and hardly a day passed without my seeing several individuals of this species. They were generally observed singly or by twos and threes, sneaking along the mountain sides or crossing the narrow valleys. They were quite shy and lost no time in plunging into dense woods as soon as they perceived us. Their howlings were often heard at night; and on one occasion I heard the doleful sound at midday—a bad omen, if we may trust the Indians.

Wolves, also members of the canid or dog family, are considerably larger, stronger and more aggressive than coyotes. A healthy wolf pack of eight to twelve individuals could run down and take an old, weakened bison bull on the plains or a bull elk in Black Hills timber.

Lieutenant Colonel Richard Dodge in his Black Hills reconnaissance report of 1876 described the wolves he saw in the Black Hills as of "enormous size, a very dark gray in color, and in considerable numbers." Where they occurred on the plains, wolves were dominant over other canids and in fact were known to kill and drive off coyotes intruding in their territory.

Wolf packs are always on the move and will travel an average of fifteen to twenty miles a day, mainly at night at a trot of eight to ten miles per hour. They generally hunt in circles inside their territory which may cover over a hundred square miles.

Using a tactic where members of a pack take turns chasing prey, they can run down large ungulates at speeds approaching forty miles per hour. During the chase, as the ungulate finally begins to tire, the wolves will move in and try to disable the prey either by severing the hamstring or by slashing the throat and severing the jugular vein.

Their sense of smell is well developed and their hearing, like all members of the dog family, is extremely acute, ranging far above the register the human ear can detect. The wolf's power, endurance, and ability to kill made it a formidable threat to slow-moving livestock and ultimately an intolerable foe to Black Hills area ranchers in the late nineteenth century.

Ronald W. Turner, in his published Ph.D. dissertation *Mammals of the Black Hills of South Dakota and Wyoming*, wrote that from the spring of 1895 to the autumn of 1897 some five hundred gray wolves were killed on the range of the Ames Cattle Company which encompassed nearly 5,500 square miles in northeastern Crook County, Wyoming (i.e., the Bear Lodge area).

Turner also wrote that another large northern Black Hills ranch with headquarters in Belle Fourche, South Dakota, reported that gray wolves *Canis lupus* were responsible for annually eliminating 3 percent of their calves, 1 percent of their cows, and 5 percent of their colts.

In 1907, about the same time all the last quarter sections on the northern plains of Montana were being homesteaded and plowed, the U.S. Forest Service reported taking 925 gray wolves out of the Bear Lodge and surrounding areas of Crook County, Wyoming. How long it took them to accomplish this task is unclear. The above statistics, however, need to be viewed with some skepticism based on today's scientific information on wolf population dynamics.

L. David Mech, considered to be an expert on timber wolves in northern Minnesota, estimated that Yellowstone National Park's 2.2 million acres could support between 100 to 150 wolves with 25 young wolves forced to disperse annually into new habitat. The entire Black Hills ecosystem, including the Bear Lodge Mountains which makes up roughly a third of it, comes close, give or take a few 100,000 acres, to being nearly the same size statistically as Yellowstone National Park. Even if you double Mech's population density number, which may be conservative, taking in the fact that the Black Hills proper was probably richer in animal protein mass made up of bison, elk, and antelope and surrounded by greater herds of accessible prey species, the 1907 forest service's number of 925 wolves still seems improbable as does the earlier estimates given by the Ames Cattle Company.

On the other hand, times were different then, wolves were certainly plentiful and literally being pushed out of every conceivable range and biological niche they had once occupied in the entire western United States. This may have created some very odd population dynamics that may have been centered on the Black Hills ecosystem as a final sanctuary.

The largest population concentrations of wolves in the early 1890s may well have been located in the Bear Lodge Mountains. Reasons for this may have been due to the fact that the last large, northern plains bison herd was concentrated north of the Wyoming Black Hills in southeastern Montana. When it was finally decimated in 1883, the disappearance of this rich protein source, along with hunting and trapping pressure on them across the northern Great Plains of Montana, Wyoming, western North Dakota and South Dakota may have forced whatever was left of the free-ranging wolf packs to move south and west, concentrating them into the then relative safe shelter of the isolated Bear Lodge Range.

By the end of the 1880s all the big game wildlife the wolves had once preyed upon disappeared out of the Black Hills and across the plains, having been shot out by market hunters and ranchers. While no accurate records that I know of give an exact account of livestock losses at that time in northeastern Wyoming and western South Dakota, livestock depredation must have been heavy as large numbers of wolves, pushed to the edge of starvation, were forced to switch from elk, deer, and bison to beef and mutton.

However, even if this scenario bears some truth, the numbers coming out of the Bear Lodge still seem implausible. Another reason for the high numbers could be the fact that wolves, coyotes, bobcats, and any other creature considered a predator of livestock in the early days were all often lumped together by trappers without concern for species. One thing, however, is certain: the kind of intense hunting and trapping pressure wolves came under just prior to the beginning of the twentieth century wiped them out of the Bear Lodge by 1910.

Over on the South Dakota side of the Black Hills the statistics appear more plausible in chronicling the wolf's demise. In 1911 bounties were paid on fifty-five gray wolves taken from the South Dakota Black Hills. Four years later, eight more wolves were taken and five more were exterminated in 1916. A pregnant female wolf with four embryos was killed near the hamlet of Dewey, South Dakota, along the southwestern edge of the Black Hills in 1917. Three years later a lone male, probably the females' mate, was also taken near Dewey. The fate of the wolf in the Black Hills was all but sealed.

In a last gasp, a lone renegade wolf gained notoriety at this time as the "Custer Wolf." The Custer Wolf was at large for seven years and ranged for sixty miles in the vicinity of Custer, South Dakota. This large rogue male was credited for killing $25,000 worth of livestock.

Despite a bounty of $500 placed on his hide, he managed to avoid the inevitable until a federal hunter named H. P. Williams arrived to hunt him down. Williams concentrated solely on the Custer Wolf from March to October 1920 when he finally succeeded in killing him.

Of the wolf, conservationist Aldo Leopold, remembering his encounters with wolves in the early part of the twentieth century, eloquently wrote in *A Sand County Almanac*:

> Every living thing pays heed to that call. To the deer, it is a reminder of the way of all flesh; to the pine, a forecast of midnight scuffles and of blood upon the snow; to the coyote, a promise of gleanings to come; to the cowman, a threat of red ink at the bank; to the hunter, a challenge of fang against bullet.
>
> Yet behind these obvious and immediate hopes and fears there lies a deeper meaning, known only to the mountain itself. Only the mountain has lived long enough to listen objectively to the howl of a wolf.
>
> In those days we never heard of passing up a chance to kill a wolf. In a second we were pumping lead into the pack. (After one such encounter) we reached the old wolf in time to watch a fierce green fire dying in her eyes. I realized then, and have known ever since, that there was something new to me in those eyes—something known only to her and the mountain.
>
> I was young then, and full of trigger-itch; I thought that because fewer wolves meant more deer, that no wolves would mean hunters' paradise. But after seeing the green fire die, I sensed that neither the wolf nor the mountain agreed with such a view.
>
> I now suspect that just as a deer herd lives in mortal fear of its wolves, so does a mountain live in mortal fear of its deer.
>
> So also with cows. The cowman who cleans his range of wolves does not realize that he is taking over the wolf's job of trimming the herd to fit the range. He has not learned to think like a mountain.
>
> We all strive for safety, prosperity, comfort, long life, and dullness. The deer strives with its supple legs, the cowman with trap and poison . . . and most of us with machines, votes and dollars, but it all comes to the same thing: peace in our time.
>
> A measure of success in this is all well enough, and perhaps is a requisite to objective thinking, but too much safety seems to yield only danger in the long run. Perhaps this is behind Thoreau's dictum: In wildness is the salvation of the world.
>
> Perhaps this is the hidden meaning in the howl of the wolf, long known among the mountains, but seldom perceived among men.

With the decimation and extirpation of the gray wolf from the Black Hills ecosystem, the coyote rapidly moved in to fill the ecological vacuum. The most cunning of opportunists and the hardest animal to trap, they took over as the dominant canid throughout the

Black Hills and are to this day steadily extending their territory east. As Waite puts it: "Coyotes win the war; when it's all over there will be a pair of coyotes and a pair of magpies and the magpies better watch their butt."

The lunch rush is over and the afternoon is getting late as we stop in Custer, walk into a local cafe, and seat ourselves at an empty table. From the kitchen, the wail of a small child intermittently punctuates the quiet of the nearly deserted restaurant. A young waitress takes our order. She is tired and out of sorts. Her days, like Waite's, probably start before first light.

Waite knows her and gives her a little good-natured teasing. She eyeballs him pretty hard at first before making a couple of verbal jabs back at him. It just makes him laugh, and by the time we have finished our lunch she is holding her baby on her hip, gossiping and pouring us a second cup of coffee. After a meal and some friendly visiting, the world has become a little more forgiving.

Over our third cup of coffee, I steer the topic back to predators in the Black Hills and ask Waite about his encounters with mountain lions. Known by at least a dozen local names in English, including painter, panther, puma, cougar, catamount—the mountain lion *(Felis concolor)* is the largest cat in North America. Once common across the continent, by the early 1900s they had been restricted for the most part to the deserts, high plateaus, and mountains of the West including the Black Hills.

Although, still officially listed as endangered in South Dakota, the big cat population in the Black Hills is slowly increasing. Both Waite and Ted Benzon, a state wildlife specialist who studies the dynamics of the deer population in the Black Hills, believe the lion population trend is up.

Lions in the Black Hills are solitary creatures that live on an established territory. Research in other mountain states found that the home range of male lions varies from 25 square miles in mountainous regions to 162 square miles in the desert chaparral habitat of Arizona. Females, particularly when they have growing kittens, tend to stay closer to the den site and therefore have a much smaller range averaging from just a few miles to 80 miles.

Lions make a complete circuit of their territory about every fifteen to eighteen days. Where territorial boundaries meet or overlap, the lion uses visual or olfactory markings to notify other cats that the territory is occupied. The most common territorial sign marking is called a scrape which a lion makes with its front paws by scratching a shallow depression four to six inches deep in the soil. It then urinates on the pile of dirt it has just made. Having left its scent marker, the cat continues in the direction it was traveling.

Other mountain lions that come across these scrapes add a bit more dirt and more urine and eventually a small mound develops. Other cat sign includes piles of feces and urine covered by organic debris as well as marks on trees where the lions have sharpened their claws. Cat sign is most often found in drainage bottoms or along ridges, the topography lions prefer to travel while on a circuit.

In the western states the prey of the lion is primarily deer with an occasional elk. Fawns tend to be selected in the spring, bucks during the fall rut and any deer during the summer and winter. To a large extent the evolution of any prey species is determined by its predators. In this regard the mountain lion has helped make the mule deer, its preferred prey, a quick, alert, and graceful creature by weeding out the old, infirm, and genetically inferior specimens and trimming the population.

The lack of understanding the significance of the balance of the predator-prey relationship resulted in one of the most spectacular cases of wildlife mis-management in the United States. It occurred on the Kaibab plateau, a high, isolated area of dry, desert country dominated by pinyon and juniper forest in northwestern Arizona.

Not long after the turn of the nineteenth century, about the same time early wildlife biologists like Aldo Leopold mistakenly believed a hunter's paradise would result from a total lack of predators, a large section of the Kaibab was set aside as a refuge to protect about four thousand mule deer. Over the course of ten years, beginning in 1907, government hunters reportedly removed 674 mountain lions, 11 wolves, 120 bobcats, and 3,000 coyotes. No deer hunting was permitted while the elimination of all the natural predators was carried out. By 1917 mule deer had increased on the Kaibab to 17,000. Eight years later in 1925, the population was estimated to be 100,000.

At this point the deer had destroyed their range. Starvation and disease became epidemic and 60,000 deer perished that winter and the next. What had once been a healthy herd with mountain lion predation became an overpopulation horror without them.

Pound for pound the mountain lion is probably the most efficient killer in the felid family. No other single animal preys on animals five times its weight.

Lions generally prefer to hunt upwind or quarter against it. They detect their prey first by scent. Once the deer is located, the stalk begins with the cat slinking cautiously along on its belly, taking advantage of every rock outcrop, log and shrub to conceal itself and get within an optimum range of twenty to thirty feet. At this point it draws its feet under the belly, extends its claws to get a good grip on the soil and tenses its muscles. Then like a spring uncoiling, it leaps upon the back of its victim.

Depending on the size of its prey, the momentum of the charge may be strong enough to knock a yearling deer off its feet. In the case of a large, strong buck or elk, the cat may be carried a distance of a hundred yards or more before it's prey goes down. In either case, one set of the big cats front claws will grip and tear into the prey's back while the jaws, with their long canine teeth, bite down through the top of the neck near the base of the prey's skull. The other front paw sharply pulls the prey's head backwards. The prey usually dies from either a broken neck or a severed spinal column, either way death is usually accomplished in a matter of seconds.

Attacks are often unsuccessful due to an obstruction which may divert the lion's jump or the prey will sense the cat before the stalk is completed. Although an adult cat can make a thirty-foot leap, clear an eight-foot obstruction in the middle of the jump and is amazingly fast for the first two hundred to three hundred yards, once the deer is on the run, the odds on a kill are greatly reduced.

After a successful attack and kill, the lion will eviscerate the carcass, ripping open the belly and feeding first on the liver, heart and lungs. It may then shear off several ribs and clean off the meat or eat part of the haunch. All cat's tongues have a raspy surface that allows them to remove the finest of meat shreds from the bone. Seven or eight pounds of meat will usually satiate the lions appetite.

Mountain lions in the Black Hills generally bury the haunch at the site of the first feeding. After each successive feeding the cat moves the remains of the kill and covers it with sticks and vegetation. It will return to this movable food cache until the meat is eaten or no longer palatable.

Lions possess enormous strength and agility. They have been seen leaping fifteen feet from the ground up into tree branches and jumping fifty feet down out of trees unhurt and bounding away. Their powerful jaws and body muscles are capable of moving a dead eight-month-old calf three miles up a very steep mountain.

Other reports describe big cats dragging eight-hundred-pound horse and steer carcasses short distances across fields and fences. In moving a heavy carcass, the lion rolls it over on its back so that all four legs stick up in the air and then bites into the chest, dragging it along on its back.

While lions breed at all times of the year, most of the births occur in the spring. The gestation period is about three months with two to three kittens being the most common litter size. The den site is usually in a cave, rock fissure, or under an overhang; the more inaccessible the better. Weaning starts after the first month and lasts until the kittens are six months old, at which time the nursery den is abandoned. The female soon takes the young kittens on extended hunting trips, staying at each kill until it is consumed. At the age of one year the kittens are almost fully grown and adept in the art of the hunt. At this time they begin to disperse and search out their own territory.

During the winter of 1986 to 1987, Ted Benzon started monitoring lion sightings in the Black Hills and plotting them on a forest service map. When he received a call of a sighting, he would go out the next day and measure the size of the tracks left in the snow.

Female lions weigh an average of 100 pounds compared to the males which average about 170. Females also generally have smaller paws and shorter strides. A heel pad greater than 2¼ inches with a 37-inch stride could be considered a male while smaller pads and shorter strides were indicative of females. Using this statistical baseline, Benzon determined the sex of the cat sighted by paw print size and stride lengths.

There were numerous sightings that winter, and a map Benzon made by plotting each sighting with a red dot showed an almost uniform, random dispersal of male and female cats spread out over the entire Black Hills.

Back about that same time, Waite recalled a lion that decided to take up residence within the city limits of Hot Springs. "He took a couple of dogs and rattled some garbage cans," Waite said, "but he eventually moved on."

In September 1984, Waite went after a cat that was working the area near Edgemont, South Dakota. "I had no idea when he might show up near Edgemont," said Waite. "He could be gone for weeks depending on the size of his territory."

Waite eventually caught what turned out to be a 160-pound male cat that December and moved him about seventy miles up into the northern Black Hills. "He probably beat me back to Edgemont," is how he described his effort, but the cat did not cause any more problems.

In 1987 Waite answered a complaint on a cat that had mauled a few colts northwest of Custer, South Dakota. He caught what he described as a young female weighing ninety pounds that had probably recently dispersed from the litter.

"The majority of complaints I get," he said, "are young cats, recently dispersed from the litter. These cats usually leave the area," said Waite, "and I can take care of most of the complaints by talking to the people and explaining the situation."

In Wyoming, mountain lions are not a threatened species and are considered a game animal. As a result two or three are shot annually on that side of the Black Hills.

Waite believes the comeback of the mountain lion in the Black Hills is due to the ban on 1080. "While mountain lions are not carrion eaters," he said, "1080 had an indirect effect on their population." Waite believes 1080 mainly affected young cats dispersing from the litter. "They lacked the hunting experience of the adults and probably got pretty hungry their first time out," he explained. These young cats were prone to taking what appeared to be and easy meal off a dead carcass with lethal effects.

The poison 1080 probably eliminated a large percentage of the young cat breeding stock with the effect that the mountain lion population during the 1960s decreased across the West. Today mountain lions range over the entire Black Hills inhabiting every good drainage with dry rocky ledges, big ravines, and canyons. They are, however, rarely seen or heard by the casual observer.

As for bears in the Black Hills the story is a different one. In pre-white settlement times prior to 1874, both Grizzly and Black bears were relatively common in the Black Hills. A trapper in 1851 mentioned that grizzly bears in the Black Hills are sometimes found roving in (family) bands like buffalo. Grinnell in 1874, Dodge in 1876, and V. Bailey in 1888 alluded to the presence of large numbers of grizzlies *(Ursus arctos horriblis)* in the Black Hills.

Grizzlies were once common across the entire northern plains, inhabiting many of the major western tributaries of the Missouri as well as that river's trench itself. The Mandans and Hidatsas, who lived on the Missouri River not far above present Bismarck, North Dakota, were reported to be"terrified" of them. Yet other Plains tribes, noting their great "power," revered them and called them "brother." To them, grizzly bear "medicine" was considered to be very potent.

Grizzlies proved to be one of the biggest threats trappers and mountain men had to contend with. Lewis and Clark's expedition encountered many of them on the plains of the upper Missouri in eastern Montana. In many cases they intentionally provoked these great beasts into fights.

Meriwether Lewis was skeptical about the tales he had heard concerning grizzlies from superstitious Indians and French traders. He believed at the beginning of his great expedition that a skilled white hunter, equipped with a new Harper's Ferry muzzle-loading rifle, should have no trouble killing one.

His first encounter on April 29, 1805, near the mouth of the Yellowstone with two adolescent grizzlies did little to change his attitude. On that occasion, two hunters with the party each picked a target and accurately fired a single rifle ball into each of the bears. One bear fled while the other reacted as the Indians had predicted; it charged. The two hunters were able to re-load and fire another round into the badly hurt animal—bringing it down.

Both Lewis and Clark inspected the dead grizzly which weighed about three hundred pounds. They noted in their journals that the tips of the yellowish/reddish fur appeared lighter than the basic strands—giving the bears, in a certain light, a "grizzled" appearance. Both men later referred to them as "grisly bears."

In that same vicinity, Lewis' journal presents a timely view of what was happening on the northern plains, three hundred miles due north of the Black Hills, nearly two centuries ago. He writes:

Game is still very abundant, we can scarcely cast our eyes in any direction without perceiving deer, elk, buffaloe or antelopes. The quantity of wolves appear to increase in the same proportion; they generally hunt in parties of six, eight or ten: they kill a great number of the antelopes at this season; the antelopes are yet meager and the females are big with young; the wolves take them most generally in attempting to swim the river (Missouri); in this manner my dog (a Newfoundland) caught one, drowned it and brought it on shore; they (pronghorn) are but clumsy swimmers, tho' on land when in good order, they are extremely fleet and durable. We have frequently seen the wolves in pursuit of the antelope in the plains; they appear to decoy a single one from a flock, and then pursue it, alternately relieving each other until they take it.

A week later and farther up river, the party of explorers and hunters came upon a full-grown grizzly standing in the water. The bear was probably fishing and content to mind its own business. Lewis, obviously impressed with a full-grown boar standing over eight feet high, writes of the animal and its subsequent death:

> It was a most tremendious looking animal, and extremely hard to kill. Notwithstanding, he had five balls through his lungs and five others in various parts, he swam more than half the distance across the (Missouri) river to a sandbar, and it was at least twenty minutes before he died; he did not attempt to attack, but fled and made the most tremendous roaring from the moment he was shot. We had no means of weighing this monster; Captain Clark thought he would weigh 500 pounds, for my own part I think the estimate too small by 100 pounds. He measured 8 feet 7.5 inches from the nose to the hind feet, 5 feet 10.5 inches around the breast. . . . his talons (claws) which were five in number on each foot were 4⅜ inches in length.

The party skinned the bear and boiled its fat down into lard for later use. Lewis then goes on to compare this grizzly to the black bear:

> This bear differs from the common black bear in several respects; its talons are much longer and more blunt, its tail shorter, its hair, which is of a reddish or gray brown, is longer, thicker and finer than that of the black bear; his liver, lungs and heart are much larger even in proportion with his size; the heart particularly was as large as that of a large ox. His maw was also ten times the size of black bear, and was filled with flesh and fish.

That experience left a large contingent of the expedition party content not to attack any more grizzlies, but other's in the group were still, as Lewis writes, "keen for action." They got it on the evening of May 14, 1805. Lewis recounts the story in his journal:

> The men in two of the rear canoes discovered a large brown bear lying in the open grounds about 300 paces from the river, and six of them went out to attack him, all good hunters; they took the advantage of a small eminence which concealed them and got within 40 paces of him unperceived, two of them reserved their fires as had been previously conscerted, the four others fired nearly at the same time and each put his bullet through him, two of the balls passed through the bulk of both lobes of his lungs, in an instant this monster ran at them with open mouth, the two who had reserved their fires discharged their pieces at him as he came towards them, both of them struck him, one only slightly and the other fortunately broke his shoulder. This however only

retarded his motion for a moment only, the men unable to reload their guns took to flight, the bear pursued and had very nearly overtaken them before they reached the river; two of the party betook themselves to a canoe and the others separated and concealed themselves among the willows, reloaded their pieces, each discharged his piece at him as they had an opportunity, they struck him several times again but the guns served only to direct the bear to them, in this manner he pursued two of them separately so close that they were obliged to throw aside their guns and pouches and throw themselves into the river altho' the bank was nearly twenty feet perpendicular; so enraged was this animal that he plunged into the river only a few feet behind the second man he had compelled to take refuge in the water, when one of those who still remained on shore shot him through the head and finally killed him.

After this hazardous encounter with the grizzly, Lewis changed his attitude and let them be. As a memento, they named the little side creek near the site of this battle Brown Bear Defeated Creek.

In the Black Hills, at the end of the nineteenth century, grizzlies were most often sighted and reported in the high mountain meadows and timber around the headwaters of Boxelder Creek in southern Lawrence County. General Custer and Colonel Ludlow shot a well-scarred old boar there on August 7, 1874. Grinnell gives this account of grizzlies in the Black Hills at that time:

Although we saw indications of the presence of large numbers of grizzlies during our march through the Black Hills, only a few were killed, chiefly from lack of time to devote to their capture. The first one killed was secured by General Custer and Colonel Ludlow. It was a very old male, the canine teeth being mere broken stumps, many of the incisors gone, and the molars worn down almost to the gums. In color it was everywhere a deep, glossy black, except on the head and on the lower body parts of the shoulders and thighs, where there was a slight sprinkling of dark gray hairs. The old veteran bore on his body the marks of many a conflict. On his back, just behind the shoulders, was a rugged scar 10 inches long and 2 wide; his face was marked in several places, and his sides and thighs were disfigured in the same manner. These scars, I am led to believe, were the result of battles with some rival during the rutting season.

Very different in appearance were an old female and two cubs that were killed later in the trip, and much farther to the eastward, by two of our Indian scouts. The cubs were about half grown, and, with the mother, were of a yellowish clay color. The inner half of each hair was deep black, but the outer extremity was a bright reddish yellow. This gave them a curious mottled appearance and induced many of those who saw them to consider them a different species from the one killed by General Custer. I saw no evidence of any great ferocity in any of the specimens killed by the party. None made any attempt at defense unless so badly wounded as to be unable to escape by flight; even the old female just referred to, continued to run after both her cubs had been disabled.

The swiftness of the grizzly is considerable, and in rough country it can easily run away from a slow horse. Even on the prairie, it requires a pretty good animal to catch them, and it took several hours' hard riding to overtake the three last mentioned.

Not surprisingly, the last reported grizzly bear killed in the Black Hills was in the Bear Lodge Mountains. What is surprising is the relatively late date, 1915.

The Black Hills also hosted a large population of black bears in pre-white settlement days. Indian informants told W. J. Hoffman, who was compiling a list of mammals found in the Grand River area of South Dakota in 1877, that the only place the black bear was encountered was in the Black Hills and the Wyoming Big Horns. Unlike the grizzly, the smaller black bears ranged only within the forested confines of the mountains.

In the year just previous to Hoffmann's report, Colonel Richard Dodge noted during his Black Hills reconnaissance that the country along Rapid and Boxelder creeks "is full of bear sign. In some places almost a quarter of an acre will be rooted up as if by hogs; small thickets of berry-bearing bushes are torn and broken; ant hills are dug into and huge logs turned over by this omnivorous monster in search of his food. . . . Seven or eight bears were killed by our whole party . . . from the little black bear to the mammoth grizzly."

A full-grown black bear is about half the size of a full-grown grizzly and, unlike the big pugnacious and sometimes ill-tempered grizzly, the black bear is relatively timid and usually avoids all human contact—usually.

On the Wyoming side of the Black Hills in Weston County, there is a grave marker. Local legend holds that this is the grave of a young prospector named Hank Mason who was killed by a black bear up Parmlee Canyon about 1900. The legend goes to say that Mason's young wife had a premonition of this disaster and, after waiting for him in a small, lonely cabin for days, went crazy when they found his mangled body and brought it back.

Black bears can be very secretive and are able to conceal them-selves and stay hidden in woodlands where no man would think of looking for them. This ability, and the fact that they are omnivorous and will kill and eat almost anything including carrion, has enabled them to survive in the hills of northern New Jersey, fifty miles away from New York City.

The black bear, like the coyote, is cunning and adaptable. When living in close proximity to humans, it becomes nocturnal in its forag-ing. However, when living in the wild, it is a diurnal creature. It's diet, while all encompassing is made up of about 75 percent vegetable mate-rial. They also possess a pronounced sense of taste that craves sweets.

From time to time signs of black bears are reported in the Black Hills. In 1966, a forest ranger reported finding huge, deep claw marks on a tree in the northern Black Hills. The claw marks reportedly began about six feet up from the base of the tree and extended to the ground; typical bear sign.

In September 1968, the *Rapid City Journal* reported that a 160-pound ewe had its throat slashed and flesh eaten from its back, shoul-ders, and hindquarters. The ewe was found five miles west of Rochford, South Dakota, on a stream bank. Beside the carcass was the unmistakable prints of black bear. That November a three-hundred-pound adult male, probably the sheep killer, was shot in that same vicinity between Black Fox and Crook's Tower.

Other sightings include a report in 1984 of a bear cub up in a tree near Pringle, South Dakota. In October 1989, Waite was called to check on a complaint of a horse killed by a bear near Deerfield Lake. Waite described the animal taken as on old horse and noted that there were bear tracks around it and bear hair on the fence.

Occasionally, someone will report seeing a bear or finding signs—such as tracks, claw marks on a tree, an old log torn apart, or pocket gopher mounds dug through. In the last twenty-five years bears have been sporadically sighted in the more remote northern and western parts of the Black Hills near the Wyoming-South Dakota state line. Sighting areas include Spearfish Canyon; along Cold Creek in western Lawrence County; in Beaver Creek valley in western Pennington County; and just across the state line at Mallo Camp in Weston County, Wyoming.

In the summer of 1992, bear sign was reported in the Bear Lodge Mountains in Wyoming and in the Spearfish Ranger District in South

Dakota. There were no reported sightings but the sign produced a lot of speculation as to where the bears were coming from. The most credible explanation is that the occasional black bears encountered in the Black Hills are escapees from the Bear Country tourist attraction south of Rapid City. Others like to speculate that maybe these strays wandered 150 miles in from the Big Horns, which does have a viable bear population, by way of the remote pine forests and breaks of southern Montana. A scant handful of black bears probably live in the Black Hills, but it is doubtful a viable reproducing population exists.

Climbing back in Waite's pickup, we drive out of Custer and head up South Dakota 89 to Sylvan Lake. At about six thousand feet we drop into the Willow Creek drainage to check on a beaver dam that has backed water up to the edge of the highway. In the middle of the new pond a small grove of aspens stand flooded in clear sparkling water. The drainage is beautiful beaver habitat with scattered stands of birch and aspen groves interspersed with a few tall pines. "I set a pair of beavers in here near the headwaters at the end of May," he tells me while pulling on his hip waders. "I knew damn well I'd be takin' 'em out before winter," he admits as he grabs his small three-pronged rake out of the back of the pickup and walks towards the beaver dam.

At the dam Waite claws at the mat of grass, supple sticks, and mud tightly woven together. The beavers have skillfully used a small granite outcrop for a dam footing on the west side. The east side is where he used the highway embankment.

In a matter of five minutes, the beaver pond, which is littered with bright, red and gold floating leaves, begins to slowly drain through the breach Waite has just created in the small dam. His sabotage done, he walks back to the pickup, lifts a Hancock trap out, slides it part way into the water, and sets it. Just below the dam, he cuts a handful of willow for the eye appeal, attaches it to the lid of the trap above the set trigger and smears a dab of castoreum on it. In a matter of twenty minutes the entire job of breaching the dam and setting the trap is done.

Climbing back into the truck as long rays of evening sunlight stream through tall trees and highlight the leaf-littered forest floor, I consider how Blair Waite will probably be moving a beaver tomorrow to another creek with tall, sweet aspens somewhere in the highest reaches of the Black Hills before most of us have had our coffee or stirred from our beds.

14

Across the Red Valley

It is a cool morning in mid-September. The air is clear and the sky a sharp, cerulean blue with a few high wisps of cirrus clouds swept out by the jet stream. On earth the aspen and ash leaves are a brilliant yellow with the cottonwood still holding back. This year autumn, like spring, is "early."

At Black Hills State University in Spearfish, South Dakota, I stop in to meet a biology instructor named Jack Lozier. Lozier said I would know he was in his office if I saw a bent-up, rusted, cream-colored Ford pickup with the grill kicked in parked in the faculty lot. It is easily the ugliest vehicle in the lot.

At sixty-two, Lozier is a large, affable man without any pretense about what he does or who he is. Lozier has been teaching courses in biology, field zoology, and natural resource conservation for twenty-five years. As he talks about being at odds with the present college administration on issues of a political nature, there is no mistaking the fact that he is a thoughtful and dedicated teacher. Today we are planning a leisurely late morning drive through the Red Valley from Spearfish, South Dakota, to Beulah, Wyoming, and then up Sand Creek to Ranch "A" to see how the fall bird migration is proceeding. Lozier has been informally keeping track of the birds and wildlife sightings here over the last dozen years. He takes his field zoology class along this route every spring. I have traveled it many times, too, and know it well. It can be a rewarding wildlife loop with its mix of grassland, woody draws, marshes, and small spring-fed lakes.

The Red Valley, also known as the Red Beds or the Racetrack, encircles the Black Hills and lies between the pine forest ridges of the foothills (Dakota Hogback) and the Black Hills proper. It is a not a valley, strictly speaking, but rather the deeply eroded bed of the soft, red shale of the Spearfish formation. The Red Beds in the northern and northwestern part of the Hills, while consisting predominately of red shale and clay, contain large quantities of gypsum strata of considerable thickness as well as in disseminated seams and veins of small size. The larger seams are usually six or eight feet in thickness.

There are numerous sink holes in the red clay and these on close examination are traced to seams of gypsum lying generally only a few feet below the surface. The gypsum, by the percolation of water, has been decomposed, dissolved, and washed away—forming vertical holes in the seam and channels of escape for the water to some lower level. Due to rain and the drainage from limited areas of the surrounding clays, these holes have become enlarged, with some attaining a diameter of fifty feet. The majority are, however, only from two to five feet in diameter and have the characteristics of sinks in limestone countries.

Both edges of the Red Valley are transition zones or ecotones where the northern Great Plains grassland biome mixes and integrates with the Rocky Mountain coniferous forest biome. This mix creates an interesting diversity of associated grassland and forest plants that many species of birds and mammals find attractive.

The northern Red Valley is about fifty miles long and lies between Sturgis, South Dakota, and Sundance, Wyoming. Its greatest constriction lies between Sturgis and Whitewood, South Dakota. On the other side of Whitewood, just west of Elkhorn Mountain, the Red Valley opens up into the broad valley referred to as the Centennial Prairie which stretches for about seven miles to Spearfish. From Spearfish the Red Valley finds its greatest expanse, stretching westward thirty miles to Sundance and Inyan Kara Mountain.

The western thirty miles of the Red Valley is about five to eight miles wide and dominated by bluestem and grama grass communities. The topography consists of low clay ridges, sinks which increase in size and frequency upon approaching the Sundance vicinity, and isolated buttes and mesas that are the eroded remnants of the Dakota hogback and the red Spearfish formation. Throughout its entire fifty-mile course the Red Valley is relatively treeless, as well as broken and scored by numerous minor drainages.

This western section of the Red Valley is interspersed with a dozen reliable artesian springs and drained by two perennial rivers. On the west end, the Redwater River flows easterly out of the Bear Lodge Range of the Black Hills, picking up a half-dozen ephemeral creeks before meandering across the Wyoming state line to the north side of the Red Valley where it bumps up against the hogback. A few miles east of where U.S. 85 crosses it, it breaches the hogback and flows north to join the Belle Fourche River just below Belle Fourche, South Dakota.

The east side of this Red Valley stretch is bounded by Spearfish Creek, which exits the Black Hills via Spearfish Canyon at the town of Spearfish. It then continues to meander north across the Red Valley floor, skirting the white outcrops of the Gypsum Springs formation (or upper Spearfish formation) for a few miles before joining the Redwater west of the U.S. 85 bridge crossing.

Occurring along both the north and south edge perimeters of the Red Valley are numerous woody draws and gulches which host plants of the eastern deciduous forest complex. The gulches on the north side of the valley that drain the hogback foothills and face south tend to be hot and arid, while the draws on the south side of the valley that face north and have cut through the Black Hills sedimentary formations (Minnekahta and Minnelusa) are deeper and cooler with more moisture and ephemeral stream flows. The cooler north-facing draws tend to be lusher and richer in biological diversity than the hotter south-facing draws.

The most extensive deciduous complex occurs at the mouths of these draws as they fan out onto the adjacent grasslands. The bottoms of these draws are comprised of deciduous trees that prefer more moisture and in the northern Hills are dominated by an overstory mixture of bur oak *(Quercus marcrocarpa)*, green ash *(Fraxinus subintergerrima)*, American elm *(Ulmus americana)* which is now nearly extinct, boxelder *(Acer negundo)*, cottonwood *(Populus deltoides)*, and peach-leaved willow *(Salix amygdaloides)*.

As the elevation increases the deciduous lowland plant elements begin to drop out and are replaced by mesophytic forest types that include ponderosa pine *(Pinus ponderosa)* and Rocky Mountain juniper *(Juniperus scopulorum)* on the driest, rockiest slopes, along with birch *(Betula papyrifera)*, ironwood/eastern hop hornbeam *(Ostrya virginiana)*, and hawthorn *(Cragaeus spp.)* on the better sites.

In the higher elevated, interior portion of the Black Hills, with the increase of moisture, cooler temperatures, and other exposure factors, Black Hills spruce *(Picea glauca)*, with interspersed aspen *(Populus tremuloides)* groves, begin to dominate the deep canyons and high meadow fringes—especially on the headwaters of Rapid, Castle, Elk, Bear Butte and Spearfish creeks.

The northern Black Hills support a more widespread deciduous forest complex than the southern Black Hills, primarily because of increased moisture and cooler temperatures. The draws and canyons of the southern Hills receive more direct solar exposure and are relatively hotter and drier. As a result, southern Black Hills slopes are dominated by local heavy stands of deerbrush *(Ceanothus spp.)*, along with Rocky Mountain juniper and mountain mahogany *(Cercocarpus montanus)*, while the draws and canyons are dry and open and tend to be dominated by grasses, scattered pines and gallery groves of cottonwoods.

The bottoms of the draws, as they fan out onto the plains in the northern Hills, have moist soils with a variety of grasses, forbs, and sedges. The dominant grasses include western wheatgrass *(Agropyrn smithii)*, needle and thread *(Stipa spp.)*, little bluestem *(Andropogon scoparius)*, prairie Junegrass *(Koeleria pyramidata)*, blue grama *(Bouteloua gracilis)*, side-oats grama *(Bouteloua curtipendula)*, and buffalo grass *(Buchloe dactyloides)*. Common forbs include asters *(Aster spp.)*, fleabanes *(Erigeron spp.)*, goldenrod *(Solidago spp.)*, sunflowers *(Helianthus spp.)*, poison ivy *(Rhus radicans)*, prickly pear *(Opuntia spp.)*, and sages *(Artmesia spp.)*.

Scattered about, either singly or more often in dense thickets near the mouth of the draws and on the adjacent grassland, are wild roses *(Rosa spp.)*, currants *(Ribes spp.)*, chokecherries *(Prunus melanocarpa)*, wild plum *(Prunus americana)*, skunkbrush *(Rhus trilobata)*, hawthorn *(Crataegus spp.)*, buffalo berry *(Shepherdia argentea)*, buckbrush/western snowberry *(Symphoricarpos occidentalis)*, and leadplant *(Amorpha canascens)*.

As might be expected, fire is also important in the lower woody draws of the Black Hills. Fire stimulates deciduous trees and shrubs to sprout and regenerate the kind of succulent new growth sought by wildlife. In woody draws, because of their moister conditions, cool fires are the general rule. Cool fires remove the old, dead debris and stimulate bur oak, boxelder, green ash, plum, and chokecherry to sucker prodigiously.

While draws and canyons with their water and riparian plant communities comprise only about 5 percent of the entire Black Hills area, they are of critical importance to the welfare of 80 percent of the native wildlife. Their natural features—which include water, shelter, shade and a variety of forage attract elk, deer, mountain lions, turkeys (introduced), coyotes, small mammals (particularly white-footed mice, pack rats, voles, rabbits, skunks), along with a host of tree- and cavity-nesting birds. Gray wolves, bison, and bear (both black and grizzly) also sought them out for shelter and food in pre-white settlement days.

About three miles north of Spearfish, Lozier and I turn west onto an unmarked county gravel road and stop near the bridge that crosses Spearfish Creek. Located downstream, a quarter mile or so on private property, is a great blue heron rookery. The rookery is in a gallery grove of century-old cottonwoods. About three dozen large, bowl-shaped nests made of sticks and coarse grass grace many of the uppermost tree crotches.

Great blue herons are one of the most ubiquitous bird species in North America. Standing at four feet with a seven-foot wingspan, they are the largest heron on the continent. They nest as far north as southeast Alaska and southern Canada and as far south as Mexico, the Galapagos Islands, and the West Indies. Often they are seen standing motionless in the shallows of lakes, ponds, marshes, wet meadows, and waterways feeding on whatever happens to walk, creep, or crawl within striking distance of their sharp, pointed bill.

Herons feed mainly on small fish (about 70 percent) which they catch crosswise in their bill. Then they maneuver the fish around and swallow it whole. They also devour frogs, lizards, snakes, crayfish, grasshoppers, dragonflies and have been known to frequently take shrews, mice, young rats, ground squirrels, and pocket gophers.

From their rookery on Spearfish Creek, they fly to feeding sites all over the northern Black Hills and out on to the plains. With their head and neck folded back on their long bodies in the shape of an "S" and the slow, majestic beat of their wide, dusky wings, they are readily identifiable flying up the canyons and draws of the northern Hills as well as over the hogback to feed in the sloughs near the mouth of the Redwater.

Since herons live and nest in all habitats, northern populations—like the one that uses the Spearfish rookery—has to annually migrate. No banding has been done on this population but Lozier guesses they winter like so many other northern plains cranes and herons on or near the Aransas National Wildlife Refuge on the Texas Gulf Coast.

A lot of research work has gone into what stimulates herons and other birds to migrate and reproduce. The urge to migrate north in the spring and reproduce is probably due to a number of factors. There is a general chain of developments that includes the lengthening of the photo period (daylight), rain, rising temperatures, and wind conditions. When all the factors come together, a heron that has been acknowledged as a leader, will initiate the beginning of the one-thousand-mile journey north to a predetermined grove of trees like this one on a small creek in the Red Valley.

The Spearfish rookery herons probably follow a traditional route north every spring, making short flights and stopping on waterways, lakes, and ponds to rest and feed. How long the journey takes depends on many variables, two of which are weather conditions and wind velocity. In the western United States herons have been clocked at flight speeds that range from 18 to 35 mph.

The herons start arriving at Spearfish Creek about the end of March. Here, the sights and sounds of the nesting colony, along with the physiological enlargement of the testis in the male and ovaries in the female, will signal the start of the reproduction cycle.

Shortly after arriving, herons pair up, mate, and begin nest-stealing behavior. This behavior includes gathering sticks as well as ransacking unguarded nests for building materials to restore an old nest or construct a new one. This obliges one bird to stay and protect the nest at all times. Males and females take turns feeding and guarding the nest site. Later they will maintain this same regime during the entire incubation period and after the eggs are hatched.

Herons have curious ways of recognizing each other as members of the same species and determining who they will mate with and who they are mated to. Courtship is carried on through a series of movements that follow in a sequential order. The proper sequence of movements triggers the next behavioral response. Both sexes must recognize the movements, know the sequence, and respond appropriately. If any of the actions are out of sequence they do not breed together. In this way species are maintained and inappropriate pairs of birds are kept from breeding, although as in all biology there are exceptions to this general rule.

In the case of water birds, which includes the families of herons and ducks, there may be as many as nine different movements, including head bobbing, tail wiggling, wing flapping, strutting, jumping, calling, and bill clacking. In the heron rookery the two most obvious displays of mate recognition are head bobbing and the clacking of bills.

Head bobbing probably establishes the pair bond while bill clack-ing serves as a reintroduction to the mate who is returning to the nest. In the spring, the hollow sound of clacking heron bills rings through the grove; I think of it as a kind of recognition greeting, something anthropomorphically similar to "honey, I'm home."

In April, the female lays an average clutch of four eggs in her rick-ety, stick nest. Both sexes take turns incubating and turning the eggs every two hours for four weeks. They also must stand guard against a host of hungry predators—owls, hawks, eagles, crows, raccoons, and snakes. At the end of the four weeks, the eggs hatch and both parents begin to take turns feeding the nestlings. This consists of regurgitat-ing food first directly into the mouths of the young and later, as the chicks grow older, into the nest. At the end of three months the young birds fledge and the nest is abandoned.

The oldest banded, wild great blue heron lived to be twenty-one years old. A great blue in the National Zoo in Washington, D.C., lived to be nearly eleven. The average life span for wild birds in this rookery with all its hazards is probably somewhere in the middle area of that range.

In the spring of 1992, Lozier and his students counted sixty-eight herons at the Spearfish Creek rookery along with twenty other species of songbirds, woodpeckers, and birds of prey that were in the process of nesting, foraging, or migrating. It makes this run of Spearfish Creek an exciting and raucous place for bird watchers.

This morning, as far as the herons are concerned, we are too late in the season. The rookery is quiet and all the nests stand stark and empty against the hard, blue September sky. Lozier believes they left a week or so ago, a little early this year. They may already be on the Platte—the premier avian waterway stop for herons and cranes on the central plains.

The only birds we see at the rookery today are three killdeer far out on an adjacent wheat stubble field, a lone turkey vulture riding the late morning thermals, and a small flock of dark-eyed juncos.

Juncos are one of the most abundantly common birds inhabiting all areas of the Black Hills all year. They are often seen flitting about on or near the ground at the edge of forest clearings and around brushy areas. Juncos belong to the largest family of all the bird fami-lies in North America, the finches. The finch family, whose Latin name, *fringillidae*, means small bird or finch, covers about eighty-three species plus eight subspecies and includes some of the finest and most beautifully plumed songbirds in North America. Species of *fringillidae* occurring in the Black Hills include the dark-eyed junco, crossbill, dickcissel, goldfinch, three species of grosbeaks, redpoll, pine siskin, two species of towhees, and fourteen species of sparrows.

Fringillids nest away from others of their kind, with each pair establishing a territory which the male defends. The female, depending on the particular species, builds a cup-like nest in a tree, bush, or on the ground. She then lays and incubates the eggs and broods the young. The male may feed the female during egg incubation and help care for the chicks.

Three species of juncos, the Oregon *(Junco hyemalis oreganus)*, the slate-colored *(Junco hyemalis hyemalis)*, and the white-winged *(Junco hyemalis aikeni)* were once all recognized as distinct species inhabiting the Black Hills. Of these three species, the white-winged was considered limited and unique to the Black Hills.

In 1973, the American Ornithologists' Union (AOU) determined that all of the above junco species were, in fact, only races or subspecies of the same bird (they all successfully interbreed). The whole group was then reclassified under the same genus and species as *Junco hyemalis*, and now are all lumped together as dark-eyed juncos.

Nonetheless, the white-winged race is considered the "nesting junco" distinct to the Black Hills ponderosa forests and it, along with its other dark-eyed junco relatives, is one of the most commonly seen birds in the high Black Hills and foothills at all seasons of the year.

In regard to nesting, female juncos are resourceful and may choose to build their nest under a log, in exposed tree roots, in or under bushes, or on an exposed rock ledge. One female built her nest in a discarded gallon syrup can and another in a tomato can laying on the forest floor near an active sawmill.

Three or four eggs are laid in May and June in the dry ponderosa forest at relatively high elevations. After the eggs hatch, the chicks, like the adults, feed on the seasons bounty, eating a preponderance of insects such as beetles, weevils, caterpillars, grasshoppers, bugs, ants, and wasps. In the fall and winter the birds migrate down to the foothills and woody draws and switch their diet from insects to berries and seed grains in season.

In his *Report of a Reconnaissance of the Black Hills*, made in the summer of 1874, Colonel Ludlow referred to *Junco hyemalis var. aikeni* as white-winged snowbirds. He wrote:

I found this species very numerous in the Black Hills near Harney Peak. They had bred in the vicinity, and I saw many broods of young, hardly fledged, on the 1st of August. On one occasion I came upon a family, the young of which had but just left the nest. They could fly but a short distance, and were of course, still under the care of their parents. On being approached, they flew a few yards and then concealed themselves behind logs, stubs, and stones, while the female, alighting on a branch near my head, uttered a quick, rolling cry, something like the sound that would be made by striking two large stones together in quick succession, but the notes duller and more prolonged. I think this is the most common bird in the more elevated portions of the Black Hills.

We leave the heron rookery and head west, turning right (north) onto the asphalt road, and then left (west) seven-tenths of a mile at the first gravel road. On the southwest corner of this junction there is a horse corral with a tree belt that hosts a variety of sparrows and starlings.

Starlings are an alien avian species first introduced to North America in 1890 by Eugene Scheifflin. Scheifflin introduced sixty pairs of starlings that first year to New York City's Central Park and more than forty the next year. The birds caught on instantly.

Starlings are an Eurasian specie that have become a well-established resident in most of the United States. They forage on the ground most of the time for food, which consists of a wide and varied host of insects, seeds, and grains. Serious bird watchers tend to find their screeching call annoying and are concerned with the fact that they are very successful in competing for the limited natural nesting cavities favored by more attractive native species—including bluebirds, flycatchers, and woodpeckers.

However, starlings are economically beneficial, particularly in places like Texas where they consume a good share of weevils, cutworms, and Japanese beetles that attack commercial crops. On the northern plains they tend to gather in large flocks around feed lots and corrals where waste grain is available. They roost together in nearby tree belts, and as a flock are capable of performing amazing aerial maneuvers that include wheeling, twisting, and turning in unison with perfect precision.

Two-tenths of a mile farther, the road bisects a wet meadow/marsh that is thick with sparrows and transient birds headed south. This morning it hosts a variety of sparrows, including vesper, chipping, and white-crowned. A red-shafted flicker also drops by, as does a crow. The red-shafted flicker is one of eight species of woodpecker, along with the sapsucker, black-backed, downy, hairy, Lewis', red-headed, and three-toed woodpeckers that inhabit the Black Hills. Woodpeckers depend on their acute hearing to detect insects and insect larvae chewing under the bark of trees. The adults of most woodpecker species eat wood-boring beetles, ants, aphids, flies, caterpillars, and bugs. Some eat acorns, pine seeds, fruit, and sap. Very few woodpecker species are migratory because their food supply of insect larvae and pupae is always available—even in the winter under the bark or in dead or rotted wood where it is unavailable to other bird species.

The red-shafted flicker, one of three flicker subspecies, is common in rural farm areas with groves of trees. It inhabits most of western North America with the Black Hills on the edge of its eastern range. It feeds mostly on the ground where ants are a favorite food. This particular dietary predilection for ants requires this specie of woodpecker to migrate south in the winter.

Crows, which are also relatively common around the foothills, are members of the family corvidae which includes the raven, jays, nutcrackers, and magpies. The latter three species are year-round residents of the Black Hills. Resident pairs and small flocks of crows tend to be localized in specific vicinities, but may forage as far as fifty miles from their home roosts. At this time of the year, large transient crow flocks from farther north begin moving through the Black Hills foothills on their way south to their winter roosts.

The corvidae family is believed to have originated in the north temperate and tropical parts of the Old World and to have spread from there to North America. Corvids are generally believed to have evolved the highest degree of intelligence among birds.

Crows are keen, wary birds that like to stay out of man's sight and just out of shotgun range. They seem to posses excellent puzzle-solving skills as well as a remarkable memory and a marked capacity to learn from experience. In 1874, Ludlow reported seeing them "occasionally in small flocks along the Little Missouri."

The pinyon, gray, and blue jays are all found in the Black Hills. Pinyon and gray jays, along with Clark's nutcracker, prefer the mature, multi-storied forest from about three thousand to five thousand feet where there is an abundance of seed cones. The blue jay prefers the lower Black Hills draws where there are oak trees and acorns, one of its preferred foods.

All corvid species are aggressive and omnivorous, eating insects, eggs, seeds, and stealing scraps of human food left unattended. Nutcrackers and jays will also frequently cache food (seeds) in the ground. In one study, a nutcracker was able to recover about 70 percent of their cached seeds—about the same percentage of squirrel cache recovery. On one occasion a nutcracker was observed digging through eight inches of snow to retrieve a seed cone it had buried.

The black-billed magpie, although raucous and omnivorous like its corvid relatives, tends to be more specialized as a meat and carrion scavenger, with a historically observed predilection for sitting on the backs of elk, deer, mountain sheep, and buffalo to pick ticks out of their hide as well as fly larvae and dead flesh from their wounds. In the days when the great elk and bison herds roamed the northern plains and Black Hills country, they were abundant. Ludlow reported the following in 1874:

> The magpie is rather common all through the country traversed by the (Custer) expedition. At the season when I first saw them, late in July and early in August, they were generally to be seen in companies of ten or a dozen, and were very noisy, hopping about through the trees, and screaming like a flock of excited jays. At other times they were more silent, and would walk up to within a few yards of me as I sat watching them, and apparently converse about me in low tones.

Today, magpies are relatively scarce in the Black Hills and like the resident crows, prefer the woody draws and the foothills. The largest flock of magpies I have ever seen numbered over two dozen individuals. I caught a glimpse of this group in a pine-wooded draw about seventy-five miles east of the Black Hills in the Badlands country south of Interior, South Dakota.

The raven, also a notorious feeder on big game and bison carrion, was formerly a nesting resident of the Black Hills and northern plains. Ludlow reported seeing ravens "almost every day on the way to the Black Hills, but never more than one pair at a time, except on one or two occasions, when we saw a pair of old ones with their newly fledged young." He also noted that "they had bred on many of the lofty buttes that we passed," adding that they were also observed in the Black Hills. Unlike magpies, ravens have completely disappeared from the northern Great Plains, nor are they present any longer in the Black Hills.

On the north side of the road, next to the marsh, winter flocks of horned larks glide and skip through a stubble field. Horned larks spend the winter in flocks out on the barren ground foraging for weed seeds and waste grain. Ludlow reported horned larks as "one of the most characteristic of the species inhabiting the high, dry plains of Dakota." He noted them in great abundance all the way from Fort Lincoln to the Black Hills, then related the following information:

> Early in July I found their nests with well-advanced eggs, and on the return march the prairies, which had been burned since we passed over them before, were fairly alive with flocks of old and young birds. When alarmed they would crouch for an instant, and then, springing from the ground, would move off with an easy gliding flight, uttering at the same time a clear, mellow whistle.

Moving west again past the marsh, the road roughly follows the old Miles City Trail. Near the top of the first ridge, on the east side of the road, are faint parallel depressions cut into the short grass sod. These depressions mark old wagon trail ruts. Looking back towards the east, further down the draw where the red clay is softer, the trail has more deeply cut and eroded the hillside.

The Miles City Trail ran 235 miles from Miles City, Montana to Spearfish and Deadwood, South Dakota. It became part of a shorter route from the gold fields of Helena, Montana, to the Black Hills and was used in the last quarter of the nineteenth century by merchants, cowboys, farmers, miners, and immigrants to the Pacific Northwest, A lot of beef on the hoof and horses were also driven over it. In the early 1880s, mail was sent via the Miles City Trail three times a week, most of the time by buckboard. Stories about the old trail are the stuff of western legend. Joe Ervine, a mail carrier, survived several blizzards on the trail by giving his horses a nose bag of oats and then wrapping himself up in a buffalo coat and robe and burrowing down into a snow bank to wait out the storm. But besides dealing with frequent blizzards and sub-zero temperatures, carriers had to deal with searing summer heat and flash floods. In the spring, stretches of the trail were graphically described "as mush clear down to China."

Also at this time, Indians gave the traveling public a hard time, frequently stealing horses and occasionally scalping a few unlucky individuals. Road agents were also busy on the trail and ran things pretty much their way. They headquartered just across the Montana state line in Alzada (formerly known in the outlaw days as Stoneville).

North of Alzada, the trail ran west of the Finger Buttes country. The Finger Buttes, located across the South Dakota line in southeastern Montana, were a last stronghold of the northern plains bison herd. In 1880, thirty thousand bison were estimated to still be free roaming there. Colonel Ludlow who passed east of that same vicinity six years earlier in 1874 noted that while "the whole country was once ranged over by enormous herds of buffalo whose trails are everywhere visible, [they] are now seldom or never found east of the Little Missouri; and the only game animals inhabiting the vast waste are antelope, numbers of which were seen during every day's march."

The Miles City Trail was tough and uncivilized, but, nonetheless, a modicum of civility was encouraged among stage passengers. One stagecoach company distributed a "Rules of Conduct" list to its passengers which would certainly have been applicable to travelers on the Miles City coaches. The list reveals, perhaps better than any description could, conditions and situations you might expect to encounter on the journey. Printed below are the rules of conduct for coach travelers:

Travelers Conduct Rules

1. Abstinence from liquor is requested, but if you must drink, share the bottle. To do otherwise makes you appear selfish and un-neighborly.
2. If ladies are present, gentlemen are urged to forego smoking cigars and pipes as the odor of same is repugnant to the Gentle Sex. Chewing tobacco is permitted, but spit WITH the wind and not against it.
3. Gentlemen must refrain from the use of rough language in the presence of Ladies and Children.
4. Buffalo robes are provided for your comfort during cold weather. Hogging robes will not be tolerated and the offender will be made to ride with the driver.
5. Don't snore loudly while sleeping or use your fellow passenger's shoulder for a pillow; he (or she) may not understand and friction may result.
6. Firearms may be kept on your person for use in emergencies. Do not fire them for pleasure or shoot at wild animals as the sound riles the horses.
7. In the event of runaway horses, remain calm. Leaping from the coach in panic will leave you injured, at the mercy of the elements, hostile Indians or hungry coyotes.

8. Forbidden topics of discussion are Stagecoach robberies and Indian uprisings.
9. Gents guilty of unchivalrous behavior toward Lady Passengers will be put off the stage. It's a long walk back. A word to the wise is sufficient.

At the curve of the road, the Miles City Trail veers west, drops down the draw, and moves out onto the flats. There are a couple of deeply eroded trenches in this draw that are indicative of an old, well-used bison trail.

About a mile north of the draw is a pleasant artesian spring. Bison like to water once a day, usually in the morning, and then graze and ruminate in the afternoon. Looking at the whole ridge line, the draw presented the easiest access up to the grass on top and, therefore, would have been the route of choice both for bison and stagecoach. Most of the old west trails that crossed the plains and wound through the western mountain passes were initially established by wild herd animals who long ago found and established where the easiest grades could be found. Indians used these established game trails both for traveling and hunting for over ten thousand years before the white men eventually graveled, graded, and paved most of them during the last half of the twentieth century.

A mile and half farther along, the gravel road leads to the artesian spring on the southwest side of the road mentioned earlier. This is one of about a dozen artesian springs that generally appear on the south side of the road. The spring weather and the marsh attract a multitude of birds and small mammals. At this time of the year, it is a staging area for flocks of blackbirds. Blackbirds are members of the Troupial family and take their name from their habit of gathering into a large flock or troupe. The family is found only in the Western Hemisphere and includes a variety of blackbirds, cowbirds, grackles, orioles, and meadowlarks—all of which are well represented in the Black Hills foothills area.

Common seasonal blackbird residents of this marsh area are the brown-headed cowbird, western meadowlark, and the red-winged blackbird. The latter is believed by many ornithologists to be the most numerous land bird in North America.

The red-winged blackbird lives in marshes and sloughs, and generally builds its nest in cattails and bushes around ponds, lakes, and sluggish streams. It feeds in open fields where it consumes weed seeds and waste grain, but, like most bird species, will also take whatever insects are plentiful and available during the season. While Ludlow reports them as "abundant along the Missouri River," he noted that only "a few were observed on the Little Missouri."

The buffalo bird, or brown-headed cowbird, was so named in the late nineteenth century by hunters and cowboys who noticed its close association with the nomadic bison herds. The buffalo bird evolved the habit of perching on the back of the great beasts, picking out parasites, or walking nearby and eating the insects they kicked up. Ludlow reported that "this species was abundant everywhere on the trip. A large number of them would often accompany the column for the greater part of the day, alighting almost under the horses' hoofs, and displaying the utmost indifference as to the presence of man."

Buffalo birds parasitize the nests of 214 species of other birds by laying an egg in the host bird's nest and leaving it for its foster parents to raise. The female will hastily lay her one egg in the nest, oftentimes returning later to pierce the host's eggs or roll them out of the nest to reduce the competition for her own young. About half of the host species the female buffalo bird picks out incubate the brown-speckled, white buffalo bird egg along with their own and raise the alien nestling. Often the larger buffalo bird nestling will crowd out or throw the smaller host nestlings from the nest. Some ornithologists theorize that the buffalo or cow bird's nest parasitism evolved as a result of the bird's habit of following the bison herds which precluded it from building and maintaining its own stationary nest. In the late summer and fall, buffalo birds find each other and gather into enormous flocks with red-winged blackbirds, Brewer's blackbirds, and grackles for the migration south.

The western meadowlark is one of the last groups of blackbirds around the marsh to migrate south. Its distinctive chuckling and sweet, flute-like song is the harbinger of spring on the Great Plains where it is a common and much loved songbird. It nests in small ground depressions and will conveniently use the sunken hoof prints left formerly by bison and later domestic livestock. It feeds primarily on insects found on the ground and migrates in species segregated groups to the southern Great Plains for the winter.

About a mile and a half farther, the road again crosses the old Miles City Trail ruts. On the north side of the road a concrete marker officially commemorates the old trail. The trail is easily observed and well established here. It was, however, in no sense a "road" as recognized in the late twentieth century. In the old coach days their was no one main track, since the driver might often break another track higher up next to the old one or take the other side of a hill if the main track was muddy or snow drifted. It is hard to imagine now, but in the late nineteenth century, the western Great Plains was all unfenced, open country as far as you could see, and drivers had the option to roll their coaches wherever they pleased.

Randomly dispersed on the hillsides and ridges on both sides of the gravel road here are huge, reddish purple sandstone boulders that, in the shadows of late evening light, present the illusion of a herd of resting bison. These boulders, remnants of the Lakota formation left on the red beds, once all fitted together and formed caps on the red knolls and ridges. Due to the wind and rain, these sandstone caps have since broken down and eroded into some interesting shapes and forms.

At the marker the Miles City Trail veers off to the northwest, crossing the road before it passes east of a group of decayed-out buildings in the near distance, known locally as the old Wahl Ranch. Past the ranch buildings the trail crosses a small, spring-fed drainage and proceeds up a shallow draw that is visible in the northwestern mid-horizon.

What appears to be an eroded trench curving up the draw marks the old trail. Once on top of the ridge, the trail continued northwesterly, dropped down and forded the Redwater, then swung around the west side of a small red butte before winding up out of sight through a wide breach of the hogback.

Near the base of the first mid-horizon ridge where it winds up the draw, a small, unmarked grave, outlined in stone in the short prairie grass, marks the last resting place of an early traveler. From the settling of the stone in the sod, the grave is probably well over a century old.

No stories survive as to who it was, but from its relatively small size it may well hold the remains of a child or small pioneer woman. The incident probably occurred sometime prior to the discovery of gold in the Black Hills. After gold was discovered, travel around the Black Hills and the northern plains became extremely dangerous for immigrants and was seldom undertaken. The Sioux, who began to understand the value of gold and could see the change that was sweeping the plains, become extremely hostile to all white travelers whom they perceived as invaders. Travel on the trail did not become relatively safe for immigrants again until 1890, following the Massacre at Wounded Knee, South Dakota.

Up above on the ridge, barely discernible, is a stone circle that appears to be a prehistoric aboriginal trail marker. West of it are old buffalo wallows and to the south evidence of a series of old artesian springs, now dry. On the next ridge to the west, a pile of stones on a red knoll vaguely resembles an arrowhead. It points in this direction. From the arrowhead knoll, looking west, a huge artesian spring called Cox Lake is visible. It lays in a wide depression surrounded by marsh, wet meadow, and prairie. The lake is sixty feet deep and crystal clear. Early travelers liked to describe it as "bottomless." Cox Lake attracts a wide variety of birds and mammals at all seasons of the year since it never freezes up, even in the coldest winter.

The wet meadow and prairie that surrounds Cox Lake are a virtual oasis for a variety of native plants and supports large, waving stands of four-foot-high big bluestem and Indian grass—two major components of the tall grass prairie that are relatively uncommon this far west, having prehistorically flourished three hundred to four hundred miles further east.

Around the vicinity of Cox Lake are fox, coyote, deer, and small herds of pronghorn. One fall I saw a gyrfalcon, an early fall migrant visitor from the northern tundra, perched on a fence post southeast of the lake. The whole area, with its water and lush grass, is a magnet for common and unusual wildlife in this arid country.

Just beyond Cox Lake the county road forks. The north fork goes down to the Redwater, while the west fork turns south and passes the McNenny Fish Hatchery. This facility primarily rears trout and takes advantage of another large Red Valley artesian spring. Above McNenny are the Mirror Lakes, both of which are spring fed and crystal clear.

East of McNenny springs on the prairie is a sharptail grouse "dancing ground." Sharptails are one of eighteen species of grouse, eight of which live exclusively in North America. Most grouse, including the sharptail, are fowl-like birds that live on the ground. All are strong, rapid fliers that can quickly cover a distance of up to three miles when threatened.

In early April, male sharptail have traditionally gathered at this dancing ground about a half hour before sunrise and sunset to perform for the females who arrive later. Following the arrival of the hens, the males inflate the air sacs in their throat and utter a hollow "booming" or cooing sound. While booming, they raise and fan their tails, and rustle and quiver their wings—challenging other males while endeavoring to attract the attention of the females. Sometimes a male will get into a fight with another male, gripping a rival with his strong, curved bill.

After courtship and copulation with the male of her choice, the female settles on a nest on the prairie about a half mile from the dancing grounds. The chicks hatch in about three weeks and are immediately lead away from the nest to an area rich in insects. The adults are great browsers and feed mainly on plant materials including wild berries, domestic grains, as well as on a host of wild native flowers along with the buds and leaves of various trees and shrubs. In the fall and early winter they gather into flocks of ten to thirty-five birds and occasionally migrate if populations are large and food is scarce.

To the north, just east of the Wyoming state line, is a low red butte which can be reached by turning west (right) off the Interstate 90 service road. It is about a quarter of a mile long and covers about a section. This butte has been deeply cut and eroded on its west- and south-facing sides by the prevailing wind and rain, while the two opposite sides are gently sloped and grass covered.

Often present in the vicinity of the butte is a small, free-roaming herd of pronghorn usually led by one buck with a harem of three to five doe. Also frequently present in the area of the butte's crest is a small flock of turkey vultures. The crest of the butte is a good place for vultures to ride up on late-morning thermals, while in the afternoon they can catch the obstruction currents or updrafts that occur when the prevailing west winds ram into that huge mass of red shale.

Turkey vultures belong to the family Cathartidae, which is Greek for "cleanser" and comes from their predilection of feeding and scavenging carrion. There are seven species in the family, including two condors and five vultures, all of which occur only in the Western Hemisphere.

The father of evolutionary biology, Charles Darwin, described turkey vultures as "disgusting birds" with their bald, scarlet heads "formed to wallow in putridity." Despite Darwin's uncomplimentary remarks, they are very useful, fastidiously clean, and considered to be the most numerous and successful birds of prey in the world.

Cathartids, in fact, do lack feathers on their head and have evolved instead rough skin that is, depending on the species, black, red, yellow, or orange. This evolutionary trait probably arose from their ancestors' habit of sticking their heads into putrid carcasses. Their naked heads help them to keep clean and cool. Cathartids are powerful and graceful fliers and are considered the perfect examples of static soaring flight being able to soar for miles at thousands of feet to look for dead animals or to watch for other vultures that might be descending to prey.

Turkey vultures are one of the few birds that have a good sense of smell as well as eyesight. In fact, they locate most of their prey with their large nostrils that can detect the smell of a dead carcass high above a forest or plain within twenty-four hours. Turkey vultures rouse themselves about mid-morning from their communal roost to catch the rising thermals as a group and patrol the skies. If one detects a dead carcass, its descent alerts the next nearest bird which goes down and, eventually, a ripple effect begins pulling all the vultures within eyesight of each other down to the carcass. Contrary to popular opinion concerning predation of wild grazing animals on the plains, most die of natural causes and their carcasses are efficiently cleaned up by these carrion birds.

In the Black Hills turkey vultures migrate south about the end of September and return in April to lay their eggs without the formality of a nest. They might deposit their egg clutch on the ground or on the floors of caves, cliffs, or in the hollows of stumps and standing trees. Cliffs are preferred since they offer the best protection from predators and the easiest access to rising updrafts.

Crossing the Wyoming state line via the service road, we turn south (left) at the first road which crosses the interstate at Beulah, Wyoming. This is the Sand Creek Road. Sand Creek heads up in the northern Black Hills and, like Spearfish Creek, is a major tributary of the Redwater. As we drop down into the Sand Creek drainage, the Minnekahta formation forms the caprock on top. Below the Minnekahta lies the crumbly, reddish orange Minnelusa formation.

The riparian area of Sand Creek is dominated almost exclusively by boxelder trees draped with vines of wild grape. Cottonwoods are sparse. Prominent are the stark white skeletons of American elms— once a beautiful and dominant tree common and abundant in most of the riparian canyons and draws of the Black Hills.

The American elms on Sand Creek, like the great majority across the Midwest, fell victim to the Dutch elm disease that swept through here in the 1970s. Dutch elm disease was first described on a tree in Holland and was inadvertently introduced into North America sometime before 1930. Soon after its introduction it made a virulent march across the continent, nearly wiping the species out.

The pathogen of this disease is an alien fungus that is transmitted by the introduced smaller European bark beetle and the native elm bark beetle, both feed on the elm's inner cambium. Using both species of beetles as vectors, the fungus sporolates after getting into the elm's xylem (water transportation system). These spores produce a substance toxic to the tree. The tree fights back by plugging up the infected vessels. If the disease transmission is widespread, however, the plugged vessels, unable to conduct water to the tree's upper tissue, effectively kill it by dehydration.

As the tree begins to dehydrate, more beetles are attracted to it since it is easier to penetrate a tree when its resistance is down. The females burrow in to lay eggs under the dying elm's bark which will serve as its feeding host for the beetle's larvae.

In the spring the young beetles emerge from under the elm bark. Unwittingly covered with the fungus *(Ophiostoma ulmi)*, they begin the process of carrying out their life cycle, starting this particularly insidious cycle again.

About four miles up the canyon is a handsome log lodge and barn known as Ranch "A." The area around this ranch was settled in 1877 following the Deadwood gold rush by George LaPlante. LaPlante, who was of French and Indian ancestry, established a fishing guide service and later a trout hatchery on Sand Creek which he operated through the 1920s.

In 1930, Moses Annenberg, a wealthy businessman, bought LaPlante's property and built the log lodge standing on the site today as a summer mansion in 1932, stamping his surname initial on it. Ten years later Annenberg sold it and for the next two decades it saw several owners who operated it variously as a nightclub, dude ranch and hunting and fishing resort. Each commercial venture in its turn failed for various reasons. In 1963, the U.S. Fish and Wildlife Service acquired the property ostensibly for its high volume of clean water that flows primarily underground through the canyon's aquifer at a relatively consistent temperature which ranges from 52 to 58 degrees.

Following the land acquisition, the federal government built a research and development complex in the mid-1960s to work specifically on rainbow trout genetics. In 1980, the genetics work was relocated and the facility became a fish diet center until 1987 when it also was relocated. The Wyoming Game and Fish Department now uses the facility to rear trout and walleye eggs. The old lodge is presently leased and operated by the South Dakota School of Mines and Technology as a retreat and conference/seminar center.

Just beyond the log barn, the canyon opens into a wide park. The west side of the canyon features high, curved walls of smooth white and red rock. This area is an excellent place to hear and see birds at all seasons of the year. In the summer and early fall a host of common hawks and small falcons, along with golden and bald eagles, are often sighted above the west wall where they launch out on the updrafts blowing down the canyon.

Ludlow noted that a single golden eagle was killed by a Ree scout at Short Pine Buttes (about sixty miles north of the Black Hills). "This bird," he noted, "is said to occur all through the country between the Missouri River and the Rocky Mountains, though it is nowhere common. It is highly prized," he added, "by the Indians, who use the tail feathers to adorn their war head-dresses. So much is this the case that two of these birds are worth a horse (i.e., $40 to $60) among the Sioux."

Lozier noted that three species of swallows—barn, cliff, and violet green, along with the white-throated swift—inhabit the rocky cliffs here. Swallows are amazing, tireless fliers that feed on a variety of insects they catch on the wing. Barn and cliff swallows build nests of mud under the overhanging canyon cliffs while the violet green nests in tree cavities and cliff crevices. When possible, all these species prefer to nest in colonies.

The white-throated swift, although similar in flight and resemblance to swallows, belongs to a different family known as Apodidae. Apodidae is derived from the Greek and means "without feet." It is an apt name for this family of small, high-speed birds with swept-back wings and legs so small and weak that if it alights on the ground it may have difficulty getting airborne again. Swifts are considered to be the fastest fliers among small birds and, literally, spend their entire life on the wing gathering insects, courting and copulating in flight. The white-throated swift, also known as the rock swift, is considered to be the fastest of swifts and possibly the fastest bird in North America.

Rock swifts have been reported dodging two-hundred-mile-per-hour stoops by falcons and have been seen copulating in the air with bodies together, pinwheeling downward. They nest in cracks and crevices in high inaccessible cliffs like those of Sand Creek Canyon.

Swallows and swifts are among the first groups of passerine birds to gather together in flocks in the fall for the migration flight to Central and South America.

The need for numerous bird species to migrate from the Black Hills is a fascinating story in itself. Migration probably evolved in various bird species near the end of the Ice Age. As the weather moderated, the ancestors of present migratory birds slowly began moving north of their wintering ranges (original homes) to breed, raise their families, and take advantage of available food resources in the north. When the weather became severe and food resources scarce, they retreated southward to wait the winter out.

Other information suggests that migratory patterns in some birds are much older than the Pleistocene Ice Age. While this past period of time had an enormous impact on bird migratory patterns, birds have undoubtedly responded to climatic and ecological changes by migrating well back into the Tertiary period. This seems evident from the fact that some species follow old watercourses that have long since disappeared or have been greatly altered by time.

Over one hundred species that summer in the United States migrate south to Mexico and Central America. Nowhere else in the world is there such an extraordinary concentration of winter migrants as in North America. Migrant residents from the north, upon reaching warmer winter climes, most often tend to occupy the forest edges and disturbed and cut-over brushy areas in tropical Mexico as opposed to the primary rain forest.

Of all the migrants from the Black Hills, the swallows, notably the barn and the cliff, travel the farthest, flying down to southern Brazil and Argentina. They generally migrate by day, feeding all the way on the wing. Other Black Hills migrants—including eagles, hawks, vultures, crows, jays, and blackbirds—also fly by day. Herons fly by day or night while most small songbirds migrate at night when they are less vulnerable to predatory birds and rest in the day.

Radar studies indicate that nocturnal migration is more the rule for birds as opposed to diurnal migration. Most nocturnal migrants fly between 1,800 to 3,000 feet above sea level, although many go much lower. All migrants fly on clear, as well as overcast nights.

During their night migratory flights, birds often utter sharp, melodious peeping and piping calls to keep in touch with each other. Small birds tend to fly alone, randomly distributed over large parts of the sky. At various intervals they will regularly flock together before dispersing again in flight.

All migrants seem to have the ability to navigate by the sun orienting their direction in relation to the position, direction and angle of sunlight. At night they navigate by the stars, again instinctively orienting themselves in the proper direction according to the season. Birds also seem able to navigate using geomagnetism—orienting themselves towards the magnetic pull of the poles.

Taking a gravel road back to Spearfish from Sand Creek, Lozier and I pause to observe an immature turkey vulture perched on a fence post. Our presence forces the big bird to jump reluctantly off his perch. Clumsily flapping his large, ungainly wings at first, he soon fixes them and soars at fence post elevation over the prairie. Neither Lozier nor I speak. We just watch the vulture dip and turn figuring it will probably be the last one we will see before winter sets in. It was at that moment I suspect we both shared the same unspoken desire; a fleeting wish that we possessed the instinct and the ability to orient ourselves to the pull of the earth, the sun, and the stars, and fly south.

15

A Conservation Legacy

Towards the end of the nineteenth century, following the free-for-all chaos of the 1876 Deadwood gold rush, unchecked logging had denuded huge portions of the Black Hills forest. During the first cutting when timber was plentiful, only the best trees were selectively cut. As timber became scarce in the following years and second cuttings were being initiated, loggers took what had been left of the remaining trees, leaving huge clear-cut areas. Henry S. Graves, a professional forester who visited the northern Black Hills in the late 1890s, reported that the hillsides were barren of trees within a radius of eight miles of Deadwood.

A great deal of waste occurred during this period of timber exploitation. Often only 50 percent of each tree cut was used with the rest discarded. Competition between fractious mining concerns exacerbated the problem as lumbermen would sometimes cut logs for the sole purpose of preventing a rival mining company from obtaining them. These surplus logs and milled lumber were often left to rot at mining operations that had been abandoned. In a government report, Graves stated:

> Probably no one who is at all familiar with the conditions of the Black Hills will deny the urgent need of protection against fires, wasteful methods of lumbering and timber frauds. The establishment of some system which will bring about such protection is the first and most necessary step in forest management. [Forestry contemplates something more] than mere police patrol and enforcement of the forest laws. It has in view the establishment of forests to take the place of those which are being cut off and the eventual utilization of the forest soil to its fullest capacity. This cannot be brought about by merely enforcing the forest

laws and keeping out fires, but requires the intelligent direction and control of lumbering with the reproduction of the forest in mind.

In the mid-1890s, Gifford Pinchot, a young eastern forester who would eventually become the first head of the United States Forest Service, observed that "the people in general knew little and cared less about forestry, and regarded the forest—like all other natural resources—as inexhaustible." In fact, at the time settlers and other residents of the Black Hills, under the auspices of the Free Timber Act of 1878, were free to exploit timber resources without charge from any unoccupied, unreserved, non-mineral, public lands within the state strictly for their own agricultural, mining, manufacturing, or domestic purposes.

In the East, however, the mood of the country was changing. An optimistic progressive movement was underway, and while those progressives held an unabiding faith in technology and efficiency, they were demanding social reform and a halt to the destruction and waste of the nation's natural resources. It was during this era—largely through the efforts of Pinchot—that the cause of scientific management of forestry resources was introduced. Pinchot espoused a "conservation" ethic that called for the proper management of forests for the production of a steady ongoing supply of lumber. Preservation proponents represented by men like John Muir, on the other hand, advocated the perpetuation of forest areas as wilderness to be maintained in a relative state of non-use. The public at the time was split over these two divergent philosophies.

During the summer of 1896, several members of the National Forestry Commission visited the Black Hills to see firsthand the nature of forestry abuses. Later that same year the full commission reported, "It is evident that without government protection these forests (of the Black Hills) so far as their productive capacity is concerned, will disappear at the end of a few years, and . . . their destruction will entail serious injury and loss to the agricultural and mining population of western North and South Dakota."

Influenced by the commission's recommendations, President Grover Cleveland signed into proclamation on February 22, 1897, the Black Hills Forest Reserve. The proclamation, in effect, removed from public use all land and timber within the Black Hills Reserve and firmly established for the first time a federal protective resource presence in the Black Hills.

A predictable howl of protest soon ensued over the omission of any provisions for the regulated use of the new reserve. Congress, faced with pressure from timber interests to abolish the entire reserve system (there were thirteen created at the time), passed the Forest Management Act of June 1897 to assure lumber consumers that the newly created reserves would continue to supply timber for their needs. The new act empowered the secretary of the interior to draft regulations under which users—including mining, lumbering, and grazing interests—could use the forest resource. The big difference was that now, instead of allowing indiscriminate cutting and grazing, government foresters would manage the land resources and select timber for harvest.

For Pinchot, the Black Hills Forest Reserve became a kind of barometer with which he sought to measure the sentiments of public opinion in regard to how his forestry conservation concepts were going. During the fall of 1897, he spent two months in the Black Hills, eventually writing back to the secretary of agriculture that "there is general change of opinion in regard to the Reserve, both among ranchers and among those interested in mining. So far I have talked with no one who was not strongly in favor of preserving the timber."

While there was support for Pinchot's conservation ethic, his statement was more a gloss than a realistic appraisal of public opinion. More objective writers of the time who made a study of the period wrote to the effect that a considerable mess had developed in the handling of the Black Hills Forest Reserve. So much commotion in fact was made of it in the newspapers that the secretary of the interior asked the Forestry Division to loan one of its trained foresters "to straighten matters out."

Pinchot sent trained forestry expert Edward M. Griffith. Griffith was given the task of working out a practical plan for the administration of the Black Hills Forest Reserve that looked both to the present and future conservation of the forest resource. The two most immediate problems Griffith observed in the Black Hills upon his arrival in 1898 were the fire hazards and the mountain pine beetles.

Fire, Griffith reported, was fairly well under control; however, he noted that the season was extremely dry. He wrote that "the forest force and the settlers were all unusually cautious and checked the forest fires at their very start." The bark beetles, however, were another matter beyond anyone's control. Griffith estimated that they had made vast and deep inroads into the northern Hills, killing over 2 million board feet of timber.

Apparently Griffith made some headway to the extent that a Missoula, Montana, newspaper reported, "Seventy-five percent of the Black Hills folk were favorable to the forest service with only 10 percent opposed." The 75 percent were enough to carry the concept of administrating national forest reserves for the purposes of conservation for all the people.

It was now time to get down to specifics. The forest reserve of the Black Hills would be the site where the first major discussion of how western forests should be regulated and managed. Pinchot's scientific forestry methods would be on trial, and as he noted in a later report, "There is no other forest in the United States in which practical forestry is more urgently needed or in which results of such importance may be more easily achieved."

In April 1898, Homestake Mining Company began to formulate its proposal for cutting trees on the Black Hills Reserve based on Pinchot's forest management principles. After a good deal of discussion over smaller issues involved in the regulated harvesting of timber between Pinchot and Homestake Mining Company managers, Timber Case #1 was finally approved and the Black Hills Forest Reserve became the first government-regulated timber cut on public forest land in the United States. Timber harvesting began at Christmastime 1899 and included eight sections of land located about four miles southwest of Nemo, South Dakota, in the drainage basin of Estes Creek.

Conditions seemed perfect to assure success of the project. Pinchot was working with a mining company that needed access to large amounts of cheap timber to maintain the profitability of its mining operation and he was also working with a seriously abused public forest that required efficient management of its remaining standing timber if it was to be able to sustain gold mining operations in the future. Both private and public managers could see the benefit of mutual cooperation.

Geography and nature also helped insure success of the new conservation ethic since the Black Hills is a highly productive ponderosa pine forest that is capable of reseeding itself relatively quickly. That biological characteristic and the fact that it is situated in an area with a strong timber demand all favored Case #1's success.

Case #1 set the precedent for government-regulated tree harvests on public lands that was essential to the conservation of western forest resources. Another federal conservation enterprise that met with unqualified success about this time was the introduction of trout to the Black Hills streams.

The story of trout in the Black Hills, or more precisely the lack of trout, begins with observations made by Colonel Ludlow, Custer's expeditionary surveyor. In his 1874 report, he notes, "We were continually looking for trout in these (Black Hills) streams, which seemed as though made expressly for that fish which requires an unfailing flow of cold, pure water. There could be no finer trout streams in the world than these, were they once stocked. As it is, we found nothing but some small chub, and a species of sucker of perhaps a pound in weight."

A dozen years later, in 1886, avid fisherman and Rapid City newspaperman, Richard Hughes also noticed the deficiency of trout in the cold, clear, spring-fed streams of the Black Hills. It was a simple fact of geography that the Black Hills was an island of the Rocky Mountain system isolated and surrounded by a vast sea of prairie grass. This isolation was responsible for the fact that cold water trout were unable to colonize Black Hills streams simply because they could not reach these streams from their major spawning areas in the high west via the warm, shallow Missouri and Cheyenne River systems. Geography, however, did not deter Hughes. Believing that Black Hills streams held great potential as a trout fishery, he persuaded his friend, Senator R. F. Pettigrew of Sioux Falls, to have the government back an experiment to stock the streams with rainbow trout.

In 1893, the first shipment of trout was ordered from the U.S. Fish Hatchery in Leadville, Colorado. The small fry were shipped in milk cans by rail from Leadville to Sidney, Nebraska, where the cans were then packed in ice and transferred to a stagecoach for the final 250-mile trip north to Rapid City. The fish were undoubtedly in poor condition when they reached their destination that summer and were eased into Rapid Creek. However, enough managed to survive and reproduce, making the experiment a success.

Six years later the U.S. Bureau of Fisheries, forerunner of the U.S. Fish and Wildlife Service, built a trout hatchery on Spearfish Creek at the mouth of Spearfish Canyon specifically to propagate trout for the Black Hills fishery.

The new facility was completed at a cost of $8,500, and that same year over 100,000 eggs from the Leadville hatchery arrived to initiate trout propagation and stocking in the Black Hills. The Spearfish facility consisted of four ponds and a two-story hatchery egg incubation building constructed in the elegant Victorian style of the period.

Following the completion of the new facility in 1899, D. C. Booth was appointed hatchery superintendent at the Spearfish facility and was assigned to manage trout fisheries both in the Black Hills as well as in Yellowstone National Park. This responsibility included making major horse and wagon expeditions annually to Yellowstone Lake, four hundred miles to the west, to spawn trout and bring the eggs back to Spearfish for incubation. Later the eggs were brought back in elaborate state of the art rail cars. Like the Black Hills Forest Reserve and Case #1, the Spearfish Hatchery proved a great success to further enhance the potential resources of the Black Hills.

The presence of the federal government was again felt in the Black Hills in 1902 when President Theodore Roosevelt signed into law the Newlands Act. The Newlands Act established the U.S. Bureau of Reclamation and set the stage for water development in the West. The bureau's primary directive was to turn arid lands into productive farmland with the help of irrigation.

In 1903, a year after the bureau's creation and with the urging of Seth Bullock, a long-time friend of Teddy Roosevelt's, the Belle Fourche Irrigation Project with Orman Dam as its centerpiece became the first land reclamation project in the United States. While not the first one completed, Belle Fourche was the first one authorized and engineered. Nothing like it, both in kind and in scope, had ever been attempted in the United States, and it almost proved a colossal fiasco.

Construction of the Belle Fourche project began in 1904 when trainloads of horses, mules and nineteenth-century, horse-drawn construction equipment—plows, dump wagons, elevated graders, and fresnoes—started arriving at the Belle Fourche railroad depot.

By today's standards the equipment seems incredibly primitive and the technology crude for such a major, sophisticated construction project. One elevated grader alone required two drivers, sixteen horses to pull it, and eight horses on a push cart behind it. A fresnoe, which was a kind of flat platform digging apparatus, required only one driver and four horses. In all cases the work was back breaking and strenuous.

An eyewitness to this dam building effort described an early construction scene of two hundred and fifty teams of horses pulling fresnoes, graders, and wheel scrapers around in four huge circles all at once. Five miles south, another crew of teamsters with heavy wagons worked at hauling sand and gravel from a pit on the Belle Fourche River up to a terrace to build concrete blocks. Sand, gravel, and lime had to be mixed by hand, using shovels and hoes, and then hauled to the forms by wheelbarrow. The finished concrete blocks were then moved to the construction site and used to face the dam. A third crew was employed in digging irrigation ditches and canals, again using only horse power.

It was estimated that the combination of all of these operations required the use of ten thousand horses and mules, either on the job or waiting as replacements. Not surprisingly, Orman and Crook, the project engineers who up until this time had built only railroad grades, went bankrupt a couple of years into the project. One story, told by a old lifelong resident of the area, was that after a particularly dry year, the contractors were simply unable to find enough forage to feed the thousands of animals required for the job.

Widdell, Finley, and Company resumed where Orman and Crook had failed. They eliminated most of the livestock by using two steam shovels mounted on flat rail cars that moved on standard width tracks to dig the reservoir and berm the dam. It was the same technology currently in use on the Panama Canal Project in Central America. As in Panama, the engineers also brought in narrow gauge steam "donkey" engines and cars to haul sand, gravel, and concrete blocks from the river to the dam.

Even with the introduction of better technology, after a few years on the project, Widdell and Finley also went broke. The project had taken more time and resources than anyone could have imagined or predicted. Two more men named Butler and Hayes took over the project and finally completed it in 1911, although project water started to flow as early as 1908.

When completed, Orman dam stretched for a mile and a quarter and stood 122 feet high. Its face shone with concrete blocks that had required thousands of man hours to construct. Perhaps not since the pyramids of Egypt or the great cathedrals of medieval Europe had such a massive engineering project been undertaken. In its scheme and scope, Belle Fourche set the precedent for the great water projects that would be associated with the agricultural transformation of the arid West.

While the Belle Fourche project was underway, Homestake Mining Company began experimenting with hydropower in Spearfish Canyon. By 1911, the powerful mining company had successfully completed a seven-mile-long water diversion tunnel from the middle of Spearfish Canyon through the mountains to the mouth of the canyon where it then employed the fall of the water to turn turbine engines. The tunnel at the time was one of the longest in the world while the turbines generated energy for some of the first electric dynamos built in the United States. Homestake's success spurred the state and federal government to seriously begin to consider hydropower in the West. The diversion, however, of huge amounts of water from Spearfish Creek seriously altered the hydrology of the whole drainage basin.

With the exploitation of mining, logging, water development, and tourism on an ever-increasing scale in the Black Hills, many local citizens began to feel the need for preserving certain areas for their aesthetic scenic value and unique natural features.

In the early 1900s, a controversy developed over who should manage a whistling hole in the ground near Hot Springs, South Dakota, known as Wind Cave. Hot Springs at the time was the only real pre-automobile tourist town in the Black Hills, having since the 1880s, with the arrival of the railroad, developed a strong trade in the mineral spa business. By the beginning of the twentieth century, various private and public interest groups were arguing over how the cave should be controlled and managed. Schemes of all kinds were proposed, including mining the cave for its unique lattice box work formations so they could be peddled as curios. A conservation ethic surfaced among a group of concerned, publicly spirited citizens who believed the federal government would make the best protector of the cave.

Congressman John F. Lacy of Iowa introduced the Wind Cave National Park bill in the House of Representatives in 1902. The bill and the proposed park represented a major shift in the concept and perception of national parks as the embodiment of American romanticism. Up until the introduction to include Wind Cave in the national park system, the term national park had been applied only to the incomparable grandeur of such places like Yosemite, Glacier, Grand Canyon, and Yellowstone. By comparison Wind Cave was considered to be "inferior," lacking the monumental size and superlative magnificence of the other parks. Lacey argued that Wind Cave would be "substantially what the Yellowstone country would be if the geysers should die. It has been excavated by hot water in the same manner that the geyser land is now being excavated in the Yellowstone."

It was a strained comparison. Wind Cave's dramatic underground past was in no way the geological equivalent of Yellowstone's dynamic present. Lacey admitted that the active forces were no longer in operation at Wind Cave and that "there is no hot water and the conditions that formerly prevailed there have ceased to exist," which was not altogether accurate either. Nonetheless, he still argued that "a series of very wonderful caves remain, and the Land Department has withdrawn this tract from settlement." He further tried to soften any objections, noting that the few claims of settlers in the area amounted to but "a few hundred acres" of the nine thousand proposed for park status. "I think it is a very meritorious proposition," he concluded, and urged that this tract of land "be reserved to the American people."

Other proponents who favored including the so-called "lesser parks" like Wind Cave in the national park system argued that the quantity of one type of feature was enough compensation for the absence of several major points of interest. To this end, Binger Hermann, commissioner of the General Land Office, quoted extensively from the reports of his surveyor who described Wind Cave as literally filled with "subterranean wonders" which included "great caverns and grotesque-looking rooms, large grottoes," along with "tons of specimens."

In the final hours park supporters argued effectively, if emotionally, that Wind Cave, like Yellowstone, was a monumental wonder; one simply needed to go underground, they maintained, to appreciate the resemblance. The proponents carried the day, and in January 1903, President Theodore Roosevelt signed the Wind Cave National Park Act into law. Again the natural features of the Black Hills acted as an important catalyst in helping shape the concept of what constituted natural beauty and should be conserved and preserved for the public as a national resource treasure. Wind Cave broke the precedent of awarding national park status to only the most monumental and inspiring western landscapes. Eventually, the park was enlarged to twenty-eight thousand acres, fenced for native wildlife, and promoted for hiking and outdoor recreation.

A few years later, a similar situation developed over on the Wyoming side of the Black Hills at Devil's Tower. Again a group of preservation-oriented conservationists sought to preserve the integrity of Devil's Tower, an imposing monolith of volcanic basalt rising 865 feet above the plains east of the Black Hills Bear Lodge Range.

In 1906, John Lacey, always the staunch conservationist, again led the charge in Congress to protect Devil's Tower by pushing through a bill entitled "An Act for the Preservation of American Antiquities." Lacey was primarily concerned with the looting of southwestern archaeological Indian sites. His bill was designed as a tool to preserve "objects of historic or scientific interest that are situated upon the lands controlled by the government of the United States."

The Antiquities Act, as it was later called, was a clear departure from previous national park legislation. Instead, it emphasized the preservation of artifacts as distinct from scenic wonders. To make the separation distinct, Lacey proposed that these new sites be designated as "national monuments." While the act did not provide for the preservation of landscapes, it did afford the president considerable discretion to broaden the impact of the legislation.

Theodore Roosevelt, the great conservation president, almost immediately used his discretion by interpreting the word "scientific" to include areas noted for their geologic (scenic), as well as man-made, significance. Using the Antiquities Act as a conservation tool, the natural features of the Black Hills again set a precedent when Roosevelt signed into law the act, in effect creating Devil's Tower as the first national monument on September 24, 1906.

In the South Dakota Black Hills, conservation received a major boost when Peter Norbeck, a native South Dakotan who operated an artesian well drilling business in Redfield, South Dakota, was elected first to the state house as a senator and later as governor in 1917. Norbeck was an adventurer and a visionary who naturally gravitated towards new ideas and innovative technology. He also developed an early love affair with the Black Hills and managed to navigate the first automobile, a Cadillac, under its own power from Fort Pierre on the Missouri River to the Black Hills.

When Norbeck drove out to the Black Hills in 1905, it was quite a feat. In that era there were no bridges or ferries across the Cheyenne River and other lesser tributaries. Norbeck at times resorted to driving over train trestles and hoping for the best. On other occasions, Norbeck's Cadillac had to be hauled out of mud holes by cowboys on horseback using lariats. All together it took Norbeck and his two traveling companions three days to reach the Black Hills. On their best day they covered eighty-seven miles. By comparison, the same trip today takes a little over three hours to drive a car the 175 miles from Fort Pierre to Rapid City.

Norbeck had that kind of spirit. He also had a lot of political savvy which, upon being elected to the state senate in 1909, he was able to put into motion. At the time a great deal of discussion focused on how to "clean up the forest" and make the management of the Black Hills Reserve more efficient. As it stood in 1900, the federal government deeded the state ownership of sections 16 and 36 of every township in the Black Hills as public school land. Public school lands were intended to generate part of the revenue necessary in financing state public education.

In January 1910, Norbeck managed to push a land trade bill through the state legislature. The bill set up a land swap with the federal government that effectively consolidated all the scattered state school sections in the Black Hills Reserve. South Dakota relinquished all rights to about 60,000 acres of timberlands within the Black Hills Reserve in exchange for 48,000 acres of forest in Custer County and 12,000 acres of grassland in Harding County. Two years later, the school lands in Custer County officially became the Custer State Forest. In the following year Norbeck boldly proposed that a wildlife preserve be established in the new state forest and then the state legislature approved it.

The land trade, one of the first of its kind between a state and the federal government, worked well for both agencies. It made the forest easier to manage while allowing Norbeck to set the foundation and precedent for one of the countries largest native wildlife preserves. The trade also set a precedent in being the first one done with clear conservation management objectives in mind.

The first animals to arrive at the Custer preserve were elk from Wyoming. Twenty-five were placed in a newly constructed seven-hundred-acre enclosure around 1913. The first bison for the preserve were purchased the following year from Scotty Philip's herd in Fort Pierre, South Dakota. The *Pierre Capitol Journal* reported the purchase in a December 14, 1914, story:

> The shipment of buffalo for the state were loaded (in rail cars) at Fort Pierre without any difficulty, and have been unloaded at the yards in Hermosa, (South Dakota) without any difficulty, from which place they will be hauled to the park in the wagon built for such transportation. While they were driven from their pasture to the yards at Fort Pierre,

it is not considered safe to attempt to drive them through the gulches between Hermosa and the park enclosure.

No mention was made in the article as to how many were purchased, all that was noted is that it took twelve days to transfer the animals from the cars at Hermosa to the park.

The first pronghorns arrived in the preserve during the spring of 1916 and included a dozen animals that had been bottle raised prior to their transfer. Few of these early human-raised animals survived long enough to reproduce, and more experimentation would be required before their reintroduction to the park would be successful.

Another experiment with wildlife in the preserve that never achieved success was the introduction of moose. In 1917 the state purchased some moose calves from the Grand Tetons area. The moose were from Victor, Idaho, and had to be pulled over Teton Pass in the winter by sled to the train depot in Jackson, Wyoming.

The first pair managed to kill themselves in the shipping crates before they arrived in South Dakota. A second shipment of moose calves did arrive in good order in smaller crates, but to no avail. They apparently did not find the Black Hills to their liking either, and soon after being freed were reported to be in Wyoming on their way back to the Tetons.

In 1916, the Custer bison herd was at 50 and the number of elk stood at 250, including 50 head that had just been introduced from Montana. Deer were also again becoming numerous in the Black Hills. Yet even with progressively more stringent game laws first initiated back in late 1890s, they were having a difficult time making a come back. Perhaps the all-time low for the struggling deer herds in the Black Hills came in 1923 when only about two thousand deer were reported in the Black Hills. All the wildlife populations were struggling due to a series of hard winters beginning in 1917 and running through 1919, then culminating with a late four-foot snowfall in 1920.

From a perspective of nearly a century, Norbeck's vision of a scenic wildlife park is one of the greatest, far-sighted conservation legacies any one South Dakotan could have left for the plants, animals, and people of the Black Hills. Following the initial creation of the Custer State Forest, Norbeck made another sound decision, this time as governor, by hiring a bright, practically oriented young man in 1918 named Cecil Clyde Gideon to act as construction foreman in the wildlife preserve. Gideon, who was from St. Cloud, Minnesota, quit school at the age of thirteen to run his own contracting business in Minneapolis. He was a natural architect and builder who learned his trade through experience. It was his outstanding work in the Twin Cities that brought him to the attention of two prominent Minneapolis architects who had been contacted by Governor Norbeck to build the State Game Lodge.

While in his late twenties, Gideon moved his family out to the Black Hills where they all lived in a tent in the park that first year. Gideon, as a state employee, earned $7.50 a day as the construction foreman and chief carpenter who was hired to oversee the park and construct the Game Lodge. His construction crew was comprised of thirty-two state penitentiary inmates who earned $1.00 per day. His daughter, Elizabeth Gideon McDonald, recalled in a *Rapid City Journal* newspaper story, nearly seventy years later, how her father, a man of small stature, was forced to carry a gun with him at all times for protection.

The Game Lodge was originally designed and built to be a meeting place and retreat for members of the State Game Commission. It was also meant to serve as the residence for the park's game keeper, which Gideon also gained title to in 1919. The first lodge was constructed of native stone and timber. The timber was taken from the park and cured in a heated garage on site. The Game Lodge officially opened on August 8, 1921, and burned to the ground that fall, two months after its completion. McDonald believes the fire was arson, and was set by a man Gideon had fired during the construction period for bootlegging whiskey to the convicts.

Undeterred, Gideon rebuilt the Game Lodge, this time buying the necessary lumber and incorporating a few new design changes. Eight months later it reopened and soon became a popular tourist attraction in the Black Hills. While it was never intended to be a tourist resort, people, nonetheless, where enormously attracted to its rustic charm and beauty and the Gideons soon became official lodge hosts. In those days the three-story main building accommodated fifty-three guests, while at other times that number could be accommodated in the nearby sleeping cabins.

As game keeper, Gideon undertook the task of enclosing the enormous park in an eight-foot-high, game-tight fence to contain the growing elk and bison herds. It was a job that Norbeck himself had begun and had spent time supervising before Gideon's arrival.

A major part of Gideon's job also included what he described as the "hazardous life" of the "'go-between' for the State Game Commission and the displaced ranchers whose grazing of state land was curtailed by my fencing the park . . ." Later, in the family memoirs, he noted that it was his responsibility to collect the grazing fees from cattlemen whose cattle heretofore had enjoyed unrestricted roaming in the Black Hills. In a terse understatement, he added, "They found it difficult to accept the new rules."

In 1921 Norbeck, the "prairie statesman," began his first term as a United States senator from South Dakota. During his earlier terms as lieutenant governor from 1915 to 1916 and as governor from 1917 to 1921, he had devoted a good deal of his time and energy into the building of the wildlife preserve. As senator he continued this work. Through his efforts mountain sheep were introduced in the preserve in 1922 with Rocky Mountain goats from Canada introduced in 1924.

Norbeck was also responsible for extending the preserve's boundaries to include grassland foothills on the southeast end as well as the towering Cathedral Spires and the Needles on the northwest end. Near the end of his tenure as governor, Norbeck convinced the state legislature to rename this beautiful 73,000-acre southern Black Hills forest and foothills wildlife preserve Custer State Park. The name change is significant for what was to become the second largest state operated park in the nation. It marked a shift in attitude from preservation to resource and recreation development for the enjoyment and edification of the general public.

Responding to this change in attitude of the early 1920s, Gideon's family hosted such business dignitaries as J. C. Penney, the Guggenheims, and the Kresges. In 1925, Gideon assisted Gutzon Borglum in evaluating sites for his proposed "Shrine of Democracy" on Mount Rushmore. Norbeck was instrumental in raising the first $200,000 at this same time to get the project started. Two years later the Gideon family hosted President Calvin Coolidge and his wife Grace for thirteen weeks at the State Game Lodge at Norbeck's invitation. Following the news of the Coolidges impending visit, Gideon and his crew quickly constructed Grace Coolidge Inn to house and feed the President's entourage of staff, secret service men, and press. When the President finally arrived, McDonald recalls "silent Cal" remarking on the front porch of the Game Lodge that "it smells like Vermont."

The President's personal assistant, Colonel Edward Starling, selected Gideon to serve as Coolidge's companion and guide because, as McDonald explained, they were both "men of few words." That summer Gideon taught Coolidge to ride horseback and fish. In spite of, or perhaps because of, the dearth of conversation, the two men were reputed to have become good friends.

Norbeck, however, had other motives than just Coolidge's well-being for inviting the President to spend the summer of 1927 at the park. During his Black Hills sojourn, the President was made intimately aware of Borglum's carving project on Mount Rushmore and his pressing need for federal funding and support. His summer in the Black Hills with Gideon was undoubtedly a major impetus in Coolidge's decision to support congressional funding for what would be designated as the Mount Rushmore National Monument during the following year.

Following Coolidge's return to Washington, Norbeck had Gideon supervise the construction of his summer home, Valhalla, that overlooked a small tributary of Iron Creek along the Needles Highway. According to Norbeck's wife Lydia, Valhalla was the perfect place for entertaining, with its winding stairs, huge living room, fireplace, and balconies on three sides. "On some afternoons," she wrote in her memoirs, "we had as many as a hundred callers."

While Norbeck had the vision of what Custer State Park was to be, it was Gideon whom he confided in implicitly to carry out the design and plan. Throughout the 1920s and into the early 1930s, they worked side by side in developing ways to allow tourists to stay and enjoy the beauty of the park. With the park well established and fenced by the end of the 1920s, Norbeck shifted his focus to making the pristine heart of the park, which included the Needles, the Cathedral Spires, and what would later become the Norbeck Wildlife Preserve, more accessible.

Throughout this later development phase, Norbeck continued to hold a strong belief in regard to preserving the integrity and pristine quality of the park as a top priority. With this as a primary objective, he and Gideon, either on horseback or walking when the going got too rough, laid out what was to become the spectacular Black Hills Needles Highway and the Iron Mountain Road. Norbeck, a true lover of wilderness in the vein of John Muir, believed that visitors should actually get out of their cars and walk the roads or at the very least drive them no faster than 20 mph.

With his enormous influence first as governor and later as a United States senator, Norbeck was able to win most of the highway battles with the civil engineers whom he referred to as "the diploma boys." Norbeck, with Gideon's advice, often had the last word on where to blast a tunnel and what particularly lovely setting the road should skirt.

As the idea of laying out roads and boring tunnels into the granitic heart of the Black Hills took hold of both Gideon and Norbeck in the late 1920s and early 1930s, reams of correspondence passed between the two men concerning alternative routes for the Iron Mountain Road. It was Norbeck who favored the one-lane tunnels on the Iron Mountain Road that would frame the sculpted presidential countenances Gutzon Borglum was chiseling out of the smooth, granite face of Mount Rushmore.

Norbeck's vision of framing tunnels, however, created an incredible road engineering challenge for Gideon. The problem was that the distance between the tunnels was relatively short, while the elevation change was significant. Since there was not enough distance for a series of climbing switchbacks between tunnels, Gideon was forced to figure out a way to loop and incline the Iron Mountain Road at the same time. In January 1932, he wrote to Norbeck that he had been trying to plan a spiral trestle beginning at the exit of the longest of the three proposed Iron Mountain Road tunnels. "Am going to send you a rough sketch," he wrote, "showing a triple spiral." After seeing the sketches of Gideon's spiral trestles, Norbeck dubbed them "whirly-jigs," while Gideon referred to them as "spiral jump-offs." Neither name stuck and they were eventually called the "pig-tail bridges."

Although Norbeck had every confidence in Gideon's ability as an experienced, practical architect and engineer, because of the expense of the spiral trestles—at the time estimated to be around $28,000 per bridge, half of which was labor—Norbeck was ready to abandon the idea.

Gideon quickly communicated back to Norbeck explaining "that he was pretty slow in this kind of work," adding that it was turning out to be "quite a job, entirely different from anything that I have had experience with due to the fact that the bridge is built on a circle and on a 5 percent grade and is also super-elevated . . . In other words," he continued, "the bridge is neither straight, level, or flat. Consequently we have encountered forces which have been very difficult to estimate."

Nonetheless, Gideon was not to be defeated. By incorporating nine thousand pounds of steel beams and long, specially cut logs for supports which he personally supervised the cutting of, Gideon succeeded in building the spiral bridges that still stand as part of the Iron Mountain Road (U.S. Alt. 16) and can be encountered near the intersection with the road to Mount Rushmore (South Dakota 244). He completed the Iron Mountain Road with its three pigtail bridges and three mountain tunnels by the summer of 1933.

In that same year and again in 1938, Thomas E. Odell, a teacher and historian from Spearfish, wrote a handful of articles for local Black Hills newspapers recommending Bear Butte for national monument status. Odell had relocated to South Dakota in 1907 at the age of thirty-one from his native Ohio. In South Dakota he was able to further his academic education, ultimately working as a school teacher for twenty-five years and completed his last school teaching assignment at the age of eighty-six. During his summers, Odell researched and wrote a history of Bear Butte which eventually culminated into a book entitled *Mato Paha: The Story of Bear Butte*.

From the standpoint that it was chosen principally for its mystical/religious implications as opposed to its natural history features, Bear Butte is unlike the other areas selected for preservation in the Black Hills by conservationists. Odell's efforts and persistence attracted other supporters, most notably a prominent Sturgis community leader and educator named R. B. (Dick) Williams who also strongly believed that the natural beauty and cultural significance of Bear Butte as a Plains Indian shrine needed to be preserved, interpreted, and protected.

The name Bear Butte is a literal translation from the Lakota Sioux term, Mato Paha. However, the original name bestowed upon it by the Cheyenne is Noaha´-vose (pronounced No-ah´ wus) which roughly translates as "mound of the vision seekers." It was on Noaha´-vose, Cheyenne tradition holds, that a young hunter who would become Sweet Medicine received a vision that would forever changed the beliefs of the Cheyenne people.

The Cheyenne are an Algonquin speaking people who, in preceding generations, dating back to the early seventeenth century, had been forced by degrees from their ancestral homelands in northern Wisconsin and Minnesota by the better-armed Ojibway, Sioux, and Cree. Eventually pushed out on to the harsh northern plains, the Cheyenne were forced to shift their lifestyle from woodland hunter/gatherers to plains gardeners and finally to nomadic plains bison hunters and warriors.

For a while, groups of Cheyenne lived on the Sheyenne River in eastern North Dakota before eventually gravitating to the Missouri River and learning the art of cultivating corn, beans, and squash from friendly Ree and Mandan Indians. Still restless and harassed by enemies from the east, the tribes vanguard pursued the great bison herds ever farther west until the main Cheyenne camps established themselves in the sheltered draws and foothills of the northern and eastern Black Hills.

Sometime before their arrival in the Black Hills, legend holds that a Council of Spirit Grandfathers convened to determine who might best help the Cheyenne people in their long, wandering struggle to survive. After great deliberation, the Council of Spirits decided a small, dark butte just outside the great circle of the pine-covered Black Hills would be the appropriate place to offer them help in the form of spiritual guidance. It also came to be that the Grandfather Bear Spirit of the Cheyenne brothers was chosen to help them by creating a powerful aura of protection and energy around the small, singular mountain.

About a generation after the Bear Spirit's endowment of Noaha´-vose, a group of Cheyenne were hunting bison on the plains north of the butte. During this hunt, a young man killed a large cow. While admiring his prize, an older man appeared, claimed the bison cow, and began butchering it. A serious fight ensued in which the young man killed the older man. Under Cheyenne law the act of killing a tribal member was justified cause for banishment from the "hoop" of the People. To live alone on the northern plains with its many dangers and without the support of the people was, in effect, a sure death sentence.

The banished young man left the tribe and eventually wandered to a small cave in a limestone outcrop on the north side of Noaha´-vose. Here he lived alone for four years and prospered with the help of the Grandfathers and Nature Spirits. During the spring of his fifth year at Noaha´-vose, the young man smelled burning grass and rushed to the entrance of his cave to see what was transpiring. A great prairie fire had swept the area, leaving only a small circle of live, unburned sweetgrass near the cave's entrance. Sweet Medicine went to the unburned spot and after giving thanks to the

Grandfathers for sparing his own life-circle, he lay down on the sweetgrass and fell asleep.

When the moon was high in the night sky, a vision of Grandfather Eagle visited him. In the vision Grandfather Eagle gave to Sweet Medicine the basis for the principles of living that he was to share with the Cheyenne people.

The essence of the principles and the message Sweet Medicine brought to the Cheyenne people were these:

1. Remember the Creator Father as the Father of all living creatures.
2. Remember to offer thanks to all the spirits for their daily help in providing such thing as fire, water, meat and corn.
3. Remember to celebrate the goodness of the Earth Mother with a ceremony in her honor in the fall to thank her for her bounty, and in the spring to ask for her blessing of fertility.
4. Remember that all is under the laws of nature and what exists in nature exists for man.
5. Foster and respect the attributes of honesty, truth, courage, strength, and compassion. Honor even your enemies in war for this proves character.
6. Do not convene the council of war without serious thought. Seek first the counsel of Grandfather Eagle.

During his vision, Sweet Medicine was also given four sacred arrows. There were two dark arrows and two light ones. One dark arrow represented war and the other peace. One light arrow represented the earth and regeneration which was for the village and the people, while the other represented the sky and the Great Spirit's love and his gift of life to them.

After giving thanks for this vision, Sweet Medicine returned to the Cheyenne people. A shaman, who had received a vision that Sweet Medicine would return with principles and ceremonies for the renewal of the people, paved the way for his message and acceptance back into the tribe. With Sweet Medicine's guidance, the Cheyenne became one of the most successful and confident hunting-warrior societies on the northern plains. Their history is filled with feats of bravery and self-sacrifice.

In September 1939, a small group of northern Cheyenne elders, accompanied by younger tribesmen, traveled from their reservation in

Lame Deer, Montana, to visit Noahá-vose. It was the first time since the late 1870s that a group of Cheyenne had journeyed to the sacred mountain of their forefathers to meditate and pray on the mountain. They were invited by a group of Sturgis citizens who sought to have the mountain preserved as a national monument.

During their sojourn, Nelson Holy Bird, eighty years old, climbed to the summit where he invoked the blessing of the Great Spirit upon the United States, while also asking Him to watch over the welfare of the nation. He then recited, as if in sorrow, the tales of the days when his tribe annually prayed at Noahá-vose.

The following year, 1940, the Bovee family, who were early homesteaders and eventual owners of a large portion of Bear Butte, formed the Bear Butte Company. The company's proposed goal was to develop the Butte as a tourist attraction. To this purpose several rough paths and eight hundred feet of wooden ladders and stairways were constructed. Burros, acquired from Custer State Park, were trained and also employed in helping tourists reach the summit. A handful of people in Sturgis, like those decades earlier in Hot Springs, where uncomfortable with the site being operated by a private sector and again launched an effort to preserve the integrity of Bear Butte. Having been unsuccessful earlier with Congress and the National Park Service, they turned this time to the South Dakota state legislature.

In 1961, the persistence of Odell and R. B. Williams finally paid off with the enactment of Chapter 307, Sessions Laws of 1961, creating Bear Butte State Park. At that time the state of South Dakota purchased one thousand acres of Sumner Bovee's land which encompassed most of Bear Butte.

Three decades later, Plains Indians meditate and raise their redstone pipes to the Great Spirit on Bear Butte. In the southern Black Hills bison roam over one hundred thousand acres of grass and timber again while elk are becoming more plentiful. Dedicated conservationists, along with sincere private citizens, non-profit conservation organizations, and public servants, have turned the tide of extinction back to one of biological diversity in the Black Hills. For all this work and these gifts there are many people, most unheralded, that deserve our gratitude.

Index